Communications
and
Society

Communications
and
Society
A Bibliography
on
Communications Technologies
and
Their Social Impact

Compiled by

Benjamin F. Shearer

and

Marilyn Huxford

Greenwood Press
Westport, Connecticut • London, England

HM
258
.S45
1983

Library of Congress Cataloging in Publication Data

Shearer, Benjamin F.
  Communications and society.

  Includes index.
  1. Mass media—Social aspects—Bibliography.
2. Communication—Social aspects—Bibliography.
3. Communication—Technological innovations—Bibliography.   I. Huxford, Marilyn.   II. Title.
Z5630.S43 1983   [HM258] 016.3022'3   83-12659
ISBN 0-313-23713-1 (lib. bdg.)

Library of Congress Catalog Card Number: 83-12659
ISBN: 0-313-23713-1

First published in 1983

Greenwood Press
A division of Congressional Information Service, Inc.
88 Post Road West, Westport, Connecticut 06881

Printed in the United States of America

10 9 8 7 6 5 4 3 2 1

Contents

Preface

Technology pervades our existence as medium and metaphor. As medium, technology is the nuts and bolts of mankind's progress, a channel for change in human interaction. As metaphor, technology may symbolize the highest reaches of civilization or the destruction of an older civilization. No matter what values may be attached to any particular technology, the fact remains that the impact of new technologies goes far beyond merely technical detail. When technologies are developed that redefine the way human beings communicate with themselves and their environment, the impact is all the more diversified.

The purpose of this selected bibliography is to explore the diversity of communications technologies and their impact on society from a humanistic perspective. Citations have been selected to introduce scholars and students in the humanities to the literature of communications technologies. As noted below, the chapters are arranged in broad subject categories to present a many-sided view of communications media.

Chapter 1.   Here are entered works that deal with mass communications theory in general and theories of film in particular. (Entry nos. 1-196.)

Chapter 2.   Here are entered works that deal with the inventors of communications technologies and their inventions as well as histories of the development of the various media. (Entry nos. 197-645.)

Chapter 3.   Here are entered works that investigate the gatekeeping functions of those who control, own, or influence mass media content. This includes works on censorship, regulation, and media bias. (Entry nos. 646-1170.)

Chapter 4.   Here are entered works that deal directly with social and cultural effects of mass communications technologies. This includes the effects mass media exposure may have on violent or aggressive behavior, learning abilities, and so forth. (Entry nos. 1171-1580.)

Chapter 5.   Here are entered works that investigate the content of the mass media to determine how they influence public opinion in general and also how public opinion and attitudes influence the content of the media. This includes works on sexual and racial stereotyping in the media. (Entry nos. 1581-1947.)

Chapter 6.   Here are entered works that investigate the use of mass media as propaganda tools and the use of the media by governments and politicians. Works that concern the effect of the media on political opinion and election results are also entered here. (Entry nos. 1948-2172.)

Chapter 7.   Here are entered works that discuss the phenomenon of mass media advertising—its history, method, aesthetics, and effects. (Entry nos. 2173-2395.)

Chapter 8.   Here are entered works that investigate the possibilities of future communications technologies and their place in the future of contemporary media. (Entry nos. 2396-2495.)

Chapter 9.   Here are entered works that deal with film and photography as art forms and the use of computers and communications technologies in the production of fine art. Works discussing the effects of technology and industrialism on literature and the views of various writers on technology are also entered here. (Entry nos. 2496-2732).

While the chapters and their subdivisions provide a general subject approach to the citations, the subject index pulls together related material from all the chapters. An author index is also provided. Citations in the subject and author indexes are to entry numbers in the text.

Acknowledgments

The collection of the Communications Library at the University of Illinois was used extensively in the initial stage of this work. Our thanks to the librarians there who went out of their way to be of assistance. We would also like to thank the library staffs of Spring Hill College, the University of South Alabama, and St. Louis University for assistance in helping us use their collections. Special thanks are due to Phyllis Picklesimer for her expert help in manuscript preparation.

Communications
and
Society

1
Theory and Process of Media: Technologies as Media and Messages

1. Akeret, Robert U. Photoanalysis: How to Interpret the Hidden Psychological Meaning of Personal and Public Photographs. Edited by Thomas Humer. New York: Wyden, 1973. (250p)

2. Allen, Don, ed. The Electric Anthology: Probes into Mass Media and Popular Culture. Dayton: Pflaum, 1975. (198p)

3. Altheide, David L. Creating Reality: How TV News Distorts Events. Beverly Hills: Sage, 1976. (222p)

4. Anderson, James A. "The equivalence of meaning among similar statements presented in the print, auval and pictorial media." Ph.D. dissertation, University of Iowa, 1965. (359p)

5. Andrae, Thomas. "The culture industry reconsidered: Adorno on film and mass culture." Jump Cut 20 (May 1979): 34-37.

6. Andrew, J. Dudley. The Major Film Theories: An Introduction. New York: Oxford University Press, 1976. (278p)

7. Avery, Robert K., et al. "Patterns of communication on talk radio." Journal of Broadcasting 22 (Winter 1978): 5-17.

8. Baggaley, Jon, et al. Psychology of the TV Image. New York: Praeger, 1980. (190p)

9. Balazs, Bela. Theory of the Film; Character and Growth of a New Art. Trans. by Edith Bone. New York: Dover, 1970. (291p)

10. Balon, Robert E. "Differential effects of three media
     in a news-gathering situation." Journalism Quarterly
     54 (Autumn 1977): 498-502, 531.

11. Barnouw, Erik. Mass Communication: Television, Radio,
     Film, Press; The Media and Their Practice in the
     United States of America. New York: Rinehart, 1956.
     (280p)

12. Baticle, Yveline. Message, média, communication; De
     lascaux a l'originateur. Paris: Magnard Université,
     1973. (221p)

13. Bazin, André. What is Cinema? Essays Selected and
     Translated by Hugh Gray. 2 vols. Berkeley: Univer-
     sity of California Press, 1967-71.

14. Belson, William A. "The effects of television on the
     reading and the buying of newspapers and magazines."
     Public Opinion Quarterly 25 (1961): 366-381.

15. Berger, René. La Mutation des signes. Paris: Denaël,
     1972. (425p)

16. Bernberg, R. E. "Prestige suggestion in art as com-
     munication." Journal of Social Psychology 38 (1953):
     23-30.

17. Bettetini, Gianfranco. The Language and Technique of
     the Film. Trans. by David Osmond-Smith. The Hague:
     Mouton, 1973. (202p)

18. Binning, Dennis W. and Tim Callan. Words, People,
     Cities, Technology. Washington: Printed by Thiel
     Press, 1971. (60p)

19. Bittner, John R. Mass Communication, An Introduction:
     Theory and Practice of Mass Media in Society. Engle-
     wood Cliffs, N.J.: Prentice-Hall, c 1977. (512p)

20. Böckelmann, Frank. Theorie der Massenkommunikation:
     Das System hergestellter Öffentlichkeit, Wirkungsfor-
     schung und Gesellschaftliche Kommunikationsverhält-
     nisse. Frankfurt a. M.: Suhrkamp, 1975. (310p)

21. Bourdin, Alain. MacLuhan; Communication, Technologie
     et Société. Paris: Editions Universitaires, 1970.
     (142p)

22. Brakhage, Stan. "Metaphors on vision." Film Culture 30
     (Fall 1963): 64p, unnumbered.

23. Bretz, R. Communication Media: Properties and Uses.
     Rand Memorandum 6070-NLM/PR. September 1969.

24. Briggs, Asa. "Word and image: changing patterns of
     communications." Daedalus 108 (Spring 1979): 133-
     149.

25. Brown, Lee. The Reluctant Reformation; On Criticizing
     the Press in America. New York: McKay, 1974. (244p)

26. Burch, Noel. Theory of Film Practice. Trans. by
     Helen R. Lane. Introd. by Annette Michelson. New
     York: Praeger, 1973. (172p)

27. Cassata, Mary B. and Molefi K. Asante. Mass Communica-
     tions: Principles and Practices. New York: Mac-
     millan, 1979. (360p)

28. Cassirer, Henry R. "From non-communication to communi-
     cation." Communication 3 (June 1978): 61-86.

29. Cavell, Stanley. The World Viewed; Reflections on the
     Ontology of Film. New York: Viking Press, 1971.
     (174p)

30. Chalfen, Richard. "Cinema naiveté: a study of home
     moviemaking as visual communication." Studies in the
     Anthropology of Visual Communication 2 (Fall 1975):
     87-103.

31. Chervy, Colin. World Communication: Threat or Promise?
     A Socio-Technical Approach. New York: Wiley-
     Interscience, 1971. (229p)

32. Citron, Michelle. "Integration: a theory of the
     science/art dichotomy in film and print." Ph.D. dis-
     sertation, University of Wisconsin—Madison, 1974.
     (72p)

33. Clarke, Arthur C. "Communications in the second century
     of the telephone." Across the Board 14 (August 1977):
     58-65.

34. Costigan, James. "Communication theory in the works of
     Marshall McLuhan." Ph.D. dissertation, Southern Illi-
     nois University, 1969. (200p)

35. Culbertson, Hugh M. "Words vs. pictures: perceived
     impact and connotative meaning." Broadcast Quarterly
     51 (Summer 1974): 226-237.

36. Dannefer, W. Dale and Nicholas Poushinsky. "Language
     and community." Journal of Communication 27 (Summer
     1977): 122-126.

37. Davison, Walter P., et al. Mass Media: Systems and
     Effects. New York: Praeger, 1976. (245p)

38. Day, Barry. "Too hot not to cool down." Sight and
     Sound 37 (Winter 1967-68): 28-32.

39. De Laurot, Edouard. "Reflections on a theory of world
     cinema." Film Culture 26 (Fall 1962): 63-70.

40. Dengler, Ralph W. "'Hot' and 'cool' catechesis: a
     content analysis of technology determinism in se-
     lected sixteenth century and twentieth century texts
     based on the general inquirer system." Ph.D. dis-
     sertation, New York University, 1972. (271p)

41. _____. "The space bias and time bias idea of Innis
     tested on catechisms." Journalism Quarterly 50
     (Autumn 1973): 502-508.

42. Dennis, Everette E. The Media Society: Evidence About
     Mass Communication in America. Dubuque: Wm. C.
     Brown, 1978. (166p)

43. Deutschmann, Paul J. "The mass media in an under-
     developed village." Journalism Quarterly 40 (1963):
     27-35.

44. Developing World and Mass Media. Prague: International
     Organization of Journalists, 1975. (128p)

45. Doblin, J. "Map of media; understanding the contexts
     for communications." Industrial Design 28 (January/
     February 1980): 35-37.

46. Dommermuth, William P. "How does the medium affect the
     message?" Journalism Quarterly 51 (Autumn 1974):
     441-447.

47. Durgnat, Raymond. "Expressing life in celluloid."
     Films and Filming 11 (May 1965): 44-48.

48. Edgerton, Gary. "Radio and motion pictures: a case
     study of media symbiosis." Mass Comm Review 8 (Win-
     ter 1980/81): 21-29.

49. Emmet, B. P. "The design of investigations into the
     effects of radio and television programmes and other
     mass communications." Journal of the Royal Sta-
     tistical Society 129 (1966): 26-59.

50. Escarpit, Robert. "Mass and the book." Sociologia
     Internationalis 17, no. 1-2 (1979): 163-174.

51. Essais sur les mass media et la culture. Paris:
     UNESCO, 1971. (119p)

52. Everitt, W. L. "Telecommunications; the resource not
     depleted by use; a historical and philosophical re-
     sume." Proceedings of the IEEE 64 (September 1976):
     1292-1299.

53. Fagen, David L. "A communication theory of aesthetics."
     Ph.D. dissertation, Stanford University, 1970. (257p)

54. Farace, V. and Lewis Donohew. "Mass communications in
     national social systems: a study of 43 variables in
     115 countries." Journalism Quarterly 42 (1965): 253-
     261.

55. Finkelstein, Sidney. Sense and Nonsense of McLuhan.
     New York: International Publishers, 1968. (122p)

56. Fiske, John and John Hartley. Reading Television.
     London: Methuen, 1978. (223p)

57. Ford, J. B. "Is there mass communication?" Sociology
     and Social Research 37 (1953): 244-250.

58. Francke, Warren T. "The normative role of McLuhan:
     Paul Revere or Benedict Arnold." Journalism Quarterly
     45 (Spring 1968): 25-30.

59. Freidson, Eliot. "Communications research and the
     concept of the mass." American Sociological Review
     18 (1953): 313-317.

60. Gelb, Phillip S. "'The communication culture,' a so-
     cial theory of communication." Ed.D. dissertation,
     Columbia University Teachers College, 1977. (701p)

61. Gessner, Robert. "The parts of cinema: a definition."
     Journal of the Society of Cinematologists 1 (1961):
     25-39.

62. Gibson, William. "Network news: elements of a theory."
     Social Text 3 (Fall 1980): 88-111.

63. Glessing, Robert J. and William P. White, comp. Mass
     Media: the invisible environment. Chicago: Sci-
     ence Research Associates, 1973. (310p)

64. Goldberg, Myron L. and A. Rodney Wellens. "A compari-
     son of nonverbal compensatory behaviors within direct
     face-to-face and television-mediated interviews."
     Journal of Applied Social Psychology 9 (May/June
     1979): 250-260.

65. Gordon, George N. Communications and Media: Con-
     structing a Cross-Discipline. New York: Hastings
     House, 1975. (209p)

66. Gouldner, Alvin W. The Dialectic of Ideology and
     Technology: The Origin, Grammar and Future of Ide-
     ology. New York: Seabury, 1976. (304p)

67.   Grossvogel, David I.   "The play of light and shadow:
      a directional error."   Yale French Studies 17 (Sum-
      mer 1956): 75-85.

68.   Hardt, Hanno.   Social Theories of the Press; Early Ger-
      man and American Perspectives.   Beverly Hills: Sage,
      1979.   (239p)

⅄69.   Harpole, Charles H.   "Ideological and technological
      determinism in deep-space cinema images: issues in
      ideology, technological history, and aesthetics."
      Film Quarterly 33 (Spring 1980): 11-22.

70.   Henderson, Brian.   "Two types of film theory."   Film
      Quarterly 24 (Spring 1971): 33-42.

71.   Hornick, Robert C.   Mass Media Use and the "Revolution
      of Rising Frustrations":   A Reconsideration of the
      Theory.   Honolulu: East-West Communication Insti-
      tute, 1974.   (27p)

72.   Houseman, John.   "How—and what—does a movie communi-
      cate?"   Quarterly of Film, Radio and Television 10
      (Spring 1956): 227-238.

73.   Hoyt, James L.   "Source-message orientation in inter-
      personal and media influence."   Journalism Quarterly
      52 (Autumn 1975): 472-476.

74.   Hurley, Neil P.   Communicaciones, teoría y estrategia.
      Santiago: Ediciones Sede Santiago Sur, Universidad
      de Chile, 1974.   (172p)

75.   Huston-Stein, Aletha and John C. Wright.   "Children and
      television: effects of the medium, its content and
      its form."   Journal of Research and Development in
      Education 13 (Fall 1979): 20-31.

76.   Hyde, Michael J.   Communication Philosophy and the
      Technological Age.   University: University of Ala-
      bama Press, 1982.   (135p)

77.   Innis, Harold A.   The Bias of Communication.   Toronto:
      University of Toronto Press, 1951.   (226p)

78.   _____.   Empire and Communication.   Oxford: Clarendon
      Press, 1950.   (198p)

79.   Jacobs, Lewis.   The Movies as Medium.   New York: Far-
      rar, Straus and Giroux, 1970.   (335p)

80.   Jarvie, Ian C.   "Seeing through movies."   Philosophy of
      the Social Sciences 8 (December 1978): 374-397.

81.   Jones, Dorothy B.   "The language of our time."   Quar-
      terly of Film, Radio and Television 10 (Winter 1955):
      167-179.

82. Kalba, Kas. The Video Implosion: Models for Reinventing
     Television. Palo Alto, CA: Aspen Institute, Program
     on Communications and Society, 1974. (46p)

83. Kemp, Weston D. Photography for Visual Communicators.
     Englewood Cliffs, NJ: Prentice-Hall, 1973. (287p)

84. Key, Wilson B. Media Sexploitation. Englewood Cliffs,
     NJ: Prentice-Hall, 1976. (234p)

85. Korobeinikov, Valery S. "Conflicts of media in modern
     industrial society." International Social Science
     Journal 32, no. 2 (1980): 238-246.

86. Kraay, Robert W. "Symbols in paradox: a theory of
     communication based on the writing of Mircea Eliade."
     Ph.D. dissertation, University of Iowa, 1977. (136p)

87. Kracauer, Siegfried. Theory of Film: The Redemption of
     Physical Reality. New York: Oxford University
     Press, 1960, 1965. (364p)

88. Lamberton, Donald M., ed. "The information revolution."
     Annals of the American Academy of Political and So-
     cial Science, vol. 412. Philadelphia, 1974. (162p)

89. Lathi, Bhagwandas P. Signals, systems and communica-
     tion. New York: Wiley, 1965. (607p)

90. Laver, F.J.M. Computers, Communications and Society.
     London and New York: Oxford University Press, 1975.
     (99p)

91. Laws, Frederick, ed. Made for Millions; A Critical
     Study of the New Media of Information and Entertain-
     ment. London: Contact Publications, 1947. (116p)

92. Lee, Alan J. The Origins of the Popular Press, 1855-
     1914. Totowa, NJ: Rowman and Littlefield, 1976.
     (310p)

93. Lehman, Maxwell and Thomas J.M. Burke, eds. Communi-
     cation Technologies and Information Flow. New York:
     Pergamon Press, 1981. (151p)

94. Lermack, Paul. "TV: the interruptible medium." Dis-
     sent 25 (Spring 1978): 186-192.

95. Lignell, E. E. The Mobile Image; Film as Environment.
     New York: Herder and Herder, 1970. (32p)

96. Lohisse, Jean. Anonymous Communication; Mass-Media in
     the Modern World. Trans. by Stephen Corrin. London:
     Allen and Unwin, 1973. (191p)

97. MacCann, Richard D., ed. Film: A Montage of Theories.
     New York: Dutton, 1966. (384p)

98. McCrone, Donald J. and Charles F. Cnudde. "Toward a
     communication theory of democratic political devel-
     opment: a causal model." American Political Science
     Review 61 (1967): 72-79.

99. Machlup, Fritz. The Production and Distribution of
     Knowledge in the United States. Princeton: Prince-
     ton University Press, 1962. (416p)

100. McLuhan, Marshall. The Gutenberg Galaxy: The Making
     of Typographic Man. Toronto: University of Toronto
     Press, 1962. (294p)

101. _____. "Radio: the tribal drum." AV Communication
     Review 12 (1964): 133-145.

102. _____. Understanding Media: The Extensions of Man.
     New York: McGraw, 1964. (359p)

103. McLuhan, Marshall and Quentin Fiore. The Medium is
     the Message: An Inventory of Effects. New York:
     Random House, 1967. (157p)

104. _____. War and Peace in the Global Village. New
     York: McGraw, 1968. (191p)

105. McQuail, Denis. Communication. London and New York:
     Longman, 1975. (229p)

106. McQuail, Denis and Sven Windahl. Communication Models
     for the Study of Mass Communications. Harlow:
     Longman, 1981. (100p)

107. Maisel, Richard. "The decline of mass media." Public
     Opinion Quarterly 37 (Summer 1973): 159-170.

108. Mander, Jerry. Four Arguments for the Elimination of
     Television. New York: Morrow, 1978. (371p)

109. Manvell, Roger. This Age of Communication: Press,
     Books, Films, Radio, TV. Glasgow and London:
     Blackie, 1966. (166p)

110. Mast, Gerald and Marshall Cohen, comp. Film Theory
     and Criticism; Introductory Readings. New York:
     Oxford University Press, 1974. (639p)

111. Meadows, Paul. "The press and the communications
     media: a technological perspective." International
     Journal of Comparative Sociology 21 (March/June
     1980): 65-73.

X112. Media and Change. Edited by J.A.F. Van Zye and K. G.
       Tomaselli. Johannesburg: McGraw-Hill, 1977. (168p)

113. Meline, Caroline W. "Does the medium matter?" Jour-
     nal of Communication 26 (Summer 1976): 81-89.

114. Mendelsohn, Harold A. "Behaviorism, functionalism,
     and mass communications policy." Public Opinion
     Quarterly 28 (Fall 1974): 379-389.

115. _____. Mass Entertainment. New Haven, CT: College
     and University Press, 1966. (203p)

116. Menon, Narayana. The Communications Revolution. New
     Delhi: National Book Trust, 1976. (89p)

117. Meringoff, Laurene K. "Influence of the medium on
     children's story apprehension." Journal of Educa-
     tional Psychology 72 (April 1980): 240-249.

118. Merrill, John C. and Ralph L. Lowenstein. Media,
     Messages, and Men; New Perspectives in Communication.
     New York: McKay, 1973, c 1971. (293p)

119. Merritt, Richard L. "Transforming international com-
     munications strategies." Political Communication
     and Persuasion 1, no. 1 (1980): 5-42.

120. Metz, Christian. Film Language; A Semiotics of the
     Cinema. Trans. by Michael Taylor. New York: Ox-
     ford University Press, 1974. (268p)

121. Mitchell, W.J.T. The Language of Images. Chicago:
     University of Chicago Press, 1980. (307p)

122. Monaco, James. How to Read a Film: The Art, Tech-
     nology, Language, History, and Theory of Film and
     Media. New York: Oxford University Press, 1977.
     (502p)

123. Mortensen, Calvin D., comp. Basic Readings in Com-
     munication Theory. New York: Harper and Row, 1973.
     (358p)

124. Morton, Patricia R. "Riesman's Theory of Social Char-
     acter Applied to Consumer-Goods Advertising." Jour-
     nalism Quarterly 44 (Summer 1967): 337-340.

125. Mousseau, Jacques, ed. Les Communications de Masse;
     L'Univers des Masse Media. Paris: Hachette, 1972.
     (506p)

126. Nevitt, Barrington. "Pipeline or grapevine: the
     changing communications environment." Technology
     and Culture 21 (April 1980): 217-226.

127. Newcomb, Horace. TV: The Most Popular Art. Garden
      City, NY: Anchor Press, 1974. (272p)

128. Nichols, Bill, ed. Movies and Methods: An Anthology.
      Berkeley: University of California Press, 1976.
      (640p)

129. Olson, David R., ed. Media and Symbols: The Forms of
      Expression, Communication, and Education. Chicago:
      National Society for the Study of Education, 1974.
      (508p)

130. Ong, Walter J. Interfaces of the Word. Ithaca:
      Cornell University Press, 1977. (352p)

131. _____. The Presence of the Word. New Haven: Yale
      University Press, 1967. (360p)

132. _____. Rhetoric, Romance and Technology. Ithaca:
      Cornell University Press, 1971 (348p)

133. Oyer, Herbert J. and E. Jane Oyer, ed. Aging and Com-
      munication. Baltimore: University Park Press, 1976.
      (302p)

134. Parmar, Shyam. Traditional Folk Media in India. New
      Delhi: Geka, 1975. (176p)

135. Perry, Ted. "The seventh art as sixth sense." Educa-
      tional Theatre Journal 21 (March 1969): 28-35.

136. Petric, Vlada. "Sight and sound: counterpoint or en-
      tity?" Filmmakers Newsletter 6 (May 1973): 27-31.

137. Petty, Richard E. et al, eds. Cognitive Responses to
      Persuasion. Hillsdale, NJ: Laurence Erlbaum, 1981.
      (476p)

138. Phelan, John M. Disenchantment: Meaning and Morality
      in the Media. New York: Hastings, 1980. (191p)

139. Piecewicz, Robert E. "Computers and society: some
      principles, theorems, and assertions." Computers
      and People 26 (April 1977): 13-16.

140. Potts, James. "Is there an international film
      language?" Sight & Sound 48 (Spring 1979): 74-81.

141. Pryluck, Calvin. "Meaning in film/video: order, time
      and ambiguity." Journal of Broadcasting 26 (Summer
      1982): 685-695.

142. Quinn, James. The Film and Television, An Aspect of
      European Culture. Leiden: Lythoff, 1968. (168p)

143. Read, Hadley. Communication: Methods for All Media.
      Urbana: University of Illinois Press, 1972. (307p)

144. Rege, G. M. "Poster as an effective medium of communi-
      cation." Social Bulletin 12 (1963): 34-39.

145. Reitberger, Reinhold and Wolfgang Fuchs. Comics:
      Anatomy of a Mass Medium. Boston: Little, Brown,
      1972. (264p)

146. Riesman, David. "The oral tradition, the written word,
      and the screen." Film Culture 2, no. 3 (1956): 1-5.

147. Robinovitch, Sidney P. "Information and Utopia: the
      aesthetic transformation of man's symbolic environ-
      ment." Ph.D. dissertation, University of Illinois,
      1970. (231p)

148. Robinson, Henry P. Pictorial Effect in Photography;
      Being Hints on Composition and Chiaroscuro for Pho-
      tographers. London: Piper and Carter, 1869. (199p)

149. Rogers, Bob. "Photography and the photographic image."
      Art Journal 38 (Fall 1978): 29-35.

150. Rollin, Roger B. "In the family: television's re-
      formation of comedy." Psychocultural Review 2 (Fall
      1978): 275-286.

151. Rosenblum, Barbara. "Style as social process." Amer-
      ican Sociological Review 43 (June 1978): 422-438.

152. Ruben, Brent D. and John Y. Kim, ed. General Systems
      Theory and Human Communication. Rochelle Park, NJ:
      Hayden, 1975. (272p)

153. Sackman, Harold. Mass Information Utilities and Social
      Excellence. Princeton: Auerbach, 1971. (284p)

154. Salt, Barry. "Film style and technology in the for-
      ties." Film Quarterly 31 (Fall 1977): 46-57.

155. Sarris, Andrew. "Notes on the Auteur Theory in 1970."
      Film Comment 6 (Fall 1970): 6-9.

156. Scanlon, T. Joseph. "Color television: new language?"
      Journalism Quarterly 44 (Summer 1967): 225-230.

157. Schramm, Wilbur L. "Information theory and mass com-
      munication." Journalism Quarterly 32 (1955): 131-146.

158. _____. Men, Messages, and Media; A Look at Human
      Communication. New York: Harper and Row, 1973.
      (341p)

159. _____. The Process and Effects of Mass Communica-
     tion. Urbana: University of Illinois Press, 1954.
     (586p)

160. Schramm, Wilbur L. and Donald F. Roberts, ed. The
     Process and Effects of Mass Communication. Rev. ed.
     Urbana: University of Illinois Press, c 1971.
     (997p)

161. Schudson, Michael. "The ideal of conversation in the
     study of mass media." Communication Research 5 (Ju-
     ly 1978): 320-329.

162. Schwartz, Barry N., ed. Human Connection and the New
     Media. Englewood Cliffs, NJ: Prentice-Hall, 1973.
     (179p)

163. Sellers, Leonard L. and William L. Rivers, ed. Mass
     Media Issues. Englewood Cliffs, NJ: Prentice-Hall,
     1977. (370p)

164. Sereno, Kenneth K. and Calvin D. Mortensen. Founda-
     tions of Communication Theory. New York: Harper
     and Row, 1970. (371p)

165. Shepardson, Philip C. "Paddy Chayefsky's Marty, a
     study of the prototype shaped by the medium." Ph.D.
     dissertation, University of Massachusetts, 1977.
     (145p)

166. Shook, Frederick. The Process of Electronic News
     Gathering. Englewood, CO: Morton, 1982. (180p)

167. Sitney, P. Adams. "The idea of morphology: the first
     of four lectures on film theory." Film Culture 53,
     54, 55 (Spring 1972): 1-24.

168. Smythe, Dallas W. "Some observations on communications
     theory." Audiovisual Communication Review 2 (1954):
     24-37.

169. Solomon, Stanley J. The Film Idea. New York: Har-
     court Brace Jovanovich, 1972. (403p)

170. Sontag, Susan. "Photography unlimited." New York Re-
     view of Books 24 (23 June 1977): 25-32.

171. Stanley, Robert H. and Charles S. Steinberg. The Media
     Environment: Mass Communications in American Society.
     New York: Hastings House, c 1976. (306p)

172. Stott, William. Documentary Expression and Thirties
     America. New York: Oxford University Press, 1973.
     (361p)

173. Taft, Robert. Photography and the American Scene; A
      Social History, 1839-1889. New York: Macmillan,
      1938. (546p)

174. Talbot, Daniel, ed. Film: An Anthology. New York:
      Simon and Schuster, 1959. (650p)

175. Trachtenberg, Alan. "The camera and Dr. Barnardo."
      Aperture 19 (1975): 68-77.

176. Tucker, William T. "Experiments in aesthetic communi-
      cations." Ph.D. dissertation, University of Illi-
      nois, 1955. (115p)

177. Tudor, Andrew. Theories of Film. New York: Viking
      Press, 1974, c 1973. (168p)

178. Tyler, Parker. The Shadow of an Airplane Climbs the
      Empire State Building; a World Theory of Film. Gar-
      den City, NY: Doubleday, 1972. (248p)

179. Vedin, Bengt-Arne. New Media Survey: A Decision-
      Maker's Guide to the Communications Explosion. Lon-
      don: Nord Media; Elms Ford, NY: Distributed in the
      U.S. by Pergamon Press, 1978. (99p)

180. Victoria, Marcos. El Cine y el teléfono. Buenos
      Aires: Editorial Américalee, 1971. (150p)

181. Walker, David. "McLuhan explains the media." Execu-
      tive 6 (August 1964): 22-27.

182. Webster, B. R. Access: Technology and Access to Com-
      munications Media. Paris: UNESCO, 1975. (54p)

183. Weingartner, Charles. "Synergistic manipulation."
      ETC 36 (Winter 1979): 371-377.

184. West, Charles. The Social and Psychological Distortion
      of Information. Chicago: Nelson-Hall, 1981. (147p)

185. White, Minor. "Lyrical and accurate; a new definition
      of the characteristics of pure photography." Image 5
      (October 1956): 172-181.

186. Whiting, John R. Photography Is a Language. Chicago:
      Ziff-Davis, 1946. (142p)

187. Wicclair, Mark R. "Film theory and Hugo Münsterberg's
      'The film: a psychological study.'" Journal of
      Aesthetic Education 12 (July 1978): 33-50.

188. Wiener, Norbert. Cybernetics, or Control and Communi-
      cation in the Animal and the Machine. New York:
      Wiley, 1948. (194p)

189.   Williams, Patrick and Joan T. Pearce. The Vital Net-
        work: A Theory of Communication and Society. West-
        port, CT: Greenwood Press, 1978. (111p)

190.   Williams, Raymond. Television: Technology and Cul-
        tural Form. London: Fontana, 1974. (160p)

191.   Williams, Raymond, ed. Contact: Human Communication
        and Its History. New York: Thames and Hudson, 1981.
        (272p)

192.   Wilson, C. Edward. "The effect of medium on loss of
        information." Journalism Quarterly 51 (Spring 1974):
        111-115.

193.   Wollen, Peter. Signs and Meaning in the Cinema. 3rd
        ed. Bloomington: Indiana University Press, 1972.
        (175p)

194.   Woodward, Kathleen, ed. The Myths of Information:
        Technology and Postindustrial Culture. Madison:
        Coda Press, 1980. (250p)

195.   Worth, Sol. "Film as a non-art: an approach to the
        study of film." American Scholar 35 (Spring 1966):
        322-334.

196.   Zettl, Herbert. Sight, Sound, Motion; Applied Modern
        Aesthetics. Belmont, CA: Wadsworth, 1973. (401p)

2
The History of Technological Development and Innovation in Communication

A. COMMUNICATIONS TECHNOLOGIES (GENERAL)

197. "AP's digital darkroom breaks new ground." Editor and Publisher 110 (16 April 1977): 15+.

198. Abramson, Norman and Franklin F. Kuo. Computer-Communication Networks. Englewood Cliffs, NJ: Prentice-Hall, 1973. (525p)

199. Appleyard, Rollo. Pioneers of Electrical Communications. London: Macmillan, 1930. (347p)

200. Barnes, Sherman B. "The beginnings of learned journalism, 1665-1730." Ph.D. dissertation, Cornell University, 1934. (338p)

201. Beck, Arnold H.W. Words and Waves. New York: McGraw-Hill, 1967. (255p)

202. Blair, C. M. "The challenge of technology in communications." Journalism Quarterly 40 (1963): 419-424.

203. Bretz, R. Media for Satellite Communication. Rand Paper 5381. February 1975. (20p)

204. Charyk, J. V. "Communications satellites." Journal of Spacecraft and Rockets 14 (July 1977): 385-394.

205. Christians, Cliff. "Home video systems: a revolution?" Journal of Broadcasting 17 (Spring 1973): 223-234.

206. Clark, Ronald W. The Scientific Breakthrough: The Impact of Modern Invention. New York: Putnam, 1974. (205p)

207. Coggeshall, Ivan S. "The compatible technologies of
      wire and radio." Proceedings of the Institute of
      Radio Engineers 50 (May 1962): 892-896.

208. Collings, Robert. A Voice from Afar: The History of
      Telecommunications in Canada. Toronto: McGraw-Hill
      Ryerson, 1977. (304p)

209. Computers and Telecommunications: Economic, Technical,
      and Social Issues. Paris: Organization for Eco-
      nomic Cooperation and Development, 1973. (222p)

210. Crawley, Chetwode G. From Telegraphy to Television;
      The Story of Electrical Communication. London:
      Warne, 1931. (212p)

211. Dennis, Ervin A. and John D. Jenkins. Comprehensive
      Graphic Arts. Indianapolis: Sams, 1974. (548p)

212. Dunlap, Orrin E. Communications in Space: From Wire-
      less to Satellite Relay. New York: Harper, 1962.
      (175p)

213. _____. Radio's 100 Men of Science; Biographical
      Narratives of Pathfinders in Electronics and Tele-
      vision. New York: Harper, 1944. (294p)

214. Edelson, B. I. and L. Pollack. "Satellite communica-
      tions." Science 195 (18 March 1977): 1125-1133.

215. Electronic Message Systems: The Technological, Market
      and Regulatory Prospects. Cambridge: Kalba Bowen
      Associates and Center for Policy Alternatives, MIT,
      1978. (243,51p)

216. Fabre, Maurice. A History of Communications. Adapted
      from the French by Peter Chastin. New York: Haw-
      thorn, 1963. (105p)

217. Farber, D. and Paul Baran. "Convergence of computing
      and telecommunications systems." Science 195 (18
      March 1977): 1166-1170.

218. Farrar, Ronald T. and John D. Stevens, ed. Mass Media
      and the National Experience; Essays in Communications
      History. New York: Harper and Row, 1971. (196p)

219. Fedida, Sam and Rex Malik. Viewdata Revolution. New
      York: Wiley, 1979. (186p)

220. "Fiftieth anniversary edition." Proceedings of the
      Institute of Radio Engineers 50 (May 1962): 529-1448.

221. Gallawa, R. L. et al. Telecommunication Alternatives
      with Emphasis on Optical Waveguide Systems. October
      1975. (116p) NTIS - COM-75-11467/8GA.

222. Gelatt, Roland. The Fabulous Phonograph: 1877-1977.
      3rd ed. New York: Macmillan, 1977. (349p)

223. Godechot, T. "The origin of mass communication media:
      the coverage of the French press during the Revolu-
      tion." Gazette; International Journal of the Science
      of the Press 8 (1962): 81-88.

224. Goldmark, Peter C. Maverick Inventor; My Turbulent
      Years at CBS. New York: Saturday Review Press, 1973.
      (278p)

225. Green, E. I. "The evolving technology of communica-
      tion." Electrical Engineering 78 (May 1959): 470-480.

226. Gumpert, Gary. "The rise of mini-comm." Journal of
      Communication 20 (September 1970): 280-290.

227. Handel, S. The Electronic Revolution. Baltimore: Pen-
      guin, 1967. (252p)

228. Head, Sydney W. and Christopher H. Sterling. Broad-
      casting in America: A Survey of Television, Radio,
      and New Technologies. 4th ed. Boston: Houghton
      Mifflin, 1982. (642p)

229. Henderson, Madeline M. and Marcia J. MacNaughton, eds.
      Electronic Communication: Technology and Impacts.
      Boulder, CO: Westview Press, for the American Asso-
      ciation for the Advancement of Science, 1980. (173p)

230. Hogben, Lancelot T. The Wonderful World of Communica-
      tion. Garden City, NY: Doubleday, 1969. (96p)

231. Hopewell, Lynn et al., ed. Computers and Communica-
      tions; FCC Planning Conference. Montval, NJ: AFIPS
      Press, 1976. (197p)

232. Howeth, Linwood S. History of Communications—Electron-
      ics in the United States Navy. Washington, D.C.:
      G.P.O., 1963. (657p)

233. International Telecommunication Union. From Semaphore
      to Satellite. Geneva, 1965. (343p)

234. Ivins, William M. How Prints Look: Photographs With a
      Commentary. Boston: Beacon Press, 1968, c 1943.
      (164p)

235. _____. Prints and Visual Communication. Cambridge:
      Harvard University Press, 1953. (190p)

236. Kesterson, Wilfred H. A History of Journalism in Cana-
      da. Toronto: McClelland and Stewart, 1976. (304p)

237. Kohlhass, H. T. "Milestones of communication progress."
      Electrical Communication 20 (1942): 143-185.

238.   Kunzle, David. The Early Comic Strip: Narrative
        Strips and Picture Stories in the European Broad-
        sheet from c. 1450 to 1825. Berkeley: University
        of California Press, 1973. (471p)

239.   Lichty, Lawrence W. and Malachai C. Topping. American
        Broadcasting; A Source Book on the History of Radio
        and Television. New York: Hastings House, 1975.

240.   Marland, Edward A. Early Electrical Communication.
        New York: Abelard-Schuman, 1964. (220p)

241.   Mayo, J. S. "Evolution of the intelligent telecommuni-
        cations network." Science 215 (12 February 1982):
        830-837.

242.   Meeting of Experts on the Use of Space Communication
        by the Mass Media, Paris, 1965. Paris: UNESCO,
        1965. (32p)

243.   Mennie, D. "Communications and microwave technology."
        IEEE Spectrum 14 (January 1977): 43-48.

244.   Nash, Deanna C. and John B. Smith. Interactive Home
        Media and Privacy. Washington, D.C.: Collingwood,
        1981. (113p)

245.   National Research Council. Telecommunications for
        Metropolitan Area: Opportunities for the 1980s.
        Washington, D.C.: National Research Council, 1978.
        (111p)

246.   Neal, Harry E. Communication From Stone Age to Space
        Age. New York: Messner, 1960. (192p)

247.   Papermaking, Art and Craft. Washington, D.C.: Library
        of Congress, 1968. (96p)

248.   Pelton, Joseph N. and Marcellus S. Snow, ed. Economic
        and Policy Problems in Satellite Communication. New
        York: Praeger, 1977. (242p)

249.   Perucca, Eligio and Vittorio Gori. "Pioneers in elec-
        trical communications." Journal of the Franklin In-
        stitute 261 (January 1956): 61-79.

250.   Pierce, John R. The Beginnings of Satellite Communi-
        cations. San Francisco: San Francisco Press, 1968.
        (61p)

251.   Pupin, Michael I. "Fifty years' progress in electrical
        communication." Science 64 (31 December 1926): 631-
        638.

252.   Read, Oliver and Walter L. Welch. From Tinfoil to
        Stereo: Evolution of the Phonograph. 2nd ed. Indi-
        anapolis: Sams, 1976. (550p)

253. Rhodes, J.G.L. "Advanced developments in telecommunication." Electronics and Power 22 (June 1976): 373-375.

254. "Satellites play major role in UPI's news distribution." Editor and Publisher 110 (30 April 1977): 52.

255. Schicke, C. A. Revolution in Sound: A Biography of the Recording Industry. Boston: Little, Brown, 1974. (246p)

256. Sigel, Efrem et al. Video Discs: The Technology, the Applications, and the Future. White Plains, NY: Knowledge Industry Publications, 1980. (183p)

257. Sivowitch, Elliot N. "A technological survey of broadcasting's 'pre-history', 1876-1920." Journal of Broadcasting 15 (Winter 1970-71): 1-20.

258. Smith, Delbert D. Communication Via Satellite: A Vision in Retrospect. Leyden; Boston: A. W. Sÿthoff, 1976. (335p)

259. Smith, R. B. "The genesis of the business press in the United States." Journal of Marketing 19 (1954): 146-151.

260. Still, Alfred. Communication Through the Ages; From Sign Language to Television. New York: Murray Hill, 1946. (201p)

261. Tyne, Gerald F. Saga of the Vacuum Tube. Indianapolis: Sams, 1977. (494p)

262. Van Trees, Harry L., ed. Satellite Communications. New York: Wiley, 1979. (665p)

263. Vries, Leonard de. The Book of Telecommunication; Telegraph, Telephone, Radio—In the Past, Present, and Future. Trans. by Karla Oosterveen. New York: Macmillan, 1962. (131p)

264. Wile, Frederick W. Emile Berliner, Maker of the Microphone. Indianapolis: Bobbs-Merrill, 1926. (353p)

265. Winkler, Stanley, ed. Computer Communications: Impacts and Implications. (First International Conference on Computer Communication.) New York: IEEE, 1972. (501p)

266. Withrow, Frank W. "Technology and the deaf learner." Journal of Educational Technology Systems 7, no. 1 (1978-1979): 3-6.

267. Woods, David L. Signaling and Communicating at Sea. New York: Arno Press, 1980. (2 vols.)

B.   BOOKS AND PRINTING

268.   Arnold, Edmund C.   Ink on Paper.   New York: Harper,
       1963.   (324p)

269.   Audin, Maurice.   Histoire de l'imprimerie; Radioscopie
       d'une ère: de Gutenberg à l'informatique.   Paris:
       Picard, 1972.   (480p)

270.   Audin, Marius.   Histoire de l'imprimerie par l'image.
       4 vols.   Paris: Jonquières, 1928-29.

271.   Bagrow, Leo.   History of Cartography.   Rev. and enl.
       by R. A. Skelton.   Trans. by D. L. Paisey.   Cam-
       bridge: Harvard University Press, 1964.   (312p)

272.   Batey, Charles.   The Printing and Making of Books; An
       Examination of Tradition With an Assessment of the
       Trends of Invention and the Development of Techniques
       Presently Discernable in the Several Crafts Devoted
       to the Making of Books.   Oxford: University Press,
       1954.   (30p)

273.   Berry, W. Turner and Edmund H. Poole.   Annals of
       Printing; A Chronological Encyclopaedia From the
       Earliest Times to 1950.   Toronto: University of
       Toronto Press, 1966.   (315p)

274.   Bloy, Colin H.   A History of Printing Ink, Balls and
       Rollers, 1440-1850.   London: Wynkyn de Worde Soci-
       ety, 1972, c 1967.   (147p)

275.   Blum, André S.   The Origins of Printing and Engraving.
       Trans. by Harry M. Lydenberg.   New York: Scribner's,
       1940.   (226p)

276.   Brooks, E. B.   "Platemaking: its history and develop-
       ment."   Inland Printer/American Lithographer 179
       (April 1977):   72.

277.   Bruno, Michael H.   "How new printing technology affects
       paper requirements."   Tappi 64 (May 1981):   41-45.

278.   _____.   "A look at new technology: trends for the
       industry."   Inland Printer/American Lithographer 180
       (January 1978):   38-43.

279.   _____.   "1977:   the new technology."   Inland Printer/
       American Lithographer 178 (January 1977):   36-41.

280.   Bühler, Curt F.   The Fifteenth Century Book: The
       Scribes, the Printers, the Decorators.   Philadelphia:
       University of Pennsylvania Press, 1960.   (195p)

281. Butler, Pierce. The Origin of Printing in Europe.
      Chicago: University of Chicago Press, 1940. (154p)

282. Carter, Thomas F. The Invention of Printing in China
      and Its Spread Westward. Rev. ed. New York: Co-
      lumbia University Press, 1931. (282p)

283. "Computer composition systems evolving rapidly." Pub-
      lishers Weekly 206 (5 August 1974): 39-40.

284. Davis, Alec. Package and Print: The Development of
      Container and Label Design. London: Faber and Fa-
      ber, 1967. (208p)

285. Diehl, Edith. Bookbinding, Its Background and Tech-
      nique. 2 vols. New York: Rinehart, 1946.

286. Diringer, David. The Alphabet: A Key to the History
      of Mankind. 2 vols. 3rd ed. New York: Funk and
      Wagnalls, 1968.

287. Doebler, P. D. "Making up pages on video screens:
      the last frontier." Publishers Weekly 209 (1 March
      1976): 74-75.

288. Durrant, W. R., et al. Machine Printing. New York:
      Hastings House, 1973. (245p)

289. Frankenthaler, M. R. "Utilizing the computer to pre-
      pare a manuscript." Scholarly Publishing 7 (January
      1976): 161-168.

290. Gaskell, Philip. A New Introduction to Bibliography.
      New York: Oxford University Press, 1972. (438p)

291. Grannis, Chandler, comp. Heritage of the Graphic Arts.
      New York: Bowker, 1972. (291p)

292. Griffith, A. K. "From Gutenberg to GRAFIX 1; new
      directions in optical character recognition." Jour-
      nal of Micrographics 9 (November 1975): 81-89.

293. Handover, P. M. Printing in London from 1476 to Modern
      Times. London: Allen and Unwin, 1960. (224p)

294. Harrison, Frederick. A Book About Books. London:
      Murray, 1943. (264p)

295. Hattery, Lowell H. and George P. Bush. Automation and
      Electronics in Publishing. Washington: Spartan,
      1965. (206p)

296. _____, ed. Technological Change in Printing and
      Publishing. Washington: Spartan, 1973. (275p)

297. Heal, Ambrose. The English Writing-Masters and Their
      Copy Books, 1570-1800. Cambridge: Cambridge Uni-
      versity Press, 1931. (225p)

298. Heuterman, Thomas H. Movable Type; Biography of
      Legh R. Freeman. Ames: Iowa State University Press,
      1979. (172p)

299. Hind, Arthur M. An Introduction to a History of Wood-
      cut. 2 vols. London: Constable, 1935.

300. _____. A Short History of Engraving and Etching.
      London: Constable, 1908. (473p)

301. Hopkins, Richard L. Origin of the American Point Sys-
      tem for Printers' Type Measurement. Terra Alta, WV:
      Hill and Dale, 1976. (100p)

302. Jennett, Sean. Pioneers in Printing: Johann Gutenberg,
      William Caxton, William Caslon, John Baskerville,
      Alois Senefelder, Frederick Koenig, Ottmar Mergen-
      thaler, Tolbert Lanston. London: Routledge and
      Paul, 1958. (196p)

303. Johnson, Elmer D. Communication: An Introduction to
      the History of Writing, Printing, Books, and Li-
      braries. 4th ed. Metuchen, NJ: Scarecrow Press,
      1973. (322p)

304. King, A. Hyatt. Four Hundred Years of Music Printing.
      London: British Museum, 1964. (48p)

305. Levarie, Norma. The Art and History of Books. New
      York: Heineman, 1968. (315p)

306. McKerrow, Ronald B. An Introduction to Bibliography
      for Literary Students. Oxford: Clarendon Press,
      1927. (358p)

307. McMurtrie, Douglas C. The Book; The Story of Printing
      and Bookmaking. New York: Covici-Friede, 1937.
      (676p)

308. Meadows, A. J., ed. Development of Science Publishing
      in Europe. New York: Elsevier, 1980. (270p)

309. Mertle, J. S. "The chronology of lithography." Modern
      Lithographer 53 (March 1957): 24-26.

310. Moran, James. The Composition of Reading Matter; A
      History From Case to Computer. London: Wace, 1965.
      (84p)

311. _____. Printing Presses: History and Development
      from the Fifteenth Century to Modern Times. Berkeley:
      University of California Press, 1973.

312. Morison, Stanley. First Principles of Typography.
      New York: Macmillan, 1936. (29p)

313. Neilly, Andrew H. "Publishing and technological de-.
      velopments: an interim report—Part 1." Computers
      and People 25 (April 1976): 24-25.

314. _____. "Publishing and technological developments:
      an interim report—Part 2." Computers and People 25
      (May 1976): 16-19.

315. Peter, John. "The new typography." Folio 5 (April
      1976): 35-37.

316. "Print technology for modern times." New Scientist 89
      (12 February 1981): 386.

317. Printing and the Mind of Man, Assembled at the British
      Museum and at Earls Court, London, 16-27 July 1963.
      (International Printing Machinery and Allied Trades
      Exhibition, 1963.) London: Bridges, 1963. (61p)

318. Proudfoot, W. B. The Origin of Stencil Duplicating.
      London: Hutchinson, 1972. (128p)

319. Simon, Oliver. Introduction to Typography. 2nd ed.
      Edited by David Bland. London: Faber and Faber,
      1963. (164p)

320. Smith, Roger H. Paperback Parnassus: The Birth, De-
      velopment, the Pending Crisis of the Modern American
      Paperbound Book. Boulder: Westview, 1975. (111p)

321. Spencer, Herbert. Pioneers of Modern Typography.
      London: Humphries, 1969. (159p)

322. Steinberg, Sigfrid H. Five Hundred Years of Printing.
      3rd ed. Harmondsworth, England and Baltimore: Pen-
      guin, 1974. (400p)

323. Strauss, Victor. The Printing Industry. New York:
      Bowker, 1967. (813p)

324. Thomas, Isaiah. The History of Printing in America.
      2 vols. Worcester: Isaiah Thomas, 1810.

325. Twyman, Michael. Printing 1770-1970: An Illustrated
      History of Its Development and Uses in England.
      London: Eyre and Spotiswoode, 1970. (283p)

326. Walker, Jerome H. "Photocomp inventor tags it 'explo-
      sion'—not revolution." Editor and Publisher 109
      (5 June 1976): 19-20.

327. Warde, Beatrice. The Crystal Goblet; Sixteen Essays on
      Typography. Selected and edited by Henry Jacob.
      London: Sylvan Press, 1955.

328. Wilson, Adrian. The Design of Books. New York:
      Reinhold, 1967. (159p)

329. Zeisler, Karl F. "The 'revolution' in printing: a
      critical appraisal." Journalism Quarterly 26 (Sep-
      tember 1949): 281-290.

                        C.   MAGAZINES

330. Allen, Frederick L. "The American magazine grows up."
      Atlantic 180 (November 1947): 77-81.

331. Bennison, Sherilyn C. "Mass magazine phenomenon: the
      German 'Illustrierte.'" Journalism Quarterly 38
      (1961): 360-362.

332. Bogart, Leo. "Magazines since the rise of television."
      Journalism Quarterly 33 (1956): 153-166.

333. Charnley, M. V. "The rise of the weekly magazine in
      Italy." Journalism Quarterly 30 (1953): 472-481.

334. Fischer, Heinz D., ed. Deutsche Zeitschriften des 17.
      bis 20. Jahrhunderts. Pullach/München: Verlag
      Dokumentation, 1973. (445p)

335. Graham, Walter J. Beginnings of English Literary Peri-
      odicals, A Study of Periodical Literature, 1665-1715.
      London: Oxford University Press, 1926. (92p)

336. Kahan, Robert S. "Magazine photography begins: an
      editorial negative." Journalism Quarterly 42 (Winter
      1965): 53-59.

337. Kronick, David A. A History of Scientific and Techni-
      cal Periodicals: The Origins and Development of the
      Scientific and Technical Press, 1665-1790. 2nd ed.
      Metuchen, NJ: Scarecrow Press, 1976. (336p)

338. Laib, J. "The trade press." Public Opinion Quarterly
      19 (1955-1956): 31-44.

339. Mott, Frank L. A History of American Magazines. 4
      vols. Cambridge: Harvard University Press, 1938.
      (Vol. 1: 1741-1850; vol. 2: 1850-1865; vol. 3:
      1865-1885; vol. 4: 1885-1905).

340. Norton, Wesley. Religious Newspapers in the Old
      Northwest to 1861; A History, Bibliography and Record
      of Opinion. Athens: Ohio University Press, 1977.
      (196p)

341. Peterson, Theodore. Magazines in the Twentieth Cen-
      tury. Urbana: University of Illinois Press, 1956.
      (457p)

342. Tassin, Algernon. The Magazine in America. New York:
      Dodd, Mead, 1916. (374p)

343. Wiles, Roy M. Serial Publication in England Before
      1750. Cambridge: University Press, 1957. (391p)

                       D. NEWSPAPERS

344. Allen, Eric W. "International origins of the news-
      paper; the establishment of periodicity in print."
      Journalism Quarterly 7 (1930): 307-319.

345. Bagdikian, Ben H. "Newspapers: learning (too slowly)
      to adapt to TV." Columbia Journalism Review 12 (No-
      vember/December 1973): 44-51.

346. "Communications satellite service for publishers."
      Editor and Publisher 109 (5 June 1976): 77-78+.

347. Cox, Harvey and David Morgan. City Politics and the
      Press; Journalists and the Governing of Merseyside.
      Cambridge, Eng.: University Press, 1973. (159p)

348. Cranford, R. J. "Effects of the teletypesetter upon
      newspaper practices." Journalism Quarterly 29
      (1952): 181-186.

349. Everett, George. "Printing technology as a barrier to
      multi-column headlines, 1850-95." Journalism Quar-
      terly 53 (Autumn 1976): 528-532.

350. "44 dailies converted to offset in 1976." Editor and
      Publisher 110 (16 April 1977): 25.

351. Gidal, Tim N. Modern Photojournalism Origin and Evo-
      lution, 1910-1933. New York: Macmillan, 1973.
      (96p)

352. Hanson, J. J. "They laughed when I sat down at the
      CRT." Folio 5 (October 1976): 57-70.

353. Howe, Ellic. Newspaper Printing in the Nineteenth
      Century. London: Printed Privately, 1943. (43p)

354. Hutt, Allen. The Changing Newspaper: Typographic
      Trends in Britain and America, 1622-1972. London:
      Gordon Fraser, 1973. (224p)

355. Isaacs, George A. The Story of the Newspaper Printing
      Press. London: Co-operative Printing Society, 1931.
      (287p)

356. Johnson, W. Thomas and L. Lee Moore. Automatic News-
      paper Composition. Boston: Nimrod, 1966. (167p)

357. Lister, Hal. The Suburban Press: A Separate Journal-
      ism. Columbia, MO: Lucas, 1975. (226p)

358. Marzio, Peter C. The Men and Machines of American
      Journalism: A Pictorial Essay from the Henry Luce
      Hall of News Reporting. Washington: National Mu-
      seum of History and Technology, 1973. (144p)

359. Mayer, Peter C. "Technical change in the typesetting
      of daily newspapers." Ph.D. dissertation, Univer-
      sity of California, Berkeley, 1969. (175p)

360. Mich, D. D. "The rise of photojournalism in the
      United States." Journalism Quarterly 24 (1947):
      202-238.

361. Morison, Stanley. The English Newspaper; Some Accounts
      of the Physical Development of Journals Printed in
      London Between 1622 and the Present Day. Cambridge:
      University Press, 1932. (335p)

362. Pickett, Calder M. "Technological developments came
      in time for gusty newspapers battles, sensationalism."
      Publisher's Auxiliary 110 (25 October 1975): 27-28.

363. _____. "Technology and the New York press in the
      19th century." Journalism Quarterly 37 (Summer 1960):
      398-407.

364. Pred, Allan R. Urban Growth and the Circulation of
      Information: The United States System of Cities,
      1790-1840. Cambridge: Harvard University Press,
      1973. (348p)

365. Pride, A. S. "The Negro newspaper in the United
      States." Gazette; International Journal of the Sci-
      ence of the Press 2 (1956): 141-149.

366. Shaaber, Matthias A. Some Forerunners of the Newspaper
      in England, 1476-1622. London: Oxford University
      Press, 1929. (368p)

367. Smith, Anthony. Goodbye, Gutenberg: The Newspaper
      Revolution of the 1980's. New York: Oxford Univer-
      sity Press, 1980. (367p)

368. Swensson, Paul. "Technology: dream—new machinery is
      boon, not bane, despite many newsroom skeptics."
      Journalism Educator 31 (April 1976): 22-23+.

369. Wendt, Lloyd. Chicago Tribune: The Rise of a Great
      American Newspaper. Chicago: Rand McNally, 1979.
      (861p)

E. TELEGRAPH AND CABLE

370. Bain, Alexander. An Account of Some Remarkable Appli-
       cations of the Electric Fluid to the Useful Arts;
       With a Vindication of His Claim to be the First In-
       ventor of the Electro-Magnetic Printing Telegraph,
       and also of the Electro-Magnetic Clock, by John Fin-
       laison. London: n.p., 1843. (127p)

371. Barty-King, Hugh. Girdle Round the Earth; The Story
       of Cable and Wireless and its Predecessors to Mark
       the Group's Jubilee, 1929-1979. London: Heinemann,
       1979. (413p)

372. Briggs, Charles F. and Augustus Maverick. The Story
       of the Telegraph, and a History of the Great Atlantic
       Cable; A Complete Record of the Inception, Progress,
       and Final Success of that Undertaking. New York:
       Rudd and Carleton, 1858. (255p)

373. Bright, Sir Charles. Imperial Telegraphic Communica-
       tion. London: P. S. King, 1911. (212p)

374. _____. Telegraphy, Aeronautics and War. London:
       Constable, 1918. (407p)

375. Chappe, Ignace V.J. Histoire de la télégraphie.
       Paris: L'auteur, 1824. (268p)

376. Clarke, Arthur C. Voice Across the Sea. London:
       Muller, 1958; New York: Harper, 1958. (220p)

377. Clarke, R. Yorke, ed. Railway Appliances in the Nine-
       teenth Century. 3rd ed. London: Clarke, 1850.
       (84p)

378. Cooke, Sir William Fothergill. The Electric Telegraph:
       Was it Invented by Professor Wheatstone? London:
       Printed for the author, and sold by W. H. Smith,
       1854. (48p)

379. _____. The Electric Telegraph: Was it Invented by
       Professor Wheatstone? A Reply to Mr. Wheatstone's
       Answer. London: Printed for the author, and sold
       by W. H. Smith, 1856. (152p)

380. Dauriac, Philippe. La Télégraphie électrique; Son
       Histoire précise, anecdotique et pittoresque, et ses
       applications en France, en Angleterre, aux Etats-
       Unis, en Belgique, en Hollande, en Suisse, en Espagne,
       en Italie, en Turquie, en Russie, en Perse, dans
       l'Inde, en Cochinchine, etc., suivie d'un guide de
       l'expéditeur de dépêches. Paris: A. Faure, 1864.
       (120p)

381. Dodd, George. Railways, Steamers and Telegraphs; A Glance at Their Recent Progress and Present State. London and Edinburgh: Chambers, 1867. (326p)

382. Eastwood, Eric, comp. Wireless Telegraphy. New York: Wiley, 1974. (391p)

383. The Electric Telegraph: An Historical Anthology. New York: Arno Press, 1977. (600p)

384. Fahie, John J. A History of Electric Telegraphy, to the Year 1837. London and New York: E. and F. N. Spon, 1884. (542p)

385. Fernandez Machado, Benito. Historia del telégrafo en Venezuela. Caracas: Impr. Nacional, 1955. (459p)

386. Fischer, Paul D. Die Telegraphie und das Völkerrecht. Leipzig: 1876. (60p)

387. Goldsmid, Sir Frederic J. Telegraph and Travel; A Narrative of the Formation and Development of Telegraphic Communication between England and India. . . . London: Macmillan, 1874. (673p)

388. Haigh, K. R. Cableships and Submarine Cables. Washington, D.C.: U.S. Undersea Cable Corp., 1968. (405p)

389. Harlow, Alvin F. Old Wires and New Waves; The History of the Telegraph, Telephone, and Wireless. New York and London: Appleton-Century, 1936. (548p)

390. Highton, Edward. The Electric Telegraph: Its History and Progress. London: J. Weale, 1852. (179p)

391. Hubbard, Geoffrey. Cooke and Wheatstone and the Invention of the Electric Telegraph. London: Routledge and K. Paul, 1965. (158p)

392. Johnston, William J., comp. Lightning Flashes and Electric Dashes, a Volume of Choice Telegraphic Literature, Humor, Fun, Wit and Wisdom. New York: Johnston, 1877. (189p)

393. Jones, Alexander. Historical Sketch of the Electric Telegraph: Including its Rise and Progress in the United States. New York: Putnam, 1852. (194p)

394. Kendall, Amos. Morse's Patent. Full exposure of Dr. Charles T. Jackson's pretensions to the invention of the American electro-magnetic telegraph. Paris: printed by A. Chaix, 1868? (80p)

395. Kieve, Jeffrey. The Electric Telegraph: A Social and Economic History. Newton Abbot: David and Charles, 1973. (310p)

396. Marland, Edward A. Early Electrical Communication.
      London and New York: Abelard-Shuman, 1964. (220p)

397. Mendez Moreno, Rafael. El Telégrafo en el destino
      nacional; Cerro de las Campanas en Querétano, 1867-
      1967. Mexico: 1967. (307p)

398. Meyer, Hugo R. The British State Telegraphs; A Study
      of the Problem of a Large Body of Civil Servants in
      a Democracy. New York and London: Macmillan, 1907.
      (408p)

399. Molella, A. P. "Electric motor, the telegraph, and
      Joseph Henry's theory of technological progress."
      Proceedings of the IEEE 64 (September 1976): 1273-
      1278.

400. Morse, Samuel F.B. Modern Telegraphy. Some Errors of
      Dates of Events and of Statements in the History of
      Telegraphy Exposed and Rectified. Paris: Printed
      by A. Chaix, 1868? (38p)

401. Parsons, Frank. The Telegraph Monopoly. Philadelphia:
      Taylor, 1899. (239p)

402. Plum, William R. The Military Telegraph During the
      Civil War in the United States, With an Exposition
      of Ancient and Modern Means of Communication, and of
      Federal and Confederate Cipher Systems. 2 vols.
      Chicago: Jansen, McClurg, 1882.

403. Prescott, George B. History, Theory, and Practice of
      the Electric Telegraph. Boston: Ticknor and Fields,
      1860. (468p)

404. Prime, Samuel I. The Life of Samuel F.B. Morse, In-
      ventor of the Electro-Magnetic Recording Telegraph.
      New York: Appleton, 1875. (776p)

405. Reid, James D. The Telegraph in America. Its Founders,
      Promoters, and Noted Men. New York: Derby, 1879.

406. A Retrospective Technology Assessment: Submarine
      Telegraphy—The Transatlantic Cable of 1866. San
      Francisco: San Francisco Press, 1979. (264p)

407. Sabine, Robert. The History and Progress of the Elec-
      tric Telegraph, With Descriptions of Some of the Ap-
      paratus. 2nd ed., with additions. New York: Lock-
      wood, 1839. (280p)

408. Scowen, F. "Transoceanic submarine telegraphy."
      Electronics and Power 23 (March 1977): 204-206.

409. Shaffners, Taleaferro P. Shaffner's Telegraph Compan-
      ion, Devoted to the Science and Art of the Morse
      American Telegraph. 2 vols. in one. New York:
      Pudney and Russell, 1854-1855.

410. Smith, Willoughby. The Rise and Extension of Submarine
      Telegraphy. London: Virtue, 1891. (390p)

411. Thompson, Robert L. Wiring a Continent, the History
      of the Telegraph Industry in the United States, 1832-
      1866. Princeton: Princeton University Press, 1947.
      (544p)

412. Vail, Alfred. The American Electro Magnetic Telegraph:
      With the Reports of Congress, and a Description of
      All Telegraphs Known, Employing Electricity or Gal-
      vanism. Philadelphia: Lea and Blanchard, 1845.
      (208p)

413. Wilson, Geoffrey. The Old Telegraphs. Totowa, NJ:
      Rowman and Littlefield, 1976. (252p)

                        F. TELEPHONE.

414. Aithen, William. Who Invented the Telephone? London
      and Glasgow: Blackie, 1939. (196p)

415. Baldwin, Francis G.C. The History of the Telephone in
      the United Kingdom. London: Chapman and Hall, 1925;
      New York: Van Nostrand, 1925. (728p)

416. Bell Telephone Laboratories, Inc. A History of En-
      gineering and Science in the Bell System: The Early
      Years, 1875-1925. New York: The Laboratories, 1975.
      (1073p)

417. Biskeborn, M. C. "Phone building blocks and precursors
      of the long distance network." Wire Journal 10 (March
      1977): 90-94.

418. Blanchard, Julian. "A pioneering attempt at multiplex
      telephony." Proceedings of the Institute of Electri-
      cal and Electronics Engineers 51 (December 1963):
      1706-1709.

419. Brooks, John N. Telephone: The First Hundred Years.
      New York: Harper and Row, c 1976. (369p)

420. Falkner, B. H. "Personal radio-telephone can go where
      you go." Communications News 14 (August 1977): 34-35.

421. Flood, J. E. "Alexander Graham Bell and the invention
      of the telephone." Proceedings of the Institution of
      Electrical Engineers 123 (December 1976): 1387-1388.

422. Gray, Elisha. Experimental Researches in Electro-
      Harmonic Telegraphy and Telephony, 1867-1878. New
      York: Russell, 1878. (96p)

423. Hanscom, C. Dean. Dates in American Telephone Tech-
      nology. New York: Bell Telephone Laboratories,
      1961. (148p)

424. Hounshell, David A. "Bell and Gray; contrasts in
      style, politics, and etiquette." Proceedings of the
      IEEE 64 (September 1976): 1305-1314.

425. _____. "Two paths to the telephone; as Alexander
      Graham Bell was developing the telephone, Elisha Gray
      was doing the same. . . ." Scientific American 244
      (January 1981): 156-163.

426. Jacob, I. "Lightwave communications: yesterday, to-
      day, and tomorrow." Bell Laboratories Record 58
      (January 1980): 2-10.

427. Jewett, Frank B. "The telephone switchboard—fifty
      years of history." Bell Telephone Quarterly 7 (July
      1928): 149-165.

428. Kingsbury, John E. The Telephone and Telephone Ex-
      changes; Their Invention and Development. London
      and New York: Longmans, Green, 1915. (558p)

429. Langdon, William C. "Myths of telephone history."
      Bell Telephone Quarterly 12 (1933): 123-140.

430. Lawson, R. "A history of automatic telephony." Post
      Office Electrical Engineers' Journal 5 (1912-1913):
      192-207.

431. Martin, William H. "Seventy-five years of the tele-
      phone: an evolution in technology." Bell System
      Technical Journal 30 (April 1951): 215-238.

432. Mims, Forrest M. "Alexander Graham Bell and the photo-
      phone: the centennial of the invention of light-wave
      communications, 1880-1980." Optics News 6, no. 1
      (1980): 8-16.

433. Osborne, H. S. "Alexander Graham Bell, 1847-1922."
      National Academy of Science, Biographical Memoirs 23
      (1945): 1-29.

434. Pier, Arthur S. Forbes: Telephone Pioneer. New York:
      Dodd, Mead, 1953. (232p)

435. Pierce, John R. Signals: The Telephone and Beyond.
      San Francisco: W. H. Freeman, 1981. (181p)

436.   Prescott, George B.   Bell's Electric Speaking Tele-
       phone: Its Invention, Construction, Application,
       Modification, and History. New York: Appleton,
       1884. (526p)

437.   _____. The Speaking Telephone, Electric Light and
       Other Recent Inventions. 2nd ed. enl. New York:
       Appleton, 1879. (616p)

438.   Rhodes, Frederick L. Beginnings of Telephony. New
       York and London: Harper, 1929. (261p)

439.   Shaw, Thomas. "The conquest of distance by wire tele-
       phony." Bell System Technical Journal 23 (October
       1944): 337-421.

440.   Taylor, Lloyd W. "The untold story of the telephone."
       American Journal of Physics 5 (December 1937): 243-
       251.

441.   The Telephone: An Historical Anthology. New York:
       Arno Press, 1977. (400p)

442.   The Telephone's First Century—and Beyond. New York:
       AT&T Co. in cooperation with Crowell, 1977. (119p)

443.   Thompson, Silvanus P. Philipp Reis, Inventor of the
       Telephone; A Biographical Sketch. London and New
       York: Spon, 1883. (182p)

444.   Watson, Thomas A. The Birth and Babyhood of the Tele-
       phone. New York: Information Dept., AT&T Co., 1940.
       (45p)

445.   _____. "How Bell invented the telephone." Pro-
       ceedings of the American Institute of Electrical En-
       gineers 34 (August 1915): 1503-1513.

446.   Webb, Herbert L. The Development of the Telephone in
       Europe. London: Electrical Press, 1911. (78p)

G.   PHOTOGRAPHY

447.   Ackerman, Carl W. George Eastman. Boston: Houghton
       Mifflin, 1930. (522p)

448.   Auer, Michel. The Illustrated History of the Camera
       From 1839 to the Present. Trans. and adapted by
       D. B. Tubbs. Boston, New York: Graphic Society,
       1975. (285p)

449.   Baier, Wolfgang. A Source Book of Photographic History.
       London: Focal Press, 1964. (704p)

450. Barclay, A. "Early high speed photography." British
      Journal of Photography 103 (16 November 1956): 588-
      593.

451. Berry, Maurice and Lo Duca. Louis Lumière, Inventeur.
      Paris: Editions Prisma, 1948. (130p)

452. Coe, Brian W. The Birth of Photography, The Story of
      the Formative Years, 1800-1900. New York: Tap-
      linger, 1977. (144p)

453. Coke, Van Deren, ed. One Hundred Years of Photographic
      History: Essays in Honor of Beaumont Newhall. Albu-
      querque: University of New Mexico Press, 1975.
      (180p)

454. Crawford, William. The Keepers of the Light: A His-
      tory and Working Guide to Early Photographic
      Processes. Dobbs Ferry, NY: Morgan and Morgan,
      1979. (319p)

455. de Haas, W.G.L. "Technology as a subject of compara-
      tive studies: the case of photography." Comparative
      Studies in Society and History 21 (July 1979): 362-
      371.

456. Eder, Joseph M. The History of Photography. Trans.
      by Edward Epstean. New York: Columbia University
      Press, 1945. (860p)

457. Fouque, Victor. The Truth Concerning the Invention of
      Photography; Nicéphore Niépce, His Life, Letters, and
      Works. Trans. by Edward Epstean. New York: Tennant
      and Ward, 1935. (163p)

458. Fuller, Kathleen. "The darkroom abolished." History
      of Photography 3 (1979): 227-231.

459. Garrett, A. E. The Advance of Photography; Its History
      and Modern Applications. London: Kegan Paul, Trench,
      Trübner, 1911. (382p)

460. Gernsheim, Helmut and Alison Gernsheim. L.G.M.
      Daguerre: The History of the Diorama and the
      Daguerreotype. 2nd rev. ed. New York: Dover,
      1968. (226p)

461. Goldberg, B. H. "Short history of electronic flash."
      Industrial Photography 27 (November 1978): 25-29.

462. Greenhill, Ralph and Andrew Birrell. Canadian pho-
      tography: 1839-1920. Toronto: Coach House; Ro-
      chester: Light Impressions, 1979. (335p)

463. Harmant, Pierre G. and Paul Marillier. "Some Thoughts
      on the World's First Photograph." Photographic
      Journal 107 (April 1967): 130-140.

464. Hepher, M. "The photo-resist story: from Niépce to
     the modern polymer chemist." Journal of Photographic
     Science 12 (July/August 1964): 181-190.

465. "History of photography in America with pen portraits
     of prominent workers." Phrenological Journal 54
     (April/May 1872): 250-258, 298-303.

466. Jahr, R. "The discovery of the gelatin dry plate."
     Photographische Industrie (1925): 1012-1013.

467. Jammes, Andre. William H. Fox Talbot, Inventor of the
     Negative-Positive Process. Trans. by Maureen Oberli-
     Turner. New York: Macmillan, 1973. (96p)

468. Jenkins, Reese V. Images and Enterprise: Technology
     and the American Photographic Industry. Baltimore:
     Johns Hopkins Press, 1975. (372p)

469. Jussim, Estelle. Visual Communication and the Graphic
     Arts: Photographic Technologies in the Nineteenth
     Century. New York: Bowker, 1974. (364p)

470. Knight, Henry. Photography in New Zealand; A Social
     and Technical History. Dunedin: McIndoe, 1971.
     (196p)

471. Lambert, Henry. "Fox-Talbot's photographic inventions."
     Photographic Journal 74 (August 1934): 430-432.

472. Lecuyer, Raymond. Histoire de la photographie. Paris:
     Baschet, 1945. (456p)

473. Leffmann, H. "The earliest apparatus and procedures of
     photography: contributions to the centenary of mod-
     ern photographic methods." Journal of the Franklin
     Institute 195 (1923): 327-336.

474. Lothrop, Eaton S. A Century of Cameras from the Col-
     lection of the International Museum of Photography
     at George Eastman House. Dobbs Ferry, NY: Morgan
     and Morgan, 1973. (150p)

475. Luther, F. Microfilm, 1839-1900. Annapolis: National
     Microfilm Association, 1959. (195p)

476. Martin, Harold. "Photography: a computer with a
     camera attached." Print 32 (September 1978): 92-94.

477. Mathews, Oliver. Early Photographs and Early Pho-
     tographers: A Survey in Dictionary Form. London:
     Reedminster, 1973. (198p)

478. Mees, C.E.K. "The modern era in photography." Photo-
     graphic Journal 79 (April 1939): 225-256.

479. Morgan, Barbara. "Birth and proliferation of the
      photographic image." Aperture 10 (1962): 56-58.

480. Naef. W. "Hercules Florence; 'inventor do photo-
      graphia.'" Artforum 14 (February 1976): 57-59.

481. "New technologies in camera design and controls are
      coming into focus." Inland Printer/American Litho-
      grapher 180 (January 1978): 51-52.

482. Newhall, Beaumont. Airborne Camera: The World From
      the Air and Outer Space. New York: Hastings House,
      1969. (144p)

483. _____. "A chronicle of the birth of photography."
      Harvard Library Bulletin 7 (Spring 1953): 208-220.

484. _____. The Daguerreotype in America. 3rd rev. ed.
      New York: Dover, 1976. (175p)

485. _____. The History of Photography from 1839 to the
      Present Day. 4th rev. and enl. ed. New York: Mu-
      seum of Modern Art, in collaboration with George
      Eastman House, 1964. (215p)

486. _____. Latent Image: The Discovery of Photography.
      Garden City, NY: Doubleday, 1967. (148p)

487. _____. "Photographic inventions of George Eastman."
      Journal of Photographic Science 3 (March/April 1955):
      33-40.

488. Norman, Daniel. "The development of astronomical pho-
      tography." Osiris 5 (1938): 560-594.

489. Olshaker, Mark. The Instant Image: Edwin Land and
      the Polaroid Experience. New York: Stein and Day,
      1978. (277p)

490. Ostroff, Eugene. "Etching, engraving and photography:
      history of photomechanical reproduction." Journal of
      Photographic Science 17 (May/June 1969): 65-80.

491. _____. "Photography and photogravure: history of
      photomechanical reproduction." Journal of Photo-
      graphic Science 17 (July/August 1969): 101-115.

492. Ott, John. My Ivory Cellar—The Story of Time-Lapse
      Photography. Chicago: Twentieth Century Press,
      1958. (157p)

493. Porter, A. "Concise chronology of instant photography,
      1947-1974." Camera 53 (October 1974): 1-2.

494. Potoniée, Georges. The History of the Discovery of
      Photography. Trans. by Edward Epstean. New York:
      Tennant and Ward, 1936. (272p)

36   Communications and Society

495. Root, Marcus A. The Camera and the Pencil; Or, the Heliographic Art, Its Theory and Practice . . . Together With Its History in the United States and Europe. New York: Appleton, 1864. (456p)

496. Schaffert, R. M. Electrophotography. London and New York: Focal Press, 1965. (463p)

497. Sipley, Louis W. Frederic E. Ives, Photo-Graphic-Arts Inventor. Philadelphia: American Museum of Photography, c 1956. (30p)

498. _____. A Half Century of Color. New York: Macmillan, 1951. (316p)

499. _____. Photography's Great Inventors. Philadelphia: American Museum of Photography, 1965. (170p)

500. Spencer, D. A. "The first hundred years of colour photography." Photographic Journal 101 (September 1961): 265-272.

501. Stenger, Erich. Fortschritte der Photographie. 2 vols. Leipzig: Akademische Verlagsgesellschaft, 1938-1940. (415p, 552p)

502. Stevens, G.W.W. "Microphotography since 1839." Photographic Journal 90B (1950): 149-156.

503. Thomas, D. B. The First Negatives; An Account of the Discovery and Early Use of the Negative-Positive Photographic Process. London: H. M. Stationery Office, 1964. (39p)

504. Wall, Edward J. The History of Three-Color Photography. Boston: American Photographic Publishing, 1925. (747p)

505. Warner, Huntington D. Reverend Hannibal Goodwin—Inventor of the Malable, Rollable Film, That Made Possible, the Roller Camera, and the Moving Pictures in Their Ever Improving Form. New York: Dombey Textile Mills, c 1921. (40p)

506. Welling, William B. "Apropos: history—origins of camera enlarging." Camera 57 (July 1978): 38-41.

507. _____. Photography in America: The Formative Years, 1839-1900. New York: Crowell, 1978. (431p)

H. FILM

508. Bardeche, Maurice and Robert Brasillach. The History
      of Motion Pictures. Trans. and ed. by Iris Barry.
      New York: Norton and Museum of Modern Art, 1938.
      (412p)

509. Barnouw, Erik. Documentary: A History of the Non-
      Fiction Film. New York: Oxford University Press,
      1974. (332p)

510. Betts, Ernest. The Film Business: A History of British
      Cinema, 1896-1972. New York: Pitman, 1973. (349p)

511. Bohn, Thomas W. and Richard L. Stromgren. Light and
      Shadows: A History of Motion Pictures. Port Wash-
      ington, NY: Alfred, 1975. (537p)

512. Bowen, H. G. "Thomas Alva Edison's early motion pic-
      ture experiments." Journal of the Society of Motion
      Picture and Television Engineers 64 (September 1955):
      508-514.

513. Card, James. "Problems of film history." Hollywood
      Quarterly 4 (Spring 1950): 279-288.

514. Casty, Alan. Development of the Film; An Interpretive
      History. New York: Harcourt Brace Jovanovich, 1973.
      (425p)

515. "Claims to motion picture invention. Great Britain:
      William Friese-Greene. France: Louis Lumiere.
      America: C. Francis Jenkins. Germany: Max Sklada-
      nowsky." Photographic Journal 66 (July 1926): 359-
      366.

516. Coe, Brian W. "Appreciations of the origins of cine-
      matography." British Kinematography 27 (December
      1955): 171-183.

517. _____. "The truth about Friese-Greene." British
      Journal of Photography 102 (9 September 1955): 446-
      448.

518. Cook, Olive. Movement in Two Dimensions; A Study of
      the Animated and Projected Pictures Which Preceded
      the Invention of Cinematography. London: Hutchin-
      son, 1963. (143p)

519. Cowie, Peter. A Concise History of the Cinema. 2
      vols. London: Zwemmer, 1971; New York: Barnes,
      1971.

520. Dickson, Antonia and W.K.L. Dickson. History of the
      Kinetograph, Kinetoscope and Kineto-Phonograph. New
      York: Bunn, 1895. (?)

521. Fielding, Raymond, ed. A Technological History of
      Motion Pictures and Television. Berkeley: Univer-
      sity of California Press, 1967. (225p)

522. Forth, Muriel (Ray Allister). Friese-Greene: Close-
      up of an Inventor. London: Marsland, 1951. (192p)

523. Fulton, Albert R. Motion Pictures: The Development
      of an Art from Silent Films to the Age of Television.
      Norman: University of Oklahoma Press, 1960. (320p)

524. Geduld, Harry M. The Birth of the Talkies: From Edi-
      son to Jolson. Bloomington: Indiana University
      Press, 1975. (337p)

525. Gill, Arthur T. "The first movie." Photographic
      Journal 109 (January 1969): 26-29.

526. Gomery, John D. "The coming of sound to the American
      cinema: a history of the transformation of an in-
      dustry." Ph.D. dissertation, University of Wiscon-
      sin—Madison, 1975. (523p)

527. Grau, Robert. The Theatre of Science; A Volume of
      Progress and Achievement in the Motion Picture In-
      dustry. New York: Blom, 1969. (378p)

528. Griffith, Richard and Arthur Mayer. The Movies. Rev.
      ed. New York: Simon and Schuster, 1970. (494p)

529. Halas, John, ed. Computer Animation. New York:
      Hastings House, 1974. (176p)

530. Hanson, W. T., Jr. "Evolution of Eastman color motion
      picture films." SMPTE Journal 90 (September 1981):
      791-794.

531. Happé, J. Bernard. Basic Motion Picture Technology.
      2nd rev. ed. New York: Hastings House, 1975. (371p)

532. Hendricks, Gordon. Beginnings of the Biograph: The
      Story of the Invention of the Mutoscope and the Bio-
      graph and Their Supplying Camera. New York: The Be-
      ginnings of the American Film, 1964. (78p)

533. _____. Eadweard Muybridge: The Father of the Mo-
      tion Picture. New York: Grossman, 1975. (271p)

534. _____. The Edison Motion Picture Myth. Berkeley
      and Los Angeles: University of California Press,
      1961. (216p)

535. _____. The Kinetoscope: America's First Commerci-
      ally Successful Motion Picture Exhibitor. New York:
      The Beginnings of the American Film, 1966. (182p)

536. Homer, W. I. "Eakins, Muybridge and the Motion Picture
      Process." Art Quarterly (Summer 1963): 194-216.

537. Jacobs, Lewis. The Rise of the American Film: A
      Critical History with an Essay, "Experimental Cinema
      in America, 1921-1947." New York: Teachers College
      Press, 1968. (631p)

538. Jenkins, C. Francis. Animated Pictures; An Exposition
      of the Historical Development of Chronophotography,
      Its Present Scientific Applications and Future Pos-
      sibilities. Washington, D.C.: Press of H. L.
      McQueen, 1898. (118p)

539. Josephson, Matthew. Edison. New York: McGraw-Hill,
      1959. (511p)

540. Kellogg, E. W. "The history of sound motion picture."
      Journal of the Society of Motion Picture and Tele-
      vision Engineers 64 (June/July/August 1955): 291-
      302, 356-374, 422-437.

541. Knight, Arthur. The Liveliest Art: A Panoramic His-
      tory of the Movies. New York: Macmillan, 1957.
      (383p)

542. Knowlton, Kenneth. "Computer-produced movies." Sci-
      ence 150 (26 November 1965): 1116-1120.

543. Lahue, Kalton C. Continued Next Week: A History of
      the Moving Picture Serial. Norman: University of
      Oklahoma Press, 1964. (293p)

544. Limbacher, James L. Four Aspects of the Film: Color,
      Sound, 3-D, and Widescreen. New York: Brussel and
      Brussel, 1968. (387p)

545. Macgowan, Kenneth. Behind the Screen: The History and
      Techniques of the Motion Picture. New York: Dela-
      corte, 1965. (528p)

546. Malkames, Don G. "Early projector mechanisms." Jour-
      nal of the Society of Motion Picture and Television
      Engineers 66 (October 1957): 628-635.

547. Marek, Kurt W. Archaeology of the Cinema. New York:
      Harcourt Brace, 1965. (264p)

548. Mast, Gerald. A Short History of the Movies. 2nd ed.
      Indianapolis: Bobbs-Merrill, 1976. (575p)

549. Noll, A. Michael. "Computer-generated 3-dimensional
      movies." Computers and Automation 14 (November 1965):
      20-23.

550. Ogle, Patrick. "Deep-focus cinematography: a techno-
      logical-aesthetic history." Filmmakers Newsletter 4
      (May 1971): 19-33.

551. Paolella, Roberto. Storia del Cinema Muto. Naples:
      Giannini, 1956. (554p)

552. _____. Storia del Cinema Sonora, 1926-1939. Naples:
      Giannini, 1966. (998p)

553. Quigley, Martin. Magic Shadows: The Story of the Ori-
      gin of Motion Pictures. New York: Biblo and Tannen,
      c 1960, 1969. (191p)

554. Ramsaye, Terry. A Million and One Nights: A History
      of the Motion Picture. New York: Simon and Schuster,
      c 1926, 1964. (868p)

555. Robinson, David. The History of World Cinema. New
      York: Stein and Day, 1973. (440p)

556. Rohr, Louis O.M. Abhandlungen zur Geschichte des
      Stereoskops von Wheatstone, Brewster, Riddell, Helm-
      holtz, Wenham, d'Alemeida und Harmer. Leipzig:
      Engelmann, 1908. (129p)

557. Rotha, Paul. Documentary Film. 3rd ed. rev. and enl.
      London: Faber and Faber, 1952. (412p)

558. Ryan, Roderick T. A History of Motion Picture Color
      Technology. New York: Focal Press, 1977. (278p)

559. Sadoul, Georges. Histoire de l'Art du Cinéma, des
      Origines à nos Jours. 4th ed. rev. and enl. Paris:
      Flammarion, 1955. (518p)

560. Sanderson, R. A. "A historical study of the develop-
      ment of American motion picture content and tech-
      niques prior to 1904." Ph.D. dissertation, Univer-
      sity of Southern California, 1961. (238p)

561. Sesonske, Alexander. "Origins of animation." Sight
      and Sound 49 (Summer 1980): 186-188.

562. Slide, Anthony. Early American Cinema. New York:
      Barnes, 1970. (192p)

563. Spottiswoode, Raymond. "The Friese-Greene controversy:
      the evidence reconsidered." Quarterly of Film, Radio
      and Television 9 (Spring 1955): 217-230.

564. Theisen, Earl. "The history of nitrocellulose as a
      film base." Journal of the Society of Motion Picture
      Engineers 20 (March 1933): 259-262.

565. Theisen, W. E. "Pioneering in the talking picture."
Journal of the Society of Motion Picture Engineers
36 (April 1941): 415-444.

566. Thomas, D. B. The First Colour Motion Pictures. London: London Science Museum, 1969. (44p)

567. _____. The Origins of the Motion Pictures. London:
H. M. Stationery Office, 1964. (32p)

568. Zajac, E. E. "Computer animation—a new scientific and
educational tool." Journal of the Society of Motion
Picture and Television Engineers 74: 1006-1008.

569. Zglinicki, Friedrich. Der Weg des Films; die Geschichte
der Kinematographie und Ihrer Vorläufer. Berlin:
Rembrandt, c 1956. (992p)

I. RADIO AND WIRELESS TELEGRAPHY

570. Aitkin, Hugh G. Syntony and Spark: The Origins of
Radio. New York: Wiley, c 1976. (347p)

571. Appleby, Thomas. Mahlon Loomis, Inventor of Radio.
Washington: Loomis Publications, 1967. (145p)

572. Armstrong, Edwin H. "Wrong roads and missed chances—
some ancient radio history." Midwest Engineer 3
(March 1951): 3-5, 21, 25.

573. Blake, George G. "Historical notes on radio telegraphy
and telephony." Wireless World 12 (1922): 253-256,
286-293.

574. _____. History of Radio Telegraphy and Telephony.
London: Radio Press, 1926. (425p)

575. Carneal, Georgette. A Conqueror of Space. New York:
Liveright, 1930. (296p)

576. Casdorph, Paul D. "Mahlon Loomis and the 'aerial telegraph.'" West Virginia History 41 (1980): 205-225.

577. Dalton, W. M. The Story of Radio. 3 vols. Bristol:
Hilger, 1975.

578. de Forest, Lee. Father of Radio. Chicago: Wilcox
and Follett, 1950. (502p)

579. Drybrough, D.A.S. "Mobile radio communication." Wireless World 82 (November 1976): 54-58; 83 (March 1977):
73-77.

580. DuBoff, Richard B. "Business demand and the develop-
      ment of the telegraph in the United States, 1844-
      1860." Business History Review 54 (1980): 459-479.

581. Epstein, Samuel and Beryl Epstein (Douglas Coe): Mar-
      coni, Pioneer of Radio. New York: Messner, 1943.
      (272p)

582. Espenschied, Lloyd. "The origin and development of
      radiotelephony." Proceedings of the Institute of
      Radio Engineers 25 (September 1937): 1101-1123.

583. Fessenden, Helen M. Fessenden—Builder of Tomorrowers.
      New York: Coward-McCann, 1940. (362p)

584. Fornatale, Peter and Joshua E. Mills. Radio in the
      Television Age. New York: Overlook Press, 1980.
      (212p)

585. Harrison, Arthur P., Jr. "Single-control tuning: an
      analysis of an innovation." Technology and Culture
      20 (1979): 296-321.

586. Herron, Edward A. Miracle of the Air Waves; A History
      of Radio. New York: Messner, 1969. (191p)

587. Hufford, George A. FM Broadcast Coverage of the Co-
      terminous United States. July 1976. (34p) NTISPB-
      257 013/36A.

588. Hammond, John H. and Ellison S. Purington. "A history
      of some foundations of modern radio-electronic tech-
      nology." Proceedings of the Institute of Radio En-
      gineers 45 (September 1957): 1191-1208.

589. "Important events in radio—peaks in the waves of wire-
      less progress, 1827-1928." Radio Service Bulletin
      141 (December 1928): 16-26.

590. Leinwoll, Stanley. From Spark to Satellite: A History
      of Radio Communication. New York: Scribner, 1979.
      (256p)

591. Lessing, Lawrence P. Man of High Fidelity: Edwin How-
      ard Armstrong. New York: Lippincott, 1956. (320p)

592. Lodge, Oliver J. "The origin or basis of wireless com-
      munication." Nature 111 (10 March 1923): 328-332.

593. Maclaurin, William R. and R. Joyce Harman. Invention
      and Innovation in the Radio Industry. New York:
      Macmillan, 1949. (304p)

594. McMahon, Morgan E., comp. Vintage Radio; Harold Green-
      wood's Historical Album Expanded with More Old Ads,
      Illustrations, and Many Photos of Wireless and Radio
      Equipment. 2nd ed. Palos Verdes Peninsula, CA:
      Vintage Radio, 1973. (263p)

595. McNicol, Donald. Radio's Conquest of Space; The Ex-
      perimental Rise in Radio Communication. New York:
      Murray Hill, 1946. (374p)

596. Marconi, Guglielmo. "The progress of electric space
      telegraphy." Proceedings of the Royal Institute of
      Great Britain 17 (1902): 195-210.

597. Morgan, Thomas O. "The contribution of Nathan B. Stub-
      blefield to the invention of wireless voice communi-
      cation." Ph.D. dissertation, Florida State Univer-
      sity, 1971. (171p)

598. Morse, A. H. Radio: Beam and Broadcast; Its Story and
      Patents. London: Benn, 1925. (192p)

599. Noble, Daniel E. "The history of land-mobile radio
      communications." Proceedings of the Institute of
      Radio Engineers 50 (May 1962): 1405-1414.

600. O'Dea, William T. Radio Communication: Its History
      and Development. London: H. M. Stationery Office,
      1934. (95p)

601. Radovsky, M. Alexander Popov: Inventor of Radio.
      Trans. by G. Yankovsky. Moscow: Foreign Languages
      Publishing House, 1957. (130p)

602. Sewall, Charles H. Wireless Telegraphy: Its Origin,
      Development, Inventions, and Apparatus. New York:
      Van Nostrand, 1903; London: Crosby, Lockwood, 1903.
      (229p)

603. Shiers, George, ed. The Development of Wireless to
      1920. New York: Arno Press, 1977. (500p)

604. Sidel, Michael K. "A historical analysis of American
      short wave broadcasting, 1916-1942." Ph.D. disserta-
      tion, Northwestern University, 1976. (278p)

605. Story, Alfred T. The Story of Wireless Telegraphy.
      London: Newnes, 1904; New York: Appleton, 1904.
      (215p)

606. Swinyard, William O. "The development of the art of
      radio receiving from the early 1920's to the present."
      Proceedings of the Institute of Radio Engineers 50
      (May 1962): 793-798.

607.   Wedlake, G.E.C.   SOS; The Story of Radio—Communication.
        New York: Crane-Russak, 1973.   (240p)

                        J.   TELEVISION

608.   Abramson, Albert.   Electronic Motion Pictures—A His-
        tory of the Television Camera.   Berkeley: University
        of California Press, 1955.   (212p)

609.   _____.   "Pioneers of television; Vladimir Kosma
        Zworykin."   SMPTE Journal 90 (July 1981): 579-590.

610.   Baird, John L.   "Television."   Journal of Scientific
        Instruments 4 (February 1927): 138-143.

611.   Barnouw, Erik.   Tube of Plenty; The Evolution of Ameri-
        can Television.   New York: Oxford University Press,
        1975.   (518p)

612.   Benson, K. B.   "Brief history of television camera
        tubes."   SMPTE Journal 90 (August 1981): 708-712.

613.   Bezencon, Marcel.   "Television via direct broadcast
        satellites."   E.B.U. Review 24 (July 1973): 14-16.

614.   Briggs, Asa.   "The tube of plenty: towards an 'age of
        television.'"   Futures 9 (December 1977): 519-525.

615.   Burns, R. W.   "J. L. Baird; success and failure."   Pro-
        ceedings of the Institution of Electrical Engineers
        126 (September 1979): 921-928.

616.   "The chronology of television."   Television and Short-
        Wave World 8 (July/August 1935):   391-393; 453-454.

617.   Eisner, Michael D.   "Old technologies."   Journal of
        Popular Culture 15 (Fall 1981): 157-163.

618.   Everson, George.   The Story of Television; The Life of
        Philo T. Farnsworth.   New York: Norton, 1949.   (266p)

619.   Exwood, M.   "Births of television."   Radio and Elec-
        tronic Engineering 46 (December 1976): 632-633.

620.   Garratt, Gerald R.M. and A. H. Mumford.   "The history
        of television."   Proceedings of the Institution of
        Electrical Engineers 99, pt. 3A (May 1952): 25-42.

621.   Goforth, K.   "Historical look at television."   Radio-
        Electronics 51 (June 1980): 43-46.

622.   Greenfield, Jeff.   "Revolution in TV watching; pro-
        gramming from satellites."   Science Digest 86 (De-
        cember 1979): 25-27.

623. Herold, E. W. "History of color television displays."
     Proceedings of the IEEE 64 (September 1976): 1331-
     1338.

624. Hewish, Mark. "Satellite television improves the
     view." New Scientist 89 (12 February 1981): 398-401.

625. Hollowell, Mary L. Cable Handbook 1976-1976; A Guide
     to Cable and New Communications Technologies. Wash-
     ington: Communications Press, 1975. (312p)

626. "How direct-broadcasting TV satellites work." New
     Scientist 89 (12 February 1981): 399.

627. "In the wake of the transistor." Electronics 53 (17
     April 1980): 275-319.

628. Jenkins, C. Francis. Vision by Radio, Radio Photo-
     graphs, Radio Photograms. Washington, D.C.: National
     Capitol Press, c 1925. (139p)

629. Jensen, A. G. "The evolution of modern television."
     Journal of the Society of Motion Picture and Tele-
     vision Engineers 63 (November 1954): 174-178.

630. Lankes, L. R. "Historical sketch of television's
     progress." Journal of the Society of Motion Picture
     and Television Engineers 51 (September 1948): 223-229.

631. Larner, E. T. Practical Television. London: Benn,
     1928. (175p)

632. Law, H. B. "Shadow mask color picture tube; how it be-
     gan." Journal of the Society of Motion Picture and
     Television Engineers 86 (April 1977): 214-221.

633. McLeod, Norman. "TV culture invasion from space."
     New Scientist 85 (28 February 1980): 645-647.

634. Mahoney, John. "How the Vietnam War changed television
     news operations." E.B.U. Review 26 (July 1975): 16-
     17.

635. Moffat, M.E.B. "Digital television via satellite."
     Wireless World 83 (July 1977): 51-54.

636. Morris, Alan. "A Report on Electronic Newsgathering by
     an American television station." E.B.U. Review 26
     (September 1975): 25-28.

637. Percy, J. D. John L. Baird—The Founder of British
     Television. London: Television Society, 1952. (16p)

638. Pitts, E, 3d and W. I. Seigal. "Fifty years of TV."
     Audio 65 (July 1981): 28-32.

639.   Shiers, George. "Early schemes for television."   IEEE
        Spectrum 7 (May 1970): 24-34.

640.   _____.   "Historical notes on television before 1900."
        Journal of the Society of Motion Picture and Tele-
        vision Engineers 86 (March 1977): 129-137.   (See Cor-
        rection in 86 (July 1977): 500.)

641.   _____.   "Rise of mechanical television."   SMPTE
        Journal 90 (June 1981): 508-521.

642.   _____, ed.   Technical Development of Television.
        New York: Arno, 1977.   (500p)

643.   Smith, Charles.   "Secrets of television in depth."
        New Scientist 93 (21 January 1982): 144-146.

644.   Taylor, John P.   "Technical automation for stations
        progresses slowly as links with business systems are
        readied."   Television/Radio Age 23 (10 May 1976): 24-
        27+.

645.   Waters, Harry F. "Video's new frontier."   Newsweek 86
        (8 December 1975): 52-57.

3
The Shaping of Mass Media Content: Media Sociology

A. MASS MEDIA (GENERAL)

646. Adler, Mortimer J. Art and Prudence, A Study in Practical Philosophy. New York: Longmans, Green, 1937. (686p)

647. Alberoni, Francesco. "Society, culture and mass communication media." Ikon 19 (1966): 29-62.

648. Aldrich, Pearl. The Impact of Mass Media. Rochelle Park, NJ: Hayden, 1975. (197p)

649. Alisky, Marvin. Latin American Media: Guidance and Censorship. Ames: Iowa University Press, 1981. (265p)

650. Anderson, David A. "The selective impact of libel law." Columbia Journalism Review 14 (May/June 1975): 38-42.

651. Angell, Norman. Let the People Know. New York: Viking Press, 1942. (245p)

652. Antitrust, the Media, and the New Technology. New York: Practising Law Institute, 1981. (568p)

653. Armstrong, David. A Trumpet to Arms: Alternative Media in America. Los Angeles: J. P. Tarcher, 1981. (384p)

654. Ashdown, Gerald. "Gertz and Firestone: a study in Constitutional policy-making." Minnesota Law Review 61, no. 4 (1976-1977): 645-690.

655.   Backman, Carl W.   "Sampling mass media content: a com-
       parison of one-stage and two-stage methods."   Ph.D.
       dissertation, Indiana University, 1954.   (118p)

656.   _____.   "Sampling media content: the use of the
       cluster design."   American Sociological Review 21
       (December 1956):   729-733.

657.   Baer, Walter S., et al.   Concentration of Mass Media
       Ownership: Assessing the State of Current Knowledge.
       Rand Report 1584-NSF.   September 1974.   (218p)

658.   Bagdikian, Ben H.   "Shaping media content: profes-
       sional, personnel and organizational structure."
       Public Opinion Quarterly 37 (Winter 1974):   569-579.

659.   Baran, Stanley J., et al.   "The FCC and the U.S. Court
       of Appeals: telecommunications policy by judicial
       decree?"   Journal of Broadcasting 23, no. 3 (1979):
       301-318.

660.   Barcus, Francis E.   "Communications content: analysis
       of the research, 1900-1958 (a content analysis of the
       content analysis)."   Ph.D. dissertation, University
       of Illinois, 1959.   (422p)

661.   Barnlund, Dean C. and Carroll Harland.   "Propinquity
       and prestige as determinants of communication net-
       works."   Sociometry 26, no. 4 (1963):   467-479.

662.   Barnouw, Erik.   A History of Broadcasting in the
       United States.   New York: Oxford University Press,
       1966-1970.   (3 volumes)

663.   Barrett, Marvin, ed.   Moments of Truth.   New York:
       Crowell, 1975.   (274p)

664.   Best, Joel.   "Social control of media content."   Jour-
       nal of Popular Culture 14 (Spring 1981):   611-617.

665.   Boyd, Douglas A.   Broadcasting in the Arab World: A
       Survey of Radio and Television in the Middle East.
       Philadelphia: Temple University Press, 1982.   (310p)

666.   Boynton, Robert P. and Deil S. Wright.   "The media, the
       masses and urban management."   Journalism Quarterly
       47 (Spring 1970):   12-19.

667.   Brady, R.   "The problem of monopoly."   Annals of the
       American Academy of Political and Social Science 254
       (November 1947):   125-136.

668.   Breed, Warren.   "Social control in the newsroom: a
       functional analysis."   Social Forces 33 (May 1955):
       326-335.

669. Brock, Gerald W. The Telecommunications Industry: the
      Dynamics of Market Structure. Cambridge: Harvard
      University Press, 1981. (336p)

670. Broom, Leonard and Shirley Reece. "Political and ra-
      cial interest: a study in content analysis." Public
      Opinion Quarterly 19 (Spring 1955): 5-19.

671. Brouwer, Martin. "Mass communication and the social
      sciences: some neglected areas." International So-
      cial Science Journal 14 (1966): 303-319.

672. Brown, E. R. "Direct broadcast satellites and freedom
      of speech." California Western International Law
      Journal 4 (1974): 374-393.

673. Bush, Chilton R. "A system of categories for general
      news content." Journalism Quarterly 37 (Spring 1960):
      206-210.

674. Carey, James T. "Changing courtship patterns in the
      popular song." American Journal of Sociology 74 (May
      1969): 720-731.

675. Carmody, Deirdre. "Challenging media monopolies."
      (31 July 1977): 21-24.

676. Carter, R. E. "Communications research and the social
      sciences." American Behavioral Scientist 4 (1960):
      8-13.

677. Cater, Douglass and Michael J. Nyhan, ed. The Future
      of Public Broadcasting. New York: Praeger, 1976.
      (372p)

678. Chafee, Zechariah. Free Speech in the United States.
      Cambridge: Harvard University Press, 1946. (634p)

679. _____. Government and Mass Communications. 2 vols.
      Chicago: University of Chicago Press, 1947. (829p)

680. Chamberlin, Bill F. "The FCC and the first principle
      of the Fairness Doctrine: a history of neglect and
      distortion." Federal Communications Law Journal 31
      (Fall 1979): 361-411.

681. Chester, Girand. "What constitutes irresponsibility on
      the air: a case study." Public Opinion Quarterly 13
      (Spring 1949): 73-82.

682. Cline, Victor B., comp. Where Do You Draw the Line?
      Provo: Brigham Young University Press, 1974. (365p)

683. Cohen, Stanley and Jack Young, ed. The Manufacture of
      News: Social Problems, Deviance and the Mass Media.
      Beverly Hills, CA: Sage, 1973. (383p)

684.   Cole, Barry and Mal Oettinger. The Regulators: The
        FCC and the Broadcast Audience. Reading, MA: Addi-
        son-Wesley, 1978. (288p)

685.   Cole, Richard R. "Top songs in the sixties: a content
        analysis of popular lyrics." American Behavioral
        Scientist 14 (January/February 1971): 389-400.

686.   Combs, James E. and Michael W. Mansfield, ed. Drama in
        Life: The Uses of Communication in Society. New
        York: Hastings House, 1976. (444p)

687.   Communication Law 1977. New York: Practicing Law In-
        stitute, 1977. (2 vols., 1062p)

688.   Compaine, Benjamin, ed. Who Owns the Media: Concen-
        tration of Ownership in the Mass Communications In-
        dustry. 2nd ed. White Plains, NY: Knowledge Indus-
        try Publications, 1982. (400p)

689.   Conteras, Eduardo et al. Cross Cultural Broadcasting.
        Paris: UNESCO, 1976. (n.p.)

690.   Control of the Direct Broadcast Satellite: Values in
        Conflict. (Aspen Institute Program on Communication
        and Society). Palo Alto, CA: 1974. (156p)

691.   Coyne, John M. "Prestige suggestion influences in
        communication analysis." Ph.D. dissertation, Stan-
        ford University, 1956. (93p)

692.   Crawley, John. "Censorship and the media." Political
        Quarterly 47 (April/June 1976): 160-168.

693.   Curran, James et al. Mass Communication and Society.
        London: Open University Press, 1977. (479p)

694.   Cusack, Mary A. "Editorializing in broadcasting."
        Ph.D. dissertation, Wayne State University, 1960.
        (273p)

695.   Cushman, Robert. The Independent Regulatory Commis-
        sions. New York: Oxford University Press, 1941.
        (780p)

696.   Dennis, Everette E. "Leaked information as property:
        vulnerability of the press to criminal prosecution."
        St. Louis University Law Journal 20, no. 4 (1975-
        1976): 610-624.

697.   _____. "Purloined information as property: a new
        First Amendment challenge." Journalism Quarterly 50
        (Autumn 1973): 456-462; 474.

698.   Denny, Reuel. The Astonished Muse. Chicago: Univer-
        sity of Chicago Press, 1957. (790p)

699. Deutschmann, Paul J. and Wayne A. Danielson. "Diffusion of knowledge of the major news story." Journalism Quarterly 37 (Summer 1960): 345-355.

700. Devlo, Kenneth S., ed. Mass Media and the Supreme Court. 2nd ed. New York: Hastings House, 1976. (400p)

701. Dexter, Lewis A. and David M. White, ed. People, Society and Mass Communications. New York: Free Press, 1964. (595p)

702. Dizard, Wilson P. "The U.S. position: DBS and free flow." Journal of Communication 30 (Spring 1980): 157-168.

703. Donohew, Lewis. "Newspaper gatekeepers and forces in the news channel." Public Opinion Quarterly 31 (Spring 1967): 61-68.

704. Drew, Dan G. and Susan H. Miller. "Sex stereotyping and reporting." Journalism Quarterly 54 (Spring 1977): 142-146.

705. Dunwoody, Sharon and Byron T. Scott. "Scientists as mass media sources." Journalism Quarterly 59 (Spring 1982): 52-59.

706. Durr, Clifford J. "Freedom of speech for whom." Public Opinion Quarterly 8 (1944): 391-406.

707. Edelstein, Alex S. "The Marshall Plan information program in Europe as an instrument of United States foreign policy, 1948-1952." Ph.D. dissertation, University of Minnesota, 1958. (468p)

708. Eisenstaat, Shmuel N. "Communication systems and social structure: an exploratory comparative study." Public Opinion Quarterly 19 (Summer 1955): 153-167.

709. Elfenbein, Julien. "Communications role in an orderly society." Journalism Quarterly 24 (June 1947): 116-121.

710. Elkin, Frederick. "Censorship and pressure groups." Phylon Quarterly 21 (Spring 1960): 71-80.

711. Emerson, Thomas I., et al. "The First Amendment and the right to know." Washington University Law Review 1 (1976): 1-36.

712. Emery, Michael C. and Curtis Smythe, comp. Readings in Mass Communication: Concepts and Issues in the Mass Media. 3rd ed. Dubuque, IA: Brown, 1977. (483p)

713. Ermann, M. David. "The operative goals of corporate phi-
      lanthropy: contributions to the Public Broadcasting
      Service, 1972-1976." Social Problems 25 (June 1978):
      504-514.

714. Ernst, Morris and William Seagle. To the Pure . . . A
      Study of Obscenity and the Censor. New York: Viking,
      1928. (336p)

715. Ettinger, Karl E. "Foreign propaganda in America." Pub-
      lic Opinion Quarterly 10 (1946): 329-342.

716. Eversole, Pam. "Concentration of ownership in the commu-
      nications industry." Journalism Quarterly 48 (Summer
      1971): 251-260, 268.

717. Fair Trial and Free Expression. (U.S. Senate. Committee
      on the Judiciary. Subcommittee on Constitutional
      Rights.) Washington, D.C.: G.P.O., 1976. (85p)

718. Fauman, S. Joseph and Harry Sharp. "Presenting the re-
      sults of social research to the public." Public Opin-
      ion Quarterly 22 (Summer 1958): 107-115.

719. Fishman, Mark. Manufacturing the News. Austin: Univer-
      sity of Texas Press, 1980. (180p)

720. Foley, Karen Sue. The Political Blacklist in the Broad-
      cast Industry: the Decade of the 1950's. New York:
      Arno, 1979. (498p)

721. Fore, William F. Image and Impact; How Man Comes Through
      in the Mass Media. New York: Friendship Press, 1970.
      (111p)

722. Francois, William E. Mass Media Law and Regulation. Co-
      lumbus: Grid Pub. Co., 1975. (470p)

723. Franklin, Marc A. Cases and Materials on Mass Media Law.
      Mineola, NY: Foundation Press, 1977. (878p)

724. Freidson, Eliot. "Communications research and the con-
      cept of the mass." American Sociological Review 18
      (June 1953): 313-317.

725. Ganley, Oswald H. and Gladys D. Ganley. To Inform or to
      Control? New York: McGraw-Hill, 1982. (250p)

726. Gans, Herbert J. "Deciding what's news: story suitabil-
      ity." Society 16 (March/April 1979): 65-77.

727. Gardiner, Harold C. Catholic Viewpoint on Censorship.
      New York: Hanover House, 1958. (192p)

728. Geiger, Louis G. "Muckrakers—then and now." Journalism
      Quarterly 43 (Autumn 1966): 469-476.

729. Gerbner, George. "Ideological perspectives and politi-
      cal tendencies in news reporting." Journalism Quar-
      terly 41 (Autumn 1964): 495-508, 516.

730. _____. Mass Media Policies in Changing Cultures.
      New York: Wiley, 1977. (291p)

731. _____. "On content analysis and critical research in
      mass communication." Audiovisual Communication Review
      6 (Spring 1958): 85-108.

732. _____, et al., ed. Communications Technology and So-
      cial Policy. New York: Wiley, 1973. (573p)

733. Gibson, George H. Public Broadcasting: The Role of the
      Federal Government, 1912-1976. New York: Praeger,
      1977. (236p)

734. Gieber, Walter. "How the 'gatekeepers' view local civil
      liberties news." Journalism Quarterly 37 (Spring
      1960): 199-205.

735. Gillmor, Donald M. "The puzzle of pornography." Jour-
      nalism Quarterly 42 (Summer 1965): 363-372.

736. Gillmor, Donald M. and Jerome A. Barron. Mass Communi-
      cation Law: Cases and Comments. 2nd ed. St. Paul,
      MN: West, 1974. (1007p)

737. Gilman, Mildred. "Truth behind the news." American
      Mercury 29 (June 1933): 139-146.

738. Gitlin, Todd. "Media sociology: the dominant para-
      digm." Theory and Society 6 (September 1978): 205-
      253.

739. Golding, Peter. The Mass Media. New York: Longmans,
      1974. (134p)

740. Goodlad, J.S.R. A Sociology of Popular Drama. London:
      Heinemann, 1971. (230p)

741. Goodrich, Herbert. "Man and society in mass-media fic-
      tion: the pattern of life in the mass media as re-
      vealed by content analysis studies." Ph.D. disserta-
      tion, University of Illinois, 1965. (494p)

742. Gormley, William T. "How cross-ownership affects news-
      gathering." Columbia Journalism Review 16 (May/June
      1977): 38-46.

743. Grams, John A. "An analysis of Federal Communications
      Commission actions in the licensing of newspaper af-
      filiated broadcasting stations." Ph.D. dissertation,
      University of Wisconsin, 1973. (332p)

744. Grant, William R. "The media and school desegregation."
      Integrated Education 14 (November/December 1976): 12-
      13.

745. Grüber, Frederick C. "Radio and television and ethical
      standards." Annals of the American Academy of Politi-
      cal and Social Science 280 (March 1952): 116-124.

746. Grunig, James, ed. Decline of the Global Village: How
      Specialization is Changing the Mass Media. Bayside,
      NY: General Hall, 1976. (297p)

747. Hall, Stuart. "Media power: the double bind." Journal
      of Communication 24 (Autumn 1975): 19-26.

748. Halloran, James D. Control or Consent? A Study of the
      Challenge of Mass Communication. New York: Sheed and
      Ward, 1963. (246p)

749. Halmos, Paul, ed. The Sociology of Mass-Media Communi-
      cators. Keele, England: University of Keele, 1969.
      (248p)

750. Hannett, Francis. "The haunting lyric: the personal
      and social significance of American popular songs."
      Psychoanalytic Quarterly 33, no. 2 (1964): 226-269.

751. Harney, Russell F. and Vernon A. Stone. "Television and
      newspaper front page coverage of a major news story."
      Journal of Broadcasting 13 (Spring 1969): 181-188.

752. Haskins, Jack B. "Cloud with a silver lining, approach
      to violence news." Journalism Quarterly 50 (Autumn
      1973): 549-552.

753. Hazard, Patrick D. "The entertainer as hero: a problem
      of the mass media." Journalism Quarterly 39 (Autumn
      1962): 436-444.

754. Heise, Juergen A. Minimum Disclosure: How the Pentagon
      Manipulates the News. New York: Norton, 1979.
      (221p)

755. Henry, Jules, et al. "Notes on the alchemy of mass mis-
      representation." Studies in Public Communication no.
      3 (Summer 1961): 59-72.

756. Hilderbrand, Robert C. Power and the People: Executive
      Management of Public Opinion in Foreign Affairs, 1897-
      1921. Chapel Hill: University of North Carolina
      Press, 1981. (262p)

757. Hirsch, Paul M. "Sociological approaches to the pop mu-
      sic phenomenon." American Behavioral Scientist 14
      (January 1971): 371-388.

758. Hofstetter, C. Richard. Bias in the News. Columbus:
      State University Press, 1976. (213p)

759. Howard, Herbert H. "Cross-media ownership of newspapers
      and TV stations." Journalism Quarterly 51 (Winter
      1974): 715-718.

760. Hubbard, J.T.W. "Business news in post-Watergate era."
      Journalism Quarterly 53 (Autumn 1976): 488-493.

761. Huffman, Denise M. "Access to the mass media: an anal-
      ysis of the underlying issues." Ph.D. dissertation,
      University of Iowa, 1975. (241p)

762. Hughes, Helen M. "The social interpretation of news."
      The Annals of the American Academy of Political and
      Social Science 219 (January 1942): 11-17.

763. Jahoda, Marie and Joseph T. Klapper. "From social book-
      keeping to social research." Public Opinion Quarterly
      16 (Winter 1952/1953): 623-630.

764. Jamieson, Donald C. The Troubled Air; A Frank, Thorough
      and Sometimes Disturbing Look at the Present State of
      Canadian Broadcasting. Fredericton: Brunswick Press,
      1966. (237p)

765. Jones, Robert L. and Roy E. Carter. "Some procedures
      for estimating 'news hole' in content analysis." Pub-
      lic Opinion Quarterly 23 (Fall 1959): 399-403.

766. Jones, William K. Cases and Materials on Electronic
      Mass Media: Radio, Television, and Cable. 2nd ed.
      Mineola, NY: Foundation Press, 1979. (545p)

767. Kecskemeti, Paul. "Totalitarian communications as a
      means of control." Public Opinion Quarterly 14 (Sum-
      mer 1950): 224-234.

768. Kerr, George D. "Canadian press censorship in WWI."
      Journalism Quarterly 59 (Summer 1982): 235-239.

769. Kline, F. Gerald. "Media time budgeting as a function
      of demographies and life style." Journalism Quarterly
      48 (Summer 1971): 211-221.

770. Klos, Thornton A. "FCC programming regulations since
      1960." Ph.D. dissertation, University of Texas at
      Austin, 1973. (283p)

771. Koop, Theodore. Weapon of Silence. Chicago: Universi-
      ty of Chicago Press, 1946. (304p)

772. Kracauer, Siegfried. "The challenge of qualitative con-
      tent analysis." Public Opinion Quarterly 16 (Winter
      1952/1953): 631-641.

773. Kriegbaum, Hillier. "Reporting science information through the mass media." Journalism Quarterly 40 (Summer 1963): 291-292.

774. Lapham, Lewis H. "Point of order." Harper's 254 (May 1977): 13-16.

775. Larson, Cedric. "Censorship of Army news during the World War, 1917-1918." Journalism Quarterly 17 (December 1940): 313-323.

776. Larson, Charles U. "A content analysis of media reporting of the Watergate hearings." Communication Research 1 (October 1974): 440-448.

777. Laver, Murray. Computers, Communications and Society. London: Oxford University Press, 1975. (99p)

778. Leonard, A. E. "Crime reporting as a police management tool." Annals of the American Academy of Political and Social Science 291 (January 1954): 127-134.

779. Lichty, Lawrence W. "The impact of FRC and FCC Commissioners' backgrounds on the regulation of broadcasting." Journal of Broadcasting 6 (Spring 1962): 97-110.

780. Lindley, William R. "Gatekeepers' avoidance of group opinion sources." Journalism Quarterly 51 (Winter 1974): 724-725.

781. Lindstrom, Carl E. "Sensationalism in the news." Journalism Quarterly 33 (Winter 1956): 9-14.

782. Liston, Robert A. The Right to Know: Censorship in America. New York: Franklin Watts, 1973. (150p)

783. Lohisse, Jean. Anonymous Communication: Mass-Media in the Modern World. Trans. from the French by Stephen Corrin. London: Allen and Unwin, 1973. (191p)

784. Luraschi, Luigi G. "Censorship at home and abroad." Annals of the American Academy of Political and Social Science 254 (November 1947): 147-152.

785. McCoy, R. E. "Banned in Boston: the development of literary censorship in Massachusetts." Ph.D. dissertation, University of Illinois, 1956. (349p)

786. McGranahan, Donald Vincent and Ivor Wayne. "German and American traits reflected in popular drama." Human Relations 1 (1948): 429-455.

787. McMahon, Robert S. "Federal regulation of the radio and television broadcast industry in the United States, 1927-1959, with special reference to the establishment and operation of workable administrative standards." Ph.D. dissertation, Ohio State University, 1959. (366p)

788. McNelly, John T. "Intermediary communicators in the
      international flow of news." Journalism Quarterly
      36 (Winter 1959): 23-26.

789. McQuail, Denis. Toward a Sociology of Mass Communica-
      tions. London: Collier and Macmillan, 1969. (122p)

790. _____, comp. Sociology of Mass Communications; Se-
      lected Readings. Harmondsworth: Penguin, 1972.
      (460p)

791. MacRorie, Ken. "Objectivity: Dead or Alive?" Jour-
      nalism Quarterly 36 (Spring 1959): 145-150.

792. Mallon, Paul. "News behind the news." Journalism
      Quarterly 13 (June 1936): 169-172.

793. Marnell, William H. The Right to Know; Media and the
      Common Good. New York: Seabury, 1973. (221p)

794. Maslog, Crispin. "Images and the mass media." Jour-
      nalism Quarterly 48 (Autumn 1971): 519-525.

795. Mass Media in Society: The Need for Research. New
      York: UNESCO Publications Center, 1970. (33p)

796. Mattelart, Armand. Multinational Corporations and the
      Control of Culture: the Ideological Apparatuses of
      Imperialism. Atlantic Highlands, NJ: Humanities
      Press, 1979. (304p)

797. The Media and Terrorism: A Seminar Sponsored by the
      Chicago Sun Times and Chicago Daily News. Chicago:
      Chicago Sun Times/Chicago Daily News, 1977. (38p)

798. Merckel, G. C. "The direct broadcast satellite: the
      need for effective international regulation." Syra-
      cuse Journal of International Law 2 (1974): 99-119.

799. Mintz, Morton and Jerry S. Cohen. Power, Inc. New
      York: Viking Press, 1976. (659p)

800. Mosco, Vincent. The Regulation of Broadcasting in the
      United States: A Comparative Analysis. Cambridge,
      Mass.: Harvard University, Program on Information
      Technologies and Public Policy, 1975. (294p)

801. Mowlana, Hamid. "Technology versus tradition: com-
      munication in the Iranian revolution." Journal of
      Communication 29 (Summer 1979): 107-112.

802. Muchnik, Melvyn M. "Free expression and political
      broadcasting on public radio and television." Ph.D.
      dissertation, University of Denver, 1973. (293p)

803. Neubauer, Mark. "The newsman's privilege after Branz-
      burg: the case for a federal shield law." UCLA Law
      Review 24, no. 1 (1976): 160-192.

804. Nelson, Harold L. Freedom of the Press from Hamilton
      to the Warren Court. Indianapolis: Bobbs Merrill,
      1967. (420p)

805. Nelson, Harold L. and Dwight L. Teeter. Law of Mass
      Communications: Freedom and Control of Print and
      Broadcast Media. 2nd ed. Mineola, NY: Foundation
      Press, 1973. (713p)

806. Osgood, Charles E., et al. The Measurement of Meaning.
      Urbana: University of Illinois Press, 1957. (342p)

807. Otto, Herbert A. "Sex and violence in contemporary
      media—three studies." Journal of Human Relations 16
      (Fourth Quarter 1968): 571-590.

808. Park, Robert E. Society: Collective Behavior, News
      and Opinion, Sociology and Modern Society. Glencoe:
      Free Press, 1955. (358p)

809. Pelton, Joseph N. and Marcellus S. Snow, ed. Economic
      and Policy Problems in Satellite Communications.
      New York: Praeger, 1977. (242p)

810. Phelan, John M. Mediaworld: Programming the Public.
      New York: Seabury Press, 1977. (169p)

811. Phillips, Charles F., ed. Telecommunications, Regula-
      tion and Public Choice: Papers Presented at a Sympo-
      sium Sponsored by Washington and Lee University with
      the Chesapeake and Potomac Telephone Company. Lex-
      ington, VA: Department of Economics, Washington and
      Lee University, 1975. (99p)

812. Pickard, P. M. I Could a Tale Unfold: Violence, Hor-
      ror, and Sensationalism in Stories for Children.
      London: Tavistock, 1961. (227p)

813. Pickerell, Albert G. "Access to news in the United
      States." Gazette; International Journal of the Sci-
      ence of the Press 4, no. 1 (1958): 65-80.

814. Pincus, Walter. "Is bigness a curse?: media monopo-
      lies." New Republic 170 (January 26, 1974): 13-14.

815. Pittman, Robert T., et al. "That monopoly of opinion."
      Masthead 26 (1975): 8-30.

816. Polich, John E. "Mass media accountability and manage-
      ment: how executives define decision factors in the
      American newsroom." Ph.D. dissertation, Stanford
      University, 1976. (308p)

817. Price, B. "Freedom of press, radio and screen." The
     Annals of the American Academy of Political and So-
     cial Science 254 (November 1947): 137.

818. Pryluck, Calvin. Sources of Meaning in Motion Pictures
     and Television. New York: Arno Press, 1976, c 1973.
     (241p)

819. Queeney, Kathryn M. "An analysis of the role of the
     United Nations in the formulation of principles gov-
     erning direct broadcast satellites." Ph.D. disser-
     tation, Ohio State University, 1975. (444p)

820. Rada, Stephen E. "Manipulating the media: a case
     study of a Chicano strike in Texas." Journalism
     Quarterly 54 (Spring 1977): 109-113.

821. Read, William H. America's Mass Media Merchants.
     Baltimore: Johns Hopkins University Press, 1976.
     (209p)

822. The Report of the U.S. Commission on Obscenity and
     Pornography. New York: Bantam, 1970. (700p)

823. Rights in Conflict: Report of the Twentieth Century
     Fund Task Force on Justice, Publicity and the First
     Amendment. New York: McGraw-Hill, 1976. (112p)

824. Riley, Matilda and John W. Riley. "A sociological
     approach to communications research." Public Opinion
     Quarterly 15 (Fall 1951): 445-460.

825. Ripley, Joseph M. "The practices and policies re-
     garding broadcasts of opinions about controversial
     issues by radio and television stations in the
     United States." Ph.D. dissertation, Ohio State Uni-
     versity, 1961. (279p)

826. Rivers, William L. "The Washington correspondents and
     government information." Ph.D. dissertation, Ameri-
     can University, 1960. (218p)

827. _____, et al. The Mass Media and Modern Society.
     2nd ed. San Francisco: Rinehart Press, 1970. (342p)

828. Roberts, Donald F. "'Printism' and non-print censor-
     ship." Catholic Library World 48 (December 1976):
     223-224.

829. The Role and Control of International Communications
     and Information. (U.S. Senate. Foreign Relations
     Committee. Subcommittee on International Relations.)
     Washington, D.C.: GPO, 1977. (89p)

830. Rowse, Arthur. Slanted News; A Case Study of the Nixon
     and Stevenson Fund Stories. Boston: Beacon Press,
     1957. (139p)

831. Rubin, Bernard, et al. Big Business and the Mass Media.
      Lexington, MA: Lexington Books, 1977. (185p)

832. Ryan, Michael. "News content, geographical origin and
      perceived media credibility." Journalism Quarterly
      50 (Summer 1973): 312-318.

833. Said, Edward W. Covering Islam: How the Media and
      the Experts Determine How We See the Rest of the
      World. New York: Pantheon Books, 1981. (186p)

834. Sanoff, A. P. "America's Press: Too Much Power for
      Too Few?" U.S. News and World Report 83 (August 15,
      1977): 27-33.

835. Schattenberg, Gus. "Social control functions of mass
      media depictions of crime." Sociological Inquiry 51,
      no. 1 (1981): 71-77.

836. Scher, Jacob. "Access to information: recent legal
      problems." Journalism Quarterly 37 (Winter 1960):
      41-52.

837. Schramm, Wilbur L. "The nature of news." Journalism
      Quarterly 26 (September 1949): 259-269.

838. Schultz, Henry E. "Censorship or self regulation."
      Journal of Educational Sociology 18 (December 1944):
      232-240.

839. Schumach, Murray. The Face on the Cutting Room Floor:
      The Story of Movie and Television Censorship. New
      York: Morrow, 1964. (305p)

840. Seiden, Martin H. Who Controls the Mass Media? Popular
      Myths and Economic Realities. New York: Basic Books,
      1974. (246p)

841. "Sex, violence, and the rules of the game." Journal of
      Communication 27 (Spring 1977): 164-210.

842. Shaw, Donald L. "News bias and the telegraph: a study
      of historical change." Journalism Quarterly 44
      (Spring 1967): 3-12.

843. Shaw, Eugene F. "Media credibility: taking the mea-
      sure of a measure." Journalism Quarterly 50 (Summer
      1973): 306-311.

844. Shuman, B. A. "Geography of censorship: a regional
      analysis of recent cases." Newsletter on Intellectual
      Freedom 26 (January 1977): 3-4+.

845. Siepmann, Charles A. Radio, Television and Society.
      New York: Oxford University Press, 1950. (410p)

846. Signitzer, Benno. Regulation of Direct Broadcasting
      from Satellites: The UN Involvement. New York:
      Praeger, 1976. (112p)

847. Silbermann, Alphons. "The sociology of mass media and
      mass communication." International Social Science
      Journal 32, no. 2 (1980): 223-237.

848. Sobel, Robert. The Manipulators: America in the Media
      Age. New York: Doubleday, 1976. (458p)

849. Sparkes, Vernone M. "Municipal agencies for the regu-
      lation of cable television: a study of current de-
      velopments and issues." Ph.D. dissertation, Indiana
      University, 1974. (189p)

850. Sparrow, John. "Freedom of expression: too much of a
      good thing?" American Scholar 46 (Spring 1977): 165-
      180.

851. Spitzer, H. M. "Presenting America in American propa-
      ganda." Public Opinion Quarterly 11 (1947): 213-221.

852. Stein, M. L. Shaping the News: How the Media Func-
      tion in Today's World. New York: Washington Square
      Press, 1974. (207p)

853. Sterling, Christopher H. "Newspaper ownership of
      broadcast stations, 1920-68." Journalism Quarterly
      46 (Summer 1969): 227-236; 254.

854. Sternberg, Beno and Evelyne Sullerot. Aspects sociaux
      de la radio et de la television. Paris: Mouton,
      1966. (138p)

855. Stoodley, Bartlett H. "Bias in reporting the FCC in-
      vestigation." Public Opinion Quarterly 24 (Spring
      1960): 92-93.

856. Taylor, Wilson L. "Gauging the mental health content
      of the mass media." Journalism Quarterly 34 (Spring
      1957): 191-201.

857. Tedlow, Richard S. Keeping the Corporate Image: Pub-
      lic Relations and Business, 1900-1950." Greenwich,
      CT: JAI Press, 1979. (233p)

858. Thayer, Lee, ed. Communication: Ethical and Moral
      Issues. New York: Gordon and Breach, 1973. (383p)

859. Thieme, V. "Broadcasting satellites and international
      law: a new communications technology and its world-
      wide legal consequences." May, 1976. (153p) NTIS-
      N76-24069/6GA.

860. Tiffen, Rodney. The News from Southeast Asia: The
      Sociology of Newsmaking. Singapore: Institute of
      Southeast Asian Studies, 1978. (206p)

861. Trotter, Edgar P. "A coorientational analysis of gate-
      keeper, audience, and publisher patterns of news se-
      lections." Ph.D. dissertation, Southern Illinois
      University, 1975. (156p)

862. Tunstall, Jeremy, comp. Media Sociology. Urbana:
      University of Illinois Press, 1970. (574p)

863. Twomey, John. "New forms of social control over mass
      media content." Studies in Public Communication
      1 (Summer 1957): 38-44.

864. Ward, N. "Feminism and censorship." Language Arts 53
      (May 1976): 536-537.

865. Waxman, Jerry J. "Local broadcast gatekeeping during
      natural disasters." Journalism Quarterly 50 (Winter
      1973): 751-758.

866. Wegner, Daniel M., et al. "Incrimination through in-
      nuendo: can media questions become public answers?"
      Journal of Personality and Social Psychology 40 (May
      1981): 822-832.

867. Wells, Alan F., ed. Mass Media and Society. Palo
      Alto, CA: National Press, 1972. (407p)

868. White, David M. "The 'gatekeeper': a case study in
      the selection of news." Journalism Quarterly 27
      (Fall 1950): 383-390.

869. Whitehead, Paul C. "Sex, violence and crime in the
      mass media." Canada's Mental Health 18, no. 2 (1970):
      20-23.

870. Whitlow, Sylvia S. "How male and female gatekeepers
      respond to news stories of women." Journalism Quar-
      terly 54 (Autumn 1977): 573-579; 609.

871. _____. "The perception of women as news principals:
      an analysis of the cognitive set of gatekeepers and
      of situational correlates." Ph.D. dissertation,
      Southern Illinois University, 1975. (358p)

872. Whitney, D. Charles and Lee B. Becker. "'Keeping the
      gates' for gatekeepers: the effects of wire news."
      Journalism Quarterly 59 (Spring 1982): 60-65.

873. Wiggins, Robert G. "Access to the mass media: public's
      right or publisher's privilege?" Ph.D. dissertation,
      Southern Illinois University, 1973. (325p)

874. William, Jack. "Twentieth-century concepts of non-commercial news media in the United States." Ph.D. dissertation, University of Illinois at Urbana-Champaign, 1972. (251p)

875. Williams, John D. "Variables in government/media interaction: freedom of information, security, and social responsibility." Ph.D. dissertation, University of Texas at Austin, 1972. (301p)

876. Wilson, H. Hubert. Pressure Group; The Campaign for Commercial Television in England. New Brunswick, NJ: Rutgers University Press, 1961. (232p)

877. Wright, Charles R. Mass Communications: A Sociological Perspective. 2nd ed. New York: Random House, 1975. (179p)

B. PRINT MEDIA

878. Abrahms, Floyd. "The press, privacy and the Constitution." New York Times Magazine, August 21, 1977: 11-13.

879. Albrecht, Milton C. "Does literature reflect common values." American Sociological Review 21 (December 1956): 722-729.

880. Allen, Frederick L. "Newspapers and the truth." The Atlantic Monthly 129 (January 1922): 44-54.

881. Almaney, Adnan. "Government control of the press in the United Arab Republic, 1952-70." Journalism Quarterly 49 (Summer 1972): 340-348.

882. Altus, William D. "Sexual role, the short story, and the writer." Journal of Psychology 47 (January 1959): 37-40.

883. Ames, William E. "Federal patronage and the Washington D.C. press." Journalism Quarterly 49 (Spring 1972): 22-30.

884. Atwood, L. Erwin, et al. "Daily newspaper contributions to community discussion." Journalism Quarterly 55 (Autumn 1980): 570-576.

885. Baker, Elizabeth F. Printers and Technology: A History of the International Printing Pressmen and Assistants' Union. New York: Columbia University Press, 1957. (545p)

886. Barlow, Reuel R. "The government and the press in Germany: Part II." Journalism Quarterly 6 (November 1929): 3-7.

887. Barr, Doris W. "A model and method for content analy-
      sis: implementation in a study of magazine covers."
      Ph.D. dissertation, University of Illinois, 1958.
      (407p)

888. Behrens, John C. The Typewriter Guerillas. Chicago:
      Nelson-Hall, 1977. (254p)

889. Berelson, Bernard and Patricia J. Salter. "Majority
      and minority Americans: an analysis of magazine fic-
      tion." Public Opinion Quarterly 10 (1946): 168-190.

890. Berkman, Aaron. "Sociology of the comic strip." Amer-
      ican Spectator 4 (June 1936): 52-53.

891. Bird, George L. "Newspaper monopoly and political in-
      dependence." Journalism Quarterly 17 (September
      1940): 207-214.

892. Brandner, Lowell and Joan Sistrunk. "The newspaper:
      molder or mirror of community values?" Journalism
      Quarterly 43 (Autumn 1966): 497-504.

893. Breed, Warren. "The newspaperman, news, and society."
      Ph.D. dissertation, Columbia University, 1952. (472p)

894. _____. "Newspapers 'opinion leaders' and the
      processes of standardization." Journalism Quarterly
      32 (Summer 1955): 277-284.

895. Bremner, John B. "An analysis of the content of Catho-
      lic diocesan newspapers in the United States." Ph.D.
      dissertation, State University of Iowa, 1965. (348p)

896. Brown, Charles H. "Press censorship in the Spanish-
      American War." Journalism Quarterly 42 (Autumn 1965):
      581-590.

897. Brown, Trevor R. "Free press fair game for South Afri-
      ca's government." Journalism Quarterly 48 (Spring
      1971): 120-127.

898. Brucker, Herbert. Communication is Power: Unchanging
      Values in a Changing Journalism. New York: Oxford
      University Press, 1973. (385p)

899. Burma, John H. "An analysis of the present Negro
      press." Social Forces 26 (December 1947): 172-180.

900. Cade, Dozier C. "Witch hunting, 1952: the role of
      the press." Journalism Quarterly 29 (Fall 1952):
      396-407.

901. Camp, Laurie. "Applying due process to gag rules and
      order." Nebraska Law Review 55, no. 3 (1975-1976):
      427-439.

902. Carter, Roy E. "Newspaper 'gatekeepers' and the source
      of news." Public Opinion Quarterly 22 (Summer 1958):
      133-144.

903. Casey, R. "Pressure groups and the press." In the
      Polls and Public Opinion, pp. 124-140. Edited by
      N. Meier and H. Saunders. New York: Holt, 1949.

904. Chomsky, Noam and Edward S. Herman. "Distortions at
      fourth hand." Nation 224 (June 25, 1977): 789-794.

905. Christian, Harry, ed. The Sociology of Journalism and
      the Press. Keele, England: University of Keele;
      Dist. of Rowman and Littlefield, Totowa, NJ: 1980.
      (395p)

906. "Comic book czar and code." America 91 (February 10,
      1954): 2-3.

907. Cony, Edward R. "Conflict-cooperation content of five
      American dailies." Journalism Quarterly 30 (Winter
      1953): 15-22.

908. Coser, Lewis, et al. Books: The Culture and Commerce
      of Publishing. New York: Basic Books, 1982. (411p)

909. Davis, F. J. "Crime news in Colorado newspapers."
      American Journal of Sociology 57 (1951): 325-330.

910. Davis, Junetta. "Sexist bias in eight newspapers."
      Journalism Quarterly 59 (Autumn 1982): 456-460.

911. Deland, Paul S. "Battling crime comics to protect
      youth." Federal Probation 19 (1905): 26-30.

912. Dennis, Everette E. "Purloined papers and information
      as property: a study of press-government conflict."
      Ph.D. dissertation, University of Minnesota, 1974.
      (335p)

913. De Volpi, A., et al. Born Secret: The H-Bomb, the
      Progressive Case and National Security. New York:
      Pergamon Press, 1981. (304p)

914. Donohew, Lewis. "Publishers and their influence
      groups." Journalism Quarterly 42 (Winter 1965):
      112-113.

915. Durocher, Aurele A. "Verbal opposition to industriali-
      zation in American magazines, 1830-1860." Ph.D. dis-
      sertation, University of Minnesota, 1955. (358p)

916. Downes, Alan J. "Optimism and pessimism in American
      magazines, 1850-1960." Ph.D. dissertation, Univer-
      sity of Washington, 1961. (238p)

917. Dudley, Bruce M. "Control of small college student
      press." Journalism Quarterly 46 (Spring 1969): 154-
      156.

918. Duscha, Julius. "A free and accessible press." Pro-
      gressive 38 (January 1974): 41-43.

919. Eggleston, Wilfrid. "Canadian magazines and the
      O'Leary Report." Gazette 7, no. 3-4 (1961): 275-282.

920. Ellis, Lewis E. Newsprint: Producers, Publishers,
      and Political Pressures. New Brunswick, NJ: Rutgers
      University Press, 1960. (520p)

921. Ellison, Jerome and Franklin Gosser. "Non-fiction
      magazine articles: a content analysis study." Jour-
      nalism Quarterly 36 (Winter 1959): 27-34.

922. Emery, Edwin. "The contemporary American daily press."
      Gazette 4, no. 1 (1958): 1-8.

923. Epstein, Matthew H. "A study of the editorial opinions
      of the New York City newspapers toward the League of
      Nations and the United Nations during the first year
      of life." Ph.D. dissertation, New York University,
      1954. (607p)

924. Erickson, John E. "Newspapers and social values: Chi-
      cago journalism, 1890-1910." Ph.D. dissertation,
      University of Illinois at Urbana-Champaign, 1973.
      (473p)

925. Eshenaur, Ruth M. "Censorship of the alternative press:
      a descriptive study of the social and political con-
      trol of radical periodicals (1964-1973)." Ph.D. dis-
      sertation, Southern Illinois University, 1975. (371p)

926. Eulau, H. "Proselytizing in the Catholic press." Pub-
      lic Opinion Quarterly 11 (1947): 189-197.

927. Evans, William B. "'Revolutionist thought' in the
      'Daily Worker' 1919-1939." Ph.D. dissertation, Uni-
      versity of Washington, 1965. (239p)

928. Fishman, Joshua A. and Gele S. Fishman. "Separatism
      and integrationism: a social-psychological analysis
      of editorial content in New York newspapers of three
      American minority groups." Genetic Psychology Mono-
      graphs 59 (May 1959): 219-261.

929. Flanagan, John T. "Folklore in the newspapers." Jour-
      nalism Quarterly 35 (Spring 1958): 205-211.

930. Fortin, Gerald A. "An analysis of the ideology of a
      French Canadian nationalist magazine: 1917-1954. A
      contribution to the sociology of knowledge." Ph.D.
      dissertation, Cornell University, 1956. (261p)

931. Fowler, Mary E. "Literature for international under-
      standing: a study of the presentation of foreign
      peoples and cultures in secondary school literature
      anthologies." Ph.D. dissertation, New York Univer-
      sity, 1954. (521p)

932. Frank, Willard C. "Error, distortion and bias in the
      Virginia gazettes, 1773-74." Journalism Quarterly
      49 (Winter 1972): 729-739.

933. Free Press-Fair Trial. (U.S. Senate Committee on the
      Judiciary. Subcommittee on Constitutional Rights.)
      Washington, D.C.: GPO, 1976. (22p)

934. Garberson, John W. "Magazine market demand for the
      factual article." Journalism Quarterly 24 (March
      1947): 31-36.

935. Gardner, Mary A. "The Inter American Press Association
      and its fight for freedom of the press." Ph.D. dis-
      sertation, University of Minnesota, 1960. (323p)

936. Gieber, Walter. "Do newspapers overplay 'negative'
      news?" Journalism Quarterly 32 (Summer 1955): 311-
      318.

937. _____. "Two communicators of the news: a study of
      the roles of sources and reporters." Social Forces
      39 (October 1960): 76-83.

938. Gillmor, Donald M. "Free press versus fair trial: a
      new era." Journalism Quarterly 41 (Winter 1964):
      27-37.

939. _____. "Freedom in press systems and the religious
      variable." Journalism Quarterly 39 (Winter 1962):
      15-26.

940. _____. "Trial by newspaper: the Constitutional
      conflict between free press and fair trial in English
      and American law." Ph.D. dissertation, University of
      Minnesota, 1961. (386p)

941. Ginglinger, Genevieve. "Basic values in 'Reader's Di-
      gest,' 'Selection' and 'Constellation.'" Journalism
      Quarterly 32 (Winter 1955): 56-61.

942. Gormley, William T. "Newspaper agendas and political
      elites." Journalism Quarterly 52 (Summer 1975): 304-
      308.

943. Gossman, Norbert J. "Political and social themes in
      the English popular novel." Public Opinion Quarterly
      20 (Fall 1956): 531-541.

944. Grotta, Gerald L. "Attitudes on newspaper accuracy
      and external controls." Journalism Quarterly 46
      (Winter 1969): 757-759.

945. _____. "Consolidation of newspapers: what happens
      to the consumer?" Journalism Quarterly 48 (Summer
      1971): 245-250.

946. Hachten, William A. "The metropolitan Sunday newspaper
      in the United States: a study of trends in content
      and practices." Ph.D. dissertation, University of
      Minnesota, 1961. (624p)

947. Hahn, Taeyoul. "Structural control of the press: an
      exploration in organizational analysis." Ph.D. dis-
      sertation, University of Minnesota, 1972. (260p)

948. Hamlin, Douglas L.B., ed. The Press and the Public.
      Toronto: University of Toronto Press, 1962. (38p)

949. Harrington, Harry F. "Can a newspaper tell the truth?"
      National Printer Journalist 40 (January 1922): 30-31.

950. Harvey, John. "The content characteristics of best-
      selling novels." Public Opinion Quarterly 17 (Spring
      1953): 91-114.

951. Hatch, Mary G. and D. L. Hatch. "Problems of married
      working women as presented by three popular working
      women's magazines." Social Forces 37 (December
      1958): 148-153.

952. Hausdorff, Don M. "Depression laughter: magazine hu-
      mor and American society, 1929-33." Ph.D. disserta-
      tion, University of Minnesota, 1963. (375p)

953. Hester, Albert L. "The Associated Press and news from
      Latin America: a gatekeeper and news flow study."
      Ph.D. dissertation, University of Wisconsin, 1972.
      (289p)

954. Hileman, Donald G. "The Kinsey Report: a study of
      press responsibility." Journalism Quarterly 30
      (Fall 1953): 434-437.

955. Hocking, William E. Freedom of the Press. Chicago:
      University of Chicago Press, 1947. (24p)

956. Houghton, Donald E. "The 'New Yorker': exponent of a
      cosmopolitan elite." Ph.D. dissertation, University
      of Minnesota, 1955. (299p)

957. Hvistendahl, J. K. "Publisher's power: functional or
      dysfunctional?" Journalism Quarterly 47 (Autumn
      1970): 472-478.

958.   Jones, David W. "The press and the politics of urban
        growth: a study of cues and constraints in the po-
        liticized newsroom." Ph.D. dissertation, Stanford
        University, 1974. (283p)

959.   Jones, Gregory. "Antitrust malaise in the newspaper
        industry." St. Mary's Law Journal 8, no. 1 (1976-
        1977): 160-174.

960.   Kelly, Susan. Access Denied; The Politics of Press
        Censorship. Beverly Hills: Sage, 1978. (80p)

961.   Kent, Ruth K. "Mental health coverage in six mass
        magazines." Journalism Quarterly 39 (Autumn 1962):
        519-522.

962.   Kingsbury, Susan M., et al. "Measuring the ethics of
        American newspapers, I: spectrum analysis of news-
        paper sensationalism." Journalism Quarterly 10 (June
        1933): 93-108.

963.   _____. "Measuring the ethics of American newspapers,
        II: news interest spectra of important papers."
        Journalism Quarterly 10 (September 1933): 181-201.

964.   _____. "Measuring the ethics of American newspapers,
        III: newspaper bias of Congressional controversies."
        Journalism Quarterly 10 (December 1933): 323-342.

965.   _____. "Measuring the ethics of American newspapers,
        IV: the headline index of newspaper bias." Journal-
        ism Quarterly 11 (June 1934): 179-199.

966.   _____. "Measuring the ethics of American newspapers,
        VI: laggards and leaders in ethical journalism."
        Journalism Quarterly 11 (September 1934): 284-300.

967.   Kolaja, Jiri. "American magazine cartoons and social
        control." Journalism Quarterly 30 (Winter 1953): 71-
        74.

968.   Lashner, Marilyn A. "Privacy and the public's right to
        know." Journalism Quarterly 53 (Winter 1976): 679-
        688.

969.   Lent, John A. "Foreign news content of United States
        and Asian print media: a literature review and prob-
        lem analysis." Gazette 22, no. 3 (1976): 169-182.

970.   Leverette, William E. "Science and values: a study of
        Edward L. Youmans' Popular Science Monthly 1872-
        1877." Ph.D. dissertation, Vanderbilt University,
        1963. (341p)

971.   Levy, Leonard W. Freedom of Speech and Press in Early
        American History: Legacy of Suppression. New York:
        Harper and Row, 1963. (353p)

972.   _____, ed. Freedom of the Press from Zenger to
        Jefferson. Indianapolis: Bobbs Merrill, 1966.
        (409p)

973.   Lewis, Felice F. Literature, Obscenity, and the Law.
        Carbondale, IL: Southern Illinois University Press,
        1976. (297p)

974.   Lewis, H. L. "The Cuban revolt story: AP, UPI and 3
        papers." Journalism Quarterly 37 (Autumn 1960):
        573-578; 646.

975.   Lewis, John N.C. Anatomy of Printing: The Influences
        of Art and History on Its Design. New York: Watson-
        Guptill, 1970. (228p)

976.   Lewkowicz, S. B. "Elton's An Exposition of the Ten
        Commandments of God (1623): a burnt book?" Biblio-
        graphical Society of American Papers 71 (April 1977):
        201-208.

977.   Lieberman, J. Ben. "Restating the concept of freedom
        of the press." Journalism Quarterly 30 (Spring
        1953): 131-138.

978.   Linneman, William R. "American life as reflected in
        illustrated humor magazines: 1877-1900." Ph.D. dis-
        sertation, University of Illinois, 1960. (315p)

979.   Lloyd, A. H. "Newspaper conscience: a study in half-
        truths." American Journal of Sociology 27 (September
        1921): 197-210.

980.   McCarthy, Eugene. "Sins of omission: the media as
        censor." Harper's 254 (June 1977): 90-92.

981.   McFadden, R. D. "Diana Trilling book is canceled by
        publisher." AB Bookman's Weekly 58 (October 11,
        1976): 1912-1918.

982.   McGrath, Edward G. "The political ideals of Life maga-
        zine." Ph.D. dissertation, Syracuse University,
        1961. (287p)

983.   Mayes, Sharon S. "Sociology, women, and fiction."
        International Journal of Women's Studies 2 (1979):
        203-220.

984.   Mazer, N. F. "Comics, cokes, and censorship." Top of
        the News 32 (January 1976): 167-170.

985.   Merrill, John C. "The image of the United States pre-
        sented by ten Mexican daily newspapers." Ph.D. dis-
        sertation, State University of Iowa, 1962. (389p)

986.   Murphy, Charles F. "A seal of approval for the comic
        books." Federal Probation 19 (1956): 19-20.

987.   Narasimhan, V. K. "Shaping of editorial policy in the
        Indian press." Journalism Quarterly 33 (Spring
        1956): 208-213.

988.   Nixon, Raymond B. "Freedom in the world's press: a
        fresh appraisal with new data." Journalism Quarterly
        42 (Winter 1965): 3-14.

989.   Nixon, Raymond B. and Jean Ward. "Trends in news-
        paper ownership and inter-media competition." Jour-
        nalism Quarterly 38 (Winter 1961): 3-14.

990.   Nixon, Raymond B. and Tae-youl Hahn. "Concentration
        of press ownership: a comparison of 32 countries."
        Journalism Quarterly 48 (Spring 1971): 5-16.

991.   Nord, David P. Newspapers and New Politics: Mid-
        western Municipal Reform, 1890-1900." Ann Arbor:
        UMI Research Press, 1981. (204p)

992.   O'Donnell, J. J. "Censorship and the publishers."
        NASSP Bulletin 59 (May 1975): 59-63.

993.   Olson, Kenneth E. "The newspaper in times of social
        change." Journalism Quarterly 12 (March 1935): 9-
        19.

994.   Otto, Herbert A. "The pornographic fringeland on the
        American newsstand." Journal of Human Relations 12
        (3rd Quarter 1964): 375-390.

995.   _____. "Sex and violence on the American news-
        stand." Journalism Quarterly 40 (Spring 1963): 19-
        26.

996.   Peck, D. C. "Government suppression of Elizabethan
        Catholic books: the cast of Leicester's Common-
        wealth." Library Quarterly 47 (April 1977): 163-
        177.

997.   Peterson, Sophia. "Foreign news gatekeepers and cri-
        teria of newsworthiness." Journalism Quarterly 56
        (Spring 1979): 116-125.

998.   Pilpel, H. F. and L. R. Rockett. "Libel, advertising
        and freedom of the press." Publishers Weekly 209
        (March 1, 1976): 46-48.

999.   Pollock, John C., et al. "Media agendas and human
        rights: the Supreme Court decision on abortion."
        Journalism Quarterly 55 (Autumn 1978): 544-548; 561.

1000.   Pruden, D. "The myth of freedom of the press." So-
        ciology of Education 19 (1945): 249-258.

1001.   Robbins, Jan C. "The paradox of press freedom: a
        study of the British experience." Journalism Quar-
        terly 44 (Autumn 1967): 428-438.

1002.   Robinson, Donald L. "Editorials of American purpose:
        a content analysis of selected newspaper editorials
        concerning international relations." Ph.D. disser-
        tation, American University, 1963. (214p)

1003.   Roche, Bruce W. "The effect of newspaper owners' non-
        media business interests on news judgments of mem-
        bers of news staffs." Ph.D. dissertation, Southern
        Illinois University, 1975. (117p)

1004.   Ross, S. S. "Is technology getting a fair shake in
        the general press?" PE—Professional Engineer 51
        (September 1981): 8-11.

1005.   Rowell, C. H. "Freedom of the press." The Annals of
        the American Academy of Political and Social Science
        185 (May 1936): 182-189.

1006.   Rubin, David M. "Reporting the corporate state: ad-
        versarity, freedom of information, public utilities,
        and the press." Ph.D. dissertation, Stanford Uni-
        versity, 1972. (280p)

1007.   Sackler, Arthur E. Federal Laws Affecting Newspapers.
        Washington, D.C.: National Newspaper Association,
        1981. (178p)

1008.   Schiller, Dan. "An historical approach to objectivity
        and professionalism in American news reporting."
        Journal of Communication 29 (Autumn 1979): 46-57.

1009.   Schlesinger, Laurence E. "Prediction of newspaper
        bias." Journal of Social Psychology 42 (1955): 35-
        42.

1010.   Schwoebel, Jean. Newsroom Democracy: The Case for
        Independence of the Press. Iowa City: Iowa Center
        for Communication Study, School of Journalism, Uni-
        versity of Iowa, 1976. (67p)

1011.   Scott, G. S. "Paperback censorship: an idea whose
        time has gone." Media and Methods 11 (May 1975):
        14-15.

1012.   Seemann, Howard L. "Keeping the gates at the Chicago
        Defender." Journalism Quarterly 48 (Summer 1971):
        275-278.

1013.   Shaw, Donald L. "Surveillance vs. constraint: press
        coverage of a social issue." Journalism Quarterly
        46 (Winter 1969): 707-712.

1014.   Shaw, Eugene F. "The press and its freedom: a pilot
        study of an American stereotype." Journalism Quar-
        terly 49 (Spring 1972): 31-42, 60.

1015.   Showalter, Stuart W. "American magazine coverage of
        the Vietnam War." Journalism Quarterly 53 (Winter
        1976): 648-652.

1016.   Siebert, Fredrick S. "The confiscated revolutionary
        press." Journalism Quarterly 13 (June 1936): 179-
        181.

1017.   _____. Freedom of the Press in England 1476-1776:
        The Rise and Decline of Government Control. Urbana:
        University of Illinois Press, 1965, c 1952. (411p)

1018.   _____. "The future of a free press." Journalism
        Quarterly 32 (Winter 1955): 6-9.

1019.   _____. "The regulation of newsbooks, 1620-1640."
        Journalism Quarterly 16 (June 1939): 151-160.

1020.   _____. "Regulation of the press in the seventeenth
        century: excerpts from the records of the Court of
        the Stationer's Company." Journalism Quarterly 13
        (December 1936): 381-393.

1021.   Stone, Gerald C. and Maxwell E. McCombs. "Tracing the
        time lag in agenda-setting." Journalism Quarterly
        58 (Spring 1981): 51-55.

1022.   Swanson, C. E. "Midcity daily: the news staff and
        its relation to control." Journalism Quarterly 26
        (March 1949): 20-28.

1023.   Taylor, Mary E. "Employed women in recent periodical
        short fiction: the fictionalized portrait of em-
        ployed women projected against a background of fac-
        tual data." Ph.D. dissertation, Indiana University,
        1955. (196p)

1024.   Teeter, Dwight L. "Press freedom and the public
        printing: Pennsylvania 1775-83." Journalism Quar-
        terly 45 (Autumn 1968): 445-451.

1025.   Thayer, Frank. Legal Control of the Press. 2nd ed.
        Brooklyn: Foundation Press, 1950. (654p)

1026.   _____. "Shifting concepts in laws affecting the
        press." Journalism Quarterly 28 (Winter 1951): 24-
        30.

1027. Thomas, Donald. A Long Time Burning: The History of
       Literary Censorship in England. London: Routledge
       and Kegan Paul, 1969. (546p)

1028. Watkins, John J. "Newsgathering and the First Amend-
       ment." Journalism Quarterly 53 (Autumn 1976): 406-
       416.

1029. Weaver, David H. "The press and government control:
       international patterns of development from 1950 to
       1966." Ph.D. dissertation, University of North
       Carolina at Chapel Hill, 1974. (272p)

1030. Weigel, Russell H. and Jeffrey J. Pappas. "Social
       science and the press: a case study and its impli-
       cations." American Psychologist 36 (May 1981): 480-
       487.

1031. White, Lee A. "The press and the public." Journalism
       Quarterly 17 (September 1940): 215-226.

1032. Wiggins, James R. "The power and responsibility of
       the press." Journalism Quarterly 37 (Winter 1960):
       29-34.

1033. Williams, J. Emlyn. "Journalism in Germany: 1933."
       Journalism Quarterly 10 (December 1933): 283-288.

C. FILM

1034. Aldgate, T. "1930's newsreels: censorship and con-
       troversy." Sight and Sound 46 (Summer 1977): 154-
       157.

1035. Bergman, Andrew. We're in the Money: Depression
       America and its Films. New York: New York Univer-
       sity Press, 1971. (200p)

1036. Bertrand, Ina. Film Censorship in Australia. St.
       Lucia: University of Queensland Press, 1978. (227p)

1037. Bouras, J. "In the realm of the censors." Film Com-
       ment 13 (January 1977): 32-33.

1038. Carmen, Ira H. Movies, Censorship and the Law. Ann
       Arbor: University of Michigan Press, 1966. (339p)

1039. The Cinema and the Protection of Youths. (Council of
       Europe. European Committee on Crime Problems.)
       Strasbourg: Council of Europe, 1968. (167p)

1040. The Cinema: Its Present Position and Future Possibil-
       ities. (National Council of Public Morals.) London:
       Williams and Norgate, 1917. (372p)

1041. Conant, Michael. Anti-Trust in the Motion Picture
      Industry. Berkeley: University of California
      Press, 1960. (240p)

1042. Dale, Edgar. The Content of Motion Pictures. New
      York: Macmillan, 1935. (234p)

1043. Elkin, Frederick. "Value implications of popular
      films." Sociology and Social Research 38 (May
      1954): 320-322.

1044. Facey, Paul W. The Legion of Decency: A Sociological
      Analysis of the Emergence and Development of a So-
      cial Pressure Group. New York: Arno Press, c 1974.
      (206p)

1045. Farber, Stephen. The Movie Rating Game. Washington,
      D.C.: Public Affairs Press, c 1972. (128p)

1046. Feldman, Charles M. "The National Board of Censorship
      (Review) of Motion Pictures, 1909-1922." Ph.D. dis-
      sertation, University of Michigan, 1975. (237p)

1047. Grace, Harry A. "A taxonomy of American crime film
      themes." Journal of Social Psychology 42 (1955):
      129-136.

1048. Huaco, George A. The Sociology of Film Art. New York:
      Basic Books, 1965. (229p)

1049. Hunnings, Neville M. Film Censors and the Law. Lon-
      don: Allen and Unwin, 1967. (474p)

1050. Inglis, Ruth A. Freedom of the Movies: A Report on
      Self-Regulation from the Commission on Freedom of
      the Press. Chicago: University of Chicago, 1947.
      (NA)

1051. Jarvie, Ian C. Movies and Society. New York: Basic
      Books, 1970. (394p)

1052. Jones, Dorothy B. "Hollywood war films." Hollywood
      Quarterly 1 (1945): 1-19.

1053. _____. "Quantitative analysis of motion picture
      content." Public Opinion Quarterly 6 (September
      1942): 411-428.

1054. _____. "Quantitative analysis of motion picture
      content." Public Opinion Quarterly 14 (Fall 1950):
      554-558.

1055. Jowett, Garth S. "The concept of history in American
      produced films: an analysis of the films made in
      the period 1950-1961." Journal of Popular Culture 3
      (Spring 1970): 799-813.

1056. _____. Film: The Democratic Art. Boston: Little,
       Brown, c 1976. (130p)

1057. Jowett, Garth S. and James M. Linton. Movies as Mass
       Communication. Beverly Hills: Sage, 1980. (149p)

1058. Kahn, Gordon. Hollywood on Trial. New York: Boni
       and Gaer, 1948. (229p)

1059. Kracauer, Siegfried. From Caligari to Hitler; A Psy-
       chological History of the German Film. Princeton:
       Princeton University Press, 1947. (361p)

1060. _____. "National types as Hollywood presents
       them." Popular Opinion Quarterly 13 (Spring 1949):
       53-72.

1061. Liehm, Antonin J. "The contemporary social film: its
       content and aesthetic character." Praxis 1 (Spring
       1975): 111-114.

1062. Linden, Kathryn B. "The film censorship struggle in
       the United States from 1926 to 1957, and the social
       values involved." Ph.D. dissertation, New York Uni-
       versity, 1972. (513p)

1063. Lunders, Leo. La Censure des films et l'admission des
       enfants en cinéma a travers le monde. Bruxelles:
       Editions du C.E.P., 1961. (508p)

1064. McCann, Richard D., ed. Film and Society. New York:
       Scribner's, 1964. (182p)

1065. McManus, J. T. and L. Kronenberger. "Motion pictures,
       the theatre, and race relations." Annals of the
       American Academy of Political and Social Science 244
       (1946): 152-158.

1066. Metzger, Charles R. "Pressure groups and the motion
       picture industry." Annals of the American Academy
       of Political and Social Science 254 (November 1947):
       110-115.

1067. Moley, Raymond. The Hays Office. New York: Bobbs-
       Merrill, 1945. (266p)

1068. Nizer, Louis. New Courts of Industry: Self-Regulation
       Under the Motion Picture Code. New York: Longacre
       Press, 1935. (344p)

1069. Phelps, Guy. Film Censorship. London: Gollancz,
       1975. (319p)

1070. Randall, Richard S. Censorship of the Movies. Madi-
       son: University of Wisconsin, 1968. (280p)

1071.   Rosten, L. C.   "Movies and propaganda."   Annals of
        the American Academy of Political and Social Science
        254 (1947): 116-124.

1072.   Sargent, John A.   "Self-regulation: the motion pic-
        ture production code, 1930-61."   Ph.D. dissertation,
        University of Michigan, 1963.   (277p)

1073.   Shain, Russell E.   An Analysis of Motion Pictures
        About War Released by the American Film Industry,
        1939-1970.   New York: Arno Press, 1976, c 1973.
        (448p)

1074.   Smith, Julian.   Looking Away; Hollywood and Vietnam.
        New York: Scribner's, 1975.   (236p)

1075.   Stevenson, Robert L. and Mark T. Grane.   "A recon-
        sideration of bias in the news."   Journalism Quar-
        terly 57 (Spring 1980): 115-121.

1076.   Turin, Kenneth and Stephen F. Zito.   Sinema: American
        Pornographic Films and the People Who Make Them.
        New York: Praeger, 1974.   (244p)

1077.   Westin, Alan F.   The Miracle Case: The Supreme Court
        and the Movies.   Indianapolis: Published for the
        ICᴰ by Bobbs-Merrill, 1961.   (38p)

1078.   Woelfel, Norman.   "The American mind and the motion
        picture."   Annals of the American Academy of Politi-
        cal and Social Science 254 (November 1947): 88-94.

1079.   Wolfenstein, Martha and Naton Leites.   Movies: A
        Psychological Study.   Glencoe: Free Press, 1950.
        (316p)

1080.   Wood, Michael.   America in the Movies.   New York: Ba-
        sic Books, 1975.   (206p)

1081.   Wright, Will.   Sixguns and Society: A Structural
        Study of the Western.   Berkeley: University of
        California Press, 1975.   (217p)

1082.   Young, Donald.   Motion Pictures: A Study in Social
        Legislation.   Philadelphia: Westbrook, 1922.   (109p)

D.   RADIO

1083.   Albig, John W.   "The content of radio programs 1925-
        1938."   Social Forces 16 (March 1938): 338-349.

1084.   Bass, Abraham Z.   "Refining the 'gatekeeper' concept:
        a UN radio case study."   Journalism Quarterly 46
        (Spring 1969): 69-72.

30000# 78   Communications and Society

1085. Buckalew, James K. "The radio news gatekeeper and
       his sources." Journalism Quarterly 51 (Winter
       1974): 602-606.

1086. Caldwell, Edward C. "Censorship of radio programs."
       Journal of Radio Law 1 (October 1931): 441-476.

1087. Harlow, Alvin F. Old Wires and New Waves. New York:
       Appleton-Century, 1936. (548p)

1088. Helffrich, Stockton. "The radio and television codes
       and the public interest." Journal of Broadcasting
       14 (Summer 1970): 267-274.

1089. Matthews, Donald C. "The public interest factor and
       management philosophy in the history and commercial
       operation of radio station WOR-AM, New York, 1922-
       1970." Ph.D. dissertation, University of Southern
       California, 1973. (328p)

1090. Miller, Neville. "Radio's of self-regulation." Pub-
       lic Opinion Quarterly 3 (October 1939): 683-688.

1091. "Radio program controls: a network of inadequacy."
       Yale Law Journal 57 (December 1947): 275-296.

1092. "Radio regulation and freedom of the air." Harvard
       Law Review 54 (April 1941): 1220-1228.

1093. Ross, Dale H. "The 'Amos 'n Andy' radio program,
       1928-1937: its history, content, and social sig-
       nificance." Ph.D. dissertation, University of Iowa,
       1974. (295p)

1094. Segal, Paul M. "Recent trends in censorship of radio
       broadcast programs." Rocky Mountain Law Review 20
       (June 1948): 366-380.

1095. Soley, Lawrence C. "An evaluation of FCC policy on
       FM ownership." Journalism Quarterly 56 (Autumn
       1979): 26-28.

1096. Summers, Havison B. Radio Censorship. New York:
       Wilson, 1939. (297p)

1097. Surlin, Stuart H. "Perceived need for minority owner-
       ship of radio stations." Journalism Quarterly 54
       (Autumn 1977): 587-591.

1098. _____. "Race, education, and fatalism: predictors
       of involvement in radio programming." Journal of
       Broadcasting 21 (Fall 1977): 413-426.

1099. Traub, James. "Radio without rules." Columbia Jour-
       nalism Review 20 (January/February 1982): 36-38.

E. TELEVISION

1100. Adams, William and Suzanne Albin. "Public information
       on social change: TV coverage of women in the work-
       force." Policy Studies Journal 8 (Spring 1980):
       717-734.

1101. Alderson, Jeremy W. "Everyman TV." Columbia Journal-
       ism Review 19 (January/February 1981): 39-42.

1102. Alley, Robert S. Television: Ethics for Hire? Nash-
       ville: Abington, 1977. (192p)

1103. Axelrad, David. "Ring around the collar—chain around
       her neck: a proposal to monitor sex role stereo-
       typing in television advertising." Hastings Law
       Journal 28, no. 1 (1976-1977): 149-190.

1104. Baehr, Helen. "The 'liberated woman' in television
       drama." Women's Studies International Quarterly 3,
       no. 1 (1980): 29-39.

1105. Bailey, Robert L. "The content of network television
       prime time special programming: 1948-1968." Jour-
       nal of Broadcasting 14 (Summer 1970): 325-336.

1106. Baran, Stanley J. and L. L. Henke. "Regulation of
       televised violence." Communication Quarterly 24
       (Fall 1976): 24-30.

1107. Bennett, William J. "Censorship for the common good."
       The Public Interest 52 (Summer 1978): 98-102.

1108. Brown, Les. Television: The Business Behind the Box.
       New York: Harcourt Brace Jovanovich, 1971. (374p)

1109. Busby, Linda J. "Defining the sex-role standard in
       network children's programs." Journalism Quarterly
       51 (Winter 1974): 690-696.

1110. Cantor, Muriel G. Prime-time Television: Content
       and Control. Beverly Hills: Sage, 1980. (143p)

1111. Cowan, Geoffrey. See No Evil; the Backstage Battle
       over Sex and Violence on Television. New York:
       Simon and Schuster, 1979. (323p)

1112. Davenport, Terry, et al., comp. The Image of Women in
       the Media. San Francisco: Carol Neuman, 2001 Cali-
       fornia St., 1975. (26p)

1113. Dominick, Joseph R., et al. "Television journalism vs.
       show business: a content analysis of eyewitness
       news." Journalism Quarterly 52 (Summer 1975): 213-
       218.

1114.   Elliott, Philip. The Making of a Television Series:
        A Case Study in the Sociology of Culture. New York:
        Hastings House, 1973. (180p)

1115.   Ellmore, R. Terry. "The licensing of television
        broadcast stations in the United States to 1972,
        with special reference to the criteria used in the
        selection of television licenses." Ph.D. disserta-
        tion, University of Southern California, 1973. (NA)

1116.   Epstein, Edward J. "The selection of reality on net-
        work news." Ph.D. dissertation, Harvard University,
        1973. (NA)

1117.   "Federal regulation of television broadcasting—are
        the prime time access rule and the family viewing
        hour in the public interest?" Rutgers Law Review
        29, no. 4 (1975-1976): 902-920.

1118.   Fernandez-Collado, Carlos F., et al. "Sexual intimacy
        and drug use in TV series." Journal of Communication
        28 (Summer 1978): 30-37.

1119.   Fore, William F. "A manual for the people: depro-
        gramming television." Christianity and Crisis 37
        (May 1977): 93-96.

1120.   Friedman, Howard S., et al. "Nonverbal communication
        on television news: the facial expressions of
        broadcasters during coverage of a presidential elec-
        tion campaign." Personality and Social Psychology
        Bulletin 6 (September 1980): 427-435.

1121.   Friendly, Fred W. The Good Guys, the Bad Guys and the
        First Amendment. New York: Random House, 1976.
        (268p)

1122.   Gandy, Oscar H., Jr. "Market power and cultural im-
        perialism." Current Research on Peace and Violence
        3, no. 1 (1980): 47-59.

1123.   Gordon, Thomas F. "An exploration into television
        violence." Educational Broadcasting Review 3 (De-
        cember 1969): 44-48.

1124.   Greenberg, Bradley S. Life on Television: Content
        Analyses of U.S. TV Drama. Norwood, NJ: Ablex,
        1980. (204p)

1125.   _____. "Three seasons of television characters:
        a demographic analysis." Journal of Broadcasting
        24 (Winter 1980): 49-60.

1126.   Grossman, Gary H. Saturday Morning TV. New York:
        Delacorte, 1981. (424p)

1127. Guerra, David M. "Network television news policy and the Nixon administration: a comparison." Ph.D. dissertation, New York University, 1974. (400p)

1128. Hachten, William A. "Policies and performance of South African television." Journal of Communication 29 (Summer 1979): 62-72.

1129. Hamilton, Robert V. and Richard H. Lawless. "Television within the social matrix." Public Opinion Quarterly 20 (Summer 1956): 393-403.

1130. Harless, James D. "Mail call: a case study of a broadcast news gatekeeper." Journalism Quarterly 51 (Spring 1974): 87-90.

1131. Head, Sydney W. "Television and social norms: an analysis of the social content of a sample of television dramas." Ph.D. dissertation, New York University, 1953. (606p)

1132. Hinton, James L., et al. "Tokenism and improving imagery of blacks in TV drama and comedy: 1973." Journal of Broadcasting 18 (Fall 1975): 423-432.

1133. Howard, Robert. "Bias in television news, a content analysis." Ph.D. dissertation, Florida State University, 1972. (152p)

1134. Kerbel, M. "Edited for television." Film Comment 13 (July and September 1977): 38-40; 34-37.

1135. Kirk, William A. "Television allocation policy: an administrative search for the public interest." Ph.D. dissertation, University of Texas, 1958. (370p)

1136. Kirkley, Donald H. A Descriptive Study of the Network Television Western During the Seasons 1955-56 to 1962-63. New York: Arno, 1979. (237p)

1137. Kittross, John M. "Television frequency allocation policy in the United States." Ph.D. dissertation, University of Illinois, 1960. (486p)

1138. Knopf, Terry A. "Media myths on violence." New Society 16 (November 12, 1970): 856-859.

1139. LeDuc, Don L. Cable Television and the FCC: A Crisis in Media Control. Philadelphia: Temple University Press, 1973. (289p)

1140. Lilley, Robert W. "Television news and the wire services: the problem of information control; a content analysis of Ohio television news." Ph.D. dissertation, Ohio University, 1974. (405p)

1141. Liss, Marsha B. and Lauri C. Reinhardt. "Aggression
       on prosocial television programs." Psychological
       Reports 46 (June 1980): 1065-1066.

1142. Lowry, Dennis T. "Agnew and the network TV news: a
       before/after content analysis." Journalism Quarterly
       48 (Summer 1971): 205-210.

1143. _____. "Gresham's Law and network TV news selec-
       tion." Journal of Broadcasting 15 (Fall 1971): 397-
       408.

1144. Malaney, Gary D. and Terry F. Buss. "AP wire reports
       vs. CBS TV news coverage of a presidential campaign."
       Journalism Quarterly 56 (Autumn 1979): 602-610.

1145. Manning, Willard G. and Bruce M. Owen. "Television
       rivalry and network power." Public Policy 24 (Win-
       ter 1976): 33-57.

1146. Mielke, Keith, et al. The Federal Role in Funding
       Children's Television Programming. 2 vols. Bloom-
       ington, IN: Institute for Communication Research,
       Department of Telecommunications, Indiana Univer-
       sity, 1975.

1147. Nestvold, Karl J. "The FCC theory of diversity as it
       applies to local news and public affairs program-
       ming on independent television stations." Ph.D.
       dissertation, University of Texas at Austin, 1972.
       (164p)

1148. Noll, Roger G., et al. Economic Aspects of Television
       Regulation. Washington: Brookings Institution,
       1973. (342p)

1149. O'Kelly, Charlotte G. "Sexism in children's tele-
       vision." Journalism Quarterly 51 (Winter 1974):
       722-724.

1150. Owen, Bruce M., et al. Television Economics. Lexing-
       ton, MA: Lexington Books, 1974. (218p)

1151. Pandiani, John A. "Crime time TV: if all we knew is
       what we saw." Contemporary Crises 2 (October 1978):
       437-458.

1152. Park, Rolla E., et al. The Role of Analysis in Regu-
       latory Decision-Making: The Case of Cable Televi-
       sion. Santa Monica: Rand, 1972. (170p)

1153. Pekurny, R. G. and L. D. Bart. "Sticks and bones: a
       survey of network affiliate decision-making." Jour-
       nal of Broadcasting 19 (Fall 1975): 427-437.

1154. Prisuta, Robert H. "The impact of media concentration
       and economic factors of broadcast public interest
       programming." Journal of Broadcasting 21, no. 3
       (Summer 1977): 321-332.

1155. Ramsey, Robert T. "Interpersonal values and communi-
       cation behavior in a commercial television station."
       Ph.D. dissertation, Bowling Green State University,
       1972. (125p)

1156. Reel, A. Frank. The Networks: How They Stole the
       Show. New York: Scribner, 1979. (208p)

1157. Regulatory Developments in Cable Television. (U.S.
       Federal Communications Commission.) Washington,
       D.C.: GPO, 1976. (26p)

1158. Reid, Pamela T. "Racial stereotyping on television:
       a comparison of the behavior of both black and
       white television characters." Journal of Applied
       Psychology 64 (October 1979): 465-471.

1159. Roucek, J. "Some sociological problems of the Ameri-
       can television." Revista Internacional de Socio-
       logica 19 (1961): 355-365.

1160. Silverman, L. Theresa, et al. "Physical contact and
       sexual behavior on prime-time TV." Journal of Com-
       munication 29 (Winter 1979): 33-43.

1161. Singer, Benjamin D. "Violence, protest and war in
       television news: the U.S. and Canada compared."
       Public Opinion Quarterly 34 (Winter 1970-1971): 611-
       616.

1162. Slaby, Ronald G., et al. "Television violence and
       its sponsors." Journal of Communications 2 (Winter
       1976): 88-96.

1163. Small, William. To Kill a Messenger: Television News
       and the Real World. New York: Hastings House,
       1970. (302p)

1164. Smythe, Dallas W. "Reality as presented by tele-
       vision." Public Opinion Quarterly 18 (Summer 1954):
       143-156.

1165. Stern, Robert H. "Television in the thirties: emerging
       patterns of technical development, industrial con-
       trol and government concern." American Journal of
       Economic Sociology 23 (July 1964): 285-301.

1166. Turow, Joseph. "Casting for TV parts: the anatomy
       of social typing." Journal of Communication 28
       (Autumn 1978): 18-24.

1167.   _____.   Entertainment, Education, and the Hard
           Sell: Three Decades of Network Children's Tele-
           vision. New York: Praeger, 1981. (153p)

1168.   Webb, Leicester. "The social control of television."
           Public Administration 19 (September 1960): 193-214.

1169.   Weigel, Russell H., et al. "Race relations on prime
           time television." Journal of Personality and Social
           Psychology 39 (November 1980): 884-893.

1170.   Wurtzel, Alan H. "The electronic neighbor: a source
           and content analysis of public access channel pro-
           gramming on a New York City cable television sys-
           tem." Ph.D. dissertation, New York University,
           1974. (184p)

4
The Social Effects of Mass Media

A. MASS MEDIA (GENERAL)

1171. Adams, John B. "Effects of reference groups and
status on opinion change." Journalism Quarterly 37
(Summer 1960): 408-412.

1172. Albert, Robert S. "The role of mass media and the
effect of aggressive film content upon children's
aggressive responses and identification choices."
Genetic Psychology Monographs 55 (1957): 221-285.

1173. Back, Kurt W. "Influence through social communication." Journal of Abnormal and Social Psychology
46 (1951): 9-23.

1174. Bailyn, L. "Mass media and children: a study of exposure habits and cognitive effects." Psychological
Monographs 73 (1959): 1-48.

1175. Baker, Robert K., et al. Mass Media and Violence: A
Report to the National Commission on the Causes and
Prevention of Violence. Washington, D.C.: GPO,
1969. (614p)

1176. Bandura, Albert. Aggression: A Social Learning Analysis. Englewood Cliffs, NJ: Prentice Hall, 1973.
(390p)

1177. Banning, Evelyn I. "Social influences on children
and youth." Review of Educational Research 25
(February 1955): 36-47.

1178. Baran, Paul. "On the impact of the new communications
media upon social values." Law and Contemporary
Problems 34 (Spring 1969): 244-254.

1179. Barrow, Lionel C. and Bruce H. Westley. "Intelligence and the effectiveness of radio and television." Audio-visual Communication Review 7 (Summer 1959): 193-208.

1180. Bauer, Raymond A. "Communication as a transaction: a comment on the concept of influence." Public Opinion Quarterly 27 (Spring 1963): 83-86.

1181. _____. "The obstinate audience: the influence process from the point of view of social communication." American Psychologist 19, no. 5 (1964): 319-328.

1182. Bauer, Raymond A. and Alice J. Bauer. "America, mass society, and the mass media." Journal of Social Issues 16, no. 3 (1960): 3-66, 85-87.

1183. Behavioral Sciences and the Mass Media. (Conference on Behavioral Sciences and the Mass Media, 1966.) New York: Russell Sage, 1968. (270p)

1184. Bergin, Allen E. "The effect of dissonant persuasive communications upon changes in a self-referring attitude." Journal of Personality 30 (1962): 423-438.

1185. Berkowitz, Leonard. "Cognitive dissonance and communication preferences." Human Relations 18, no. 4 (1965): 361-372.

1186. _____, ed. Advances in Experimental Social Psychology. 5 (1970): 1-31.

1187. Birch, H. G. "The effect of socially disapproved labeling upon a well-structured attitude." Journal of Abnormal and Social Psychology 40 (1945): 301-310.

1188. Bittner, John R. Mass Communication, An Introduction: Theory and Practice. Englewood Cliffs, NJ: Prentice-Hall, 1977. (512p)

1189. Bogart, Leo. "Violence in the mass media." Television Quarterly 8 (Summer 1969): 36-47.

1190. Bogart, Leo and Frank E. Orenstein. "Mass media and community identity in an interurban setting." Journalism Quarterly 42 (Spring 1965): 179-188.

1191. Bowman, J. S. and K. Hanaford. "Mass media and the environment since Earth Day." Journalism Quarterly 54 (Spring 1977): 160-165.

1192. Breed, Warren. "Mass communication and socio-cultural integration." Social Forces 37 (December 1958): 109-116.

1193. Bryan, James H. and Tanis Schwartz. "Effects of film
       material upon children's behavior." Psychological
       Bulletin 75 (January 1971): 50-59.

1194. Burnet, Mary, ed. The Mass Media in a Violent World.
       (International Symposium on the Impact of Violence
       in the Mass Media.) Paris: UNESCO, 1971. (44p)

1195. Carter, Richard F. "On reactions to mass media con-
       tent." Audiovisual Communication Review 8 (July/
       August 1960): 210-213.

1196. Cassata, Mary B. and Molefi K. Asante, ed. The Social
       Uses of Mass Communication. Buffalo: SUNY at Buf-
       falo, Communication Research Center, Department of
       Communication, 1977. (92p)

1197. Casty, Alan, ed. Mass Media and Mass Man. New York:
       Holt, Rinehart and Winston, 1968. (260p)

1198. Chu, Godwin C. "Culture, personality and persuasibil-
       ity." Ph.D. dissertation, Stanford University, 1964.
       (178p)

1199. Cipolla, John M. "Communication systems and social
       change." Ph.D. dissertation, University of Iowa,
       1976. (169p)

1200. Clark, Wesley C. "The impact of mass communication in
       America." Annals of the American Academy of Politi-
       cal and Social Science 378 (July 1968): 68-74.

1201. Clarke, Peter. "Some proposals for continuing research
       on youth and mass media." American Behavioral Sci-
       entist 14 (January 1971): 313-322.

1202. Clutterbuck, Richard. The Media and Political Vio-
       lence. London: Macmillan, 1981. (191p)

1203. Colle, Royal D. "Negro image in the mass media: a
       case study in social change." Journalism Quarterly
       45 (Spring 1968): 55-60.

1204. Comstock, George A. "Types of portrayal and aggres-
       sive behavior." Journal of Communication 27, no. 3
       (Summer 1977): 189-198.

1205. Conway, M. Margaret. "The news media in children's
       political socialization." Public Opinion Quarterly
       45 (Summer 1981): 164-178.

1206. Courtright, John A. and Stanley J. Baran. "The acqui-
       sition of sexual information by young people." Jour-
       nalism Quarterly 57 (Spring 1980): 107-114.

1207. Cowlan, Bert. "Thinking small: some comments on the
       role of mass media for economic and social develop-
       ment." Educational Broadcasting International 6
       (June 1973): 79-83.

1208. Curran, James, et al. Mass Communication and Society.
       London: Edward Arnold in association with the Open
       University Press, 1977. (479p)

1209. Dabbs, James M., Jr. "Self-esteem, communicator
       characteristics, and attitude change." Journal of
       Abnormal and Social Psychology 69, no. 2 (1964):
       173-181.

1210. Daniels, Les. Living in Fear: A History of Horror
       in the Mass Media. New York: Scribners, 1975.
       (248p)

1211. Danish, Roy. "The American family and mass communica-
       tions." Marriage and Family Living 25 (August
       1963): 305-310.

1212. Daudt, H. "Effects of media exposure in the Elmira
       study." Gazette 3, no. 4 (1957): 321-328.

1213. Davis, Keith and Edward E. Jones. "Changes in inter-
       personal perception as a means of reducing cogni-
       tive dissonance." Journal of Abnormal and Social
       Psychology 61 (1960): 402-410.

1214. Davison, W. Phillips. "On the effects of communica-
       tion." Public Opinion Quarterly 23 (Fall 1959):
       343-360.

1215. _____, et al. Mass Media: Systems and Effects.
       2nd ed. New York: Holt, Rinehart and Winston,
       1982. (284p)

1216. DeFleur, Melvin L. "Mass communication and social
       change." Social Forces 44 (1966): 314-326.

1217. De Sola Pool, Ithiel, ed. The Social Impact of the
       Telephone. Cambridge: MIT Press, 1981. (502p)

1218. Denisoff, R. Serge and Richard A. Peterson, ed. The
       Sounds of Social Change; Studies in Popular Culture.
       Chicago: Rand McNally, 1972. (332p)

1219. Dienstbier, Richard A. "Sex and violence: can re-
       search have it both ways?" Journal of Communication
       27 (Summer 1977): 176-188.

1220. Donohew, Lewis. "Communication and readiness for
       change in Appalachia." Journalism Quarterly 44
       (Winter 1967): 679-687.

1221. Donohue, G. A., et al. "Mass media functions, know-
       ledge and social control." Journalism Quarterly 50
       (Winter 1973): 652-659.

1222. Downs, H. "Rating the media." Center Magazine 11
       (March 1978): 17-22.

1223. Drabman, Ronald S. and Margaret H. Thomas. "Does me-
       dia violence increase children's toleration of real-
       life aggression." Developmental Psychology 10 (May
       1974): 418-421.

1224. Elliott, Philip and Peter Golding. "Mass communica-
       tion and social change," in Sociology and Develop-
       ment, ed. E. de Radt and G. Williams. London:
       Tavistock, 1974. (374p)

1225. Ellis, Glenn T. "The effect of aggressive cartoons
       on children's behavior." Ph.D. dissertation, Mis-
       sissippi State University, 1971. (49p)

1226. Emery, Edwin. The Press and America: An Interpretive
       History of the Mass Media. 3rd ed. Englewood
       Cliffs, NJ: Prentice-Hall, 1972. (788p)

1227. "Entertainment—the great leveler." Forbes 120 (Sep-
       tember 15, 1977): 41-48.

1228. Fauconnier, Guido. Mass Media and Society: An Intro-
       duction to the Scientific Study of Mass Communica-
       tion: Concepts, Intentions, Effects. Trans. by
       Leon Coetzee. Leuven: Universitaire Pers, 1975.
       (222p)

1229. Fisk, George. "Media influence reconsidered." Public
       Opinion Quarterly 23 (Spring 1959): 83-91.

1230. Frandsen, Kenneth D. "Effects of threat appeals and
       media of transmission." Speech Monographs 30 (June
       1963): 101-104.

1231. Frank, Josette. "Chills and thrills in radio, movies
       and comics." Child Study 25 (Spring 1948): 42-48.

1232. _____. Comics, Radio, Movies and Children. Wash-
       ington: Public Affairs Committee, 1949. (32p)

1233. Fraser, John. Violence in the Arts. London: Cam-
       bridge University Press, 1974. (192p)

1234. Ganguly, S. N. "Communication, identity, and human
       development." Communication 2 (September 1976):
       221-244.

1235. Gerbner, George, et al., ed. Communications Technol-
       ogy and Social Policy: Understanding the New "Cul-
       tural Revolution." New York: Wiley, 1973. (573p)

1236.   Gerson, Walter M.   "Mass media and socialization be-
        havior: Negro-white differences." Social Forces
        45 (1966): 40-50.

1237.   Goldhamer, H. and R. Westrum.   The Social Effects of
        Communication Technology. Rand Report 486-RSF.
        May 1970. (38p)

1238.   Goldstein, Michael and Harold S. Kant. Pornography
        and Sexual Deviance: A Report of the Legal and Be-
        havioral Institute. Berkeley: University of Cal-
        ifornia Press, 1973. (194p)

1239.   Goldstein, Naomi S.   "The effect of animated cartoons
        on hostility in children." Ph.D. dissertation, New
        York University, 1957. (136p)

1240.   Gordon, Thomas F.   "The effect of viewing physical
        consequences of violence on perceptions and aggres-
        siveness." Ph.D. dissertation, Michigan State Uni-
        versity, 1973. (NA)

1241.   Gormley, William T.   The Effects of Newspaper-Tele-
        vision Cross-Ownership on News Homogeneity. Chapel
        Hill, NC: Institute for Research in Social Science,
        University of North Carolina, 1976. (276p)

1242.   Graham, Hugh D. and Ted R. Garr.   A History of Vio-
        lence in America. New York: Praeger, 1969. (822p)

1243.   Hacker, Frederick J.   "Terror and terrorism: modern
        growth industry and mass entertainment." Terrorism
        4, no. 1-4 (1980): 143-159.

1244.   Halloran, James D.   The Effects of Mass Communication.
        Leicester: University of Leicester Press, 1964.
        (83p)

1245.   _____.   Mass Media and Socialization. Leeds:
        Kavanagh, 1976. (130p)

1246.   Haring, Ardyce.   "Communication and change in communi-
        ty development." Journalism Quarterly 49 (Autumn
        1972): 512-518, 530.

1247.   Hart, Lance R.   "Immediate effects of exposure to
        filmed cartoon aggression on boys." Ph.D. disserta-
        tion, Emory University, 1971. (87p)

1248.   Haselden, K. Morality and the Mass Media. Nashville:
        Boardman Press, 1968. (192p)

1249.   Hornick, Robert C. Mass Media Use and the "Revolution
        of Rising Frustrations": A Reconsideration of the
        Theory. Honolulu: East-West Center, 1974. (27p)

1250. Hoshino, Kanehiro. "Mass communication and delinquen-
       cy." Journal of Educational Sociology 25 (October
       1970): 89-104.

1251. Howitt, Dennis and Guy Cumberbatch. Mass Media, Vio-
       lence and Society. New York: Wiley, 1975. (167p)

1252. Hoyt, James L. "Effect of media violence 'justifica-
       tion' on aggression." Journal of Broadcasting 14
       (Fall 1970): 455-464.

1253. Hubbard, Jeffrey C., et al. "Mass media influences
       on public conceptions of social problems." Social
       Problems 23 (October 1975): 22-34.

1254. Hyman, Herbert H. "Mass communication and socializa-
       tion." Public Opinion Quarterly 37 (Winter 1974):
       524-538.

1255. Katz, Elihu. "Can authentic cultures survive new
       media." Journal of Communication 27 (Spring 1977):
       113-121.

1256. Katz, Elihu and David Foulkes. "On the use of the
       mass media as 'escape.'" Public Opinion Quarterly
       26 (Fall 1962): 377-388.

1257. Katz, Elihu and Tamas Szecsko, eds. Mass Media and
       Social Change. London: Sage, 1981. (1271p)

1258. Klapper, Joseph T. The Effects of Mass Communication.
       Glencoe: Free Press, 1960. (302p)

1259. _____. The Effects of Mass Media. New York: Co-
       lumbia University, Bureau of Applied Social Research,
       1949. (192p)

1260. _____. "What we know about the effects of mass
       communications: the brink of hope." Public Opin-
       ion Quarterly 21 (Winter 1957/1958): 453-474.

1261. Knopf, Terry A. "Media myths on violence." Columbia
       Journalism Review 9 (Spring 1970): 17-23.

1262. Kraus, Sidney. "Modifying prejudice: attitude change
       as a function of the race of the communicator."
       Audiovisual Communication Review 10 (January/Febru-
       ary 1962): 14-22.

1263. _____, et al. "Mass media and the fallout contro-
       versy." Public Opinion Quarterly 27 (Summer 1963):
       191-205.

1264. Kurth, E. "Fernsehen und Verhaltens Störungen."
       Zeitschrift für Psychologie 170 (164): 261-269.

1265. Lang, Gladys E. and Kurt Lang. "Some pertinent ques-
       tions on collective violence and the news media."
       Journal of Social Issues 28 (1972): 93-110.

1266. Larsen, Otto N. Violence and the Mass Media. New
       York: Harper, 1968. (310p)

1267. Lovibond, S. H. "The effect of media stressing crime
       and violence upon children's attitudes." Social
       Problems 15 (Summer 1967): 91-100.

1268. Lyness, Paul I. "The place of the mass media in the
       lives of boys and girls." Journalism Quarterly 29
       (Winter 1952): 43-54.

1269. McAlister, Alfred, et al. "Psychology in action;
       mass communication and community organization for
       public health education." American Psychologist 35
       (April 1980): 375-379.

1270. McCarthy, Elizabeth D., et al. "Violence and behavior
       disorders." Journal of Communication 25 (Autumn
       1975): 71-85.

1271. McCormack, Thelma. "Machismo in media research: a
       critical review of research on violence and porno-
       graphy." Social Problems 25 (June 1978): 544-555.

1272. McDonald, Arthur S. "Television, books, and school
       marks." Education Digest 25 (February 1960): 4-6.

1273. McLeod, Jack, et al. "Alienation and uses of mass
       media." Public Opinion Quarterly 29 (Winter 1965/
       1966): 583-594.

1274. McLuhan, Marshall. "Effects of the improvements of
       communication media." Journal of Economic History
       20 (1960): 566-575.

1275. Mass Media Hearings; A Report. (U.S. National Commis-
       sion on the Causes and Prevention of Violence.)
       Washington, D.C.: GPO, 1969. (463p)

1276. Mehling, Reuben. "Attitude changing effect of news
       and photo combinations." Journalism Quarterly 36
       (Spring 1959): 189-198.

1277. Meier, Kurt Von. "Violence: art and the American
       way!" Artscanada 25 (April 1968): 19-24.

1278. Meier, Richard L. "Communications and social change."
       Behavioral Science 1 (1956): 43-58.

1279. Mendelsohn, Harold A. "Measuring the process of com-
       munications effect." Public Opinion Quarterly 26
       (Fall 1962): 411-416.

1280.   _____. "Socio-psychological perspectives on the
         mass media and public anxiety." Journalism Quar-
         terly 40 (Autumn 1963): 511-516.

1281.   Meyer, Timothy P. and James A. Anderson. "Media vio-
         lence research: interpreting the findings." Jour-
         nal of Broadcasting 17 (Fall 1973): 447-458.

1282.   Mishra, Vishwa M. "Mass media variables related to
         urbanization and modernization in developing areas."
         Journalism Quarterly 48 (Autumn 1971): 513-518.

1283.   Mosse, Hilde L. "The influence of mass media on the
         sex problems of teenagers." Journal of Sex Research
         2 (April 1966): 27-35.

1284.   Murphy, Lawrence W. "Cultural values in the study of
         journalism." Journalism Quarterly 7 (December
         1930): 328-342.

1285.   Muson, Howard. Media Violence. New York: Harper and
         Row, 1972. (64p)

1286.   Mussen, P. and E. Rutherford. "Effects of aggressive
         cartoons on children's aggressive play." Journal of
         Abnormal and Social Psychology 62 (1961): 461-464.

1287.   Oglesbee, Frank W. "The basis for Marshall McLuhan's
         concepts of the effects of television viewing."
         Ph.D. dissertation, University of Missouri, Colum-
         bia, 1969. (137p)

1288.   Okanes, Marion M. "Expected behavior of sources as a
         predictor of attitude change through communications."
         Ph.D. dissertation, Cornell University, 1956.
         (194p)

1289.   Parsons, Talcott and Winston White. "Commentary I:
         the mass media and the structure of American soci-
         ety." Journal of Social Issues 16, no. 3 (1960):
         67-77.

1290.   Peck, Robert. "Anthropology and mass communication
         research." Sociologus 17 (1967): 97-114.

1291.   Pember, Don R. Mass Media in America. Chicago:
         Science Research Associates, 1974. (380p)

1292.   Pfuhl, H. E. "The relationship of mass media to re-
         ported delinquent behavior." Ph.D. dissertation,
         Washington State University, 1960.

1293.   Phillips, David P. "Suicide, motor vehicle fatalities,
         and the mass media: evidence toward a theory of
         suggestion." American Journal of Sociology 84
         (March 1979): 1150-1174.

1294. Pool, Ithiel de Sola, ed. The Social Impact of the
       Telephone. Cambridge, MA: MIT Press, 1977. (502p)

1295. Preston, M. I. "Children's reactions to movie hor-
       rors and radio crime." Journal of Pediatrics 19
       (1941): 147-168.

1296. Real, Michael R. Mass-Mediated Culture. Englewood
       Cliffs, NJ: Prentice-Hall, 1977. (289p)

1297. Renshaw, Samuel, et al. Children's Sleep. New York:
       Macmillan, 1933. (242p)

1298. Roberts, Donald F. and Christine M. Bachen. "Mass
       communication effects." Annual Review of Psychology
       32 (1981): 307-356.

1299. Royal Commission on Violence in the Communication In-
       dustry. Report. Toronto: The Commission, 1977.
       (7 volumes).

1300. Schiller, Herbert I. Communication and Cultural Dom-
       ination. White Plains, NY: International Arts and
       Sciences Press, 1976. (127p)

1301. Schramm, Wilbur L. "The effects of mass communica-
       tions: a review." Journalism Quarterly 26 (Decem-
       ber 1949): 397-409.

1302. Seldes, George. Even the Gods Can't Change History.
       Secaucus, NJ: Lyle Stuart, 1976. (352p)

1303. Short, John, et al. The Social Psychology of Tele-
       communications. New York: Wiley, 1976. (195p)

1304. Simon, Rita J. and Thomas Eimermann. "The jury finds
       not guilty: another look at media influence on the
       jury." Journalism Quarterly 48 (Summer 1971): 343-
       344.

1305. Singer, Benjamin D. Social Functions of the Telephone.
       Palo Alto, CA: R & E Research Associates, 1981.
       (114p)

1306. Singer, Jerome L., ed. The Control of Aggression and
       Violence: Cognitive and Physiological Factors. New
       York: Academic Press, 1971. (171p)

1307. Singh, Indu B. and B. N. Sahay. Communication Beha-
       vior and Social Change. New Delhi: Bookhive, 1972.
       (152p)

1308. Smythe, Dallas W. "The dimensions of violence."
       Audio-Visual Communications Review 3 (Winter 1955):
       58-63.

1309. Stein, Jay W. Mass Media, Education, and a Better
       Society. Chicago: Nelson-Hall, 1979. (164p)

1310. Stephens, Lowndes F. "Media exposure and moderniza-
       tion among the Appalachian poor." Journalism Quar-
       terly 49 (Summer 1972): 247-257, 262.

1311. Suicide et Mass Media. (3 Reunion du Groupment d'E-
       tudes et de Prevention du Suicide.) Paris: Masson
       & Cie, 1972. (127p)

1312. Symposium on Human Rights and Mass Communications.
       Strasbourg: Council of Europe, 1968. (118p)

1313. Tarde, Gabriel de. On Communication and Social In-
       fluence. Chicago: University of Chicago Press,
       1969. (324p)

1314. Tragner, Robert E. "Adolescent audience system reac-
       tions to mass media messages regarding drug educa-
       tion." Ph.D. dissertation, University of Minnesota,
       1972. (334p)

1315. Treacy, David P. "The effects of mass communication:
       a survey and critique." Ph.D. dissertation, Uni-
       versity of Illinois, 1966. (261p)

1316. Tumin, Melvin M. "Exposure to mass media and readi-
       ness for desegregation." Public Opinion Quarterly
       21 (Summer 1957): 237-251.

1317. "The violence profile: an exchange of views." Jour-
       nal of Broadcasting 21, no. 3 (Summer 1977): 273-
       303.

1318. Wertham, Frederic. Seduction of the Innocent. New
       York: Rinehart, 1954. (400p)

1319. Wicklein, John. Electronic Nightmare: The New Com-
       munications and Freedom. New York: Viking, 1979,
       1981. (282p)

1320. Wilensky, Harold L. "Mass society and mass culture."
       American Sociological Review 29 (April 1964): 173-
       179.

1321. Winick, Charles, ed. Deviance and Mass Media. Bever-
       ly Hills: Sage, 1978. (309p)

1322. Wood, Michael. "The iconography of violence." New
       Society 42 (13 October 1977): 66-68.

B. PRINT MEDIA

1323. Bender, Lauretta and R. S. Laurie. "Effects of comic
       books on the ideology of children." American Jour-
       nal of Orthogenics 11 (1941): 540-550.

1324. _____. "The psychology of children's reading and
       the comics." Journal of Educational Psychology 18
       (December 1944): 223-341.

1325. Bogardus, Emory S. "Sociology of the cartoon." So-
       ciology and Social Research 30 (November 1945):
       139-147.

1326. Brinton, James E. and L. Norman McKown. "Effects of
       newspaper reading on knowledge and attitudes."
       Journalism Quarterly 38 (Spring 1961): 187-195.

1327. Carter, John and Percy H. Muir. Printing and the
       Mind of Man: The Impact of Print on Five Centuries
       of Western Civilization. New York: Holt, 1967.
       (280p)

1328. "Comic books and delinquency." America 91 (April 24,
       1954): 86.

1329. Davidson, Sol M. "Culture and the comic strips."
       4 vols. Ph.D. dissertation, New York University,
       1959. (1006p)

1330. Edelstein, Alex S. and Jerome L. Nelson. "Violence in
       the comic cartoon." Journalism Quarterly 46 (Summer
       1969): 355-358.

1331. Engle, Gerald, et al. "Projective responses to a news
       article: a study in aspects of bias." Journal of
       Psychology 46 (October 1958): 309-317.

1332. Escarpit, Robert. The Book Revolution. London:
       Harrap, 1966. (160p)

1333. Febvre, Lucien and H. J. Martin. The Coming of the
       Book: The Impact of Printing, 1450-1800. Trans.
       by Geoffrey Nowell-Smith and David Wootton. London:
       N.L.B., 1976. (378p)

1334. Fox, C. "Development of social reportage in English
       periodical illustration during the 1840's and early
       1850's." Past and Present no. 74 (February 1977):
       90-111.

1335. Freeman, T. "Heinrich Hoffmann's Struwwelpeter: an
       inquiry into the effects of violence in children's
       literature." Journal of Popular Culture 10 (Spring
       1977): 808-820.

1336.   Gardiner, Harold C.   "Comic books: cultural threat?"
        America 91 (June 19, 1954): 319-321.

1337.   _____. "Comic books: moral threat?" America 91
        (June 26, 1954): 340-342.

1338.   Gerbner, George.   "The social role of the confession
        magazine."   Social Problems 6 (Summer 1958): 29-40.

1339.   Gieber, Walter.   "The 'lovelorn' columnist and her
        social role."   Journalism Quarterly 37 (Autumn
        1960): 499-514.

1340.   Hoult, Thomas F.   "Comic books and juvenile delin-
        quency."   Sociology and Social Research 33 (March
        1949): 279-284.

1341.   Hutchison, Bruce D.   "Comic strip violence, 1911-
        1966."   Journalism Quarterly 46 (Summer 1969): 358-
        362.

1342.   "Juvenile delinquency: crime comics."   Congressional
        Digest 33 (December 1954): 293+.

1343.   Kielbowicz, Richard B.   "The limits of the press as
        an agent of reform: Minneapolis, 1900-1905."
        Journalism Quarterly 59 (Spring 1982): 21-27, 170.

1344.   Le Coq, Jean Pierre.   "Dynamic social forces of lit-
        erature."   Sociology and Social Research 31 (Novem-
        ber 1946): 117-126.

1345.   Lehmann, Oskar.   Die Deutschen Moralischen Wochen-
        schriften des Achtzehnten Jahrhunderts als Päda-
        gogische Reformschriften.   Leipzig: Richter, 1893.
        (86p)

1346.   Mott, Frank L.   Golden Multitudes: The Story of Best
        Sellers in the United States.   New York: Macmillan,
        1947.   (357p)

1347.   Motto, Jerome A.   "Newspaper influence on suicide: a
        controlled study."   Archives of General Psychiatry
        23 (August 1970): 143-148.

1348.   Phillips, David P.   "Airplane accident fatalities in-
        crease just after newspaper stories about murder and
        suicide."   Science 201 (August 1978): 748-750.

1349.   Rosaldo, Renato.   "Cultural impact of the printed
        word; a review article."   Comparative Studies in
        Society and History 23 (July 1981): 508-513.

1350.   Schmidt, Dorothy.   "Magazines, technology, and Ameri-
        can culture."   Journal of American Culture 3 (Spring
        1980): 3-16.

1351. Smith, A.C.H., et al. Paper Voices, the Popular
       Press and Social Change, 1935-1965. Totowa, NJ:
       Rowman and Littlefield, 1975. (262p)

1352. Smith, Richard L. "The rise of the mass press in
       19th century France." Journalism Quarterly 53
       (Spring 1976): 94-99.

1353. Tan, Alexis S. and Kermit J. Scruggs. "Does exposure
       to comic book violence lead to aggression in chil-
       dren?" Journalism Quarterly 57 (Winter 1980): 579-
       583.

1354. Tannenbaum, Percy H. "The effect of headlines on the
       interpretation of news stories." Journalism Quar-
       terly 30 (Spring 1953): 189-197.

1355. Tebbel, John. The Media in America. New York:
       Crowell, 1975. (422p)

1356. Thrasher, Frederic M. "The comics and delinquency:
       cause or scapegoat." Journal of Educational Socio-
       logy 23 (1949): 196-205.

1357. _____. "Do the crime comic books promote juvenile
       delinquency?" Congressional Digest 33 (December
       1954): 303+.

1358. "Violence in literature." (Symposium.) American
       Scholar 37 (Summer 1968): 482-496.

1359. Waples, Douglas. People and Print; The Social Aspects
       of Reading in the Depression. Chicago: University
       of Chicago Press, 1938. (228p)

C. FILM

1360. Bandura, Albert, et al. "Imitation of film—mediated
       aggressive models." Journal of Abnormal and Social
       Psychology 66, no. 1 (1963): 3-11.

1361. Berkowitz, Leonard and Edna Rawlings. "Effects of
       film violence on inhibitions against subsequent
       aggression." Journal of Abnormal and Social Psy-
       chology 66, no. 5 (1963): 405-412.

1362. Berkowitz, Leonard, et al. "Film violence and subse-
       quent aggressive tendencies." Public Opinion Quar-
       terly 27 (Summer 1963): 217-229.

1363. Bloom, Samuel W. "A social psychological study of mo-
       tion picture audience behavior: a case study of the
       Negro image in mass communication." Ph.D. disserta-
       tion, University of Wisconsin, 1956. (439p)

1364.   Blumer, Herbert. Movies and Conduct. New York:
        Macmillan, 1933. (257p)

1365.   Blumer, Herbert and Philip M. Hanser. Movies, Delin-
        quency and Crime. New York: Macmillan, 1933.
        (233p)

1366.   Charters, Wervett W. Motion Pictures and Youth.
        New York: Macmillan, 1933. (66p)

1367.   DeLauretis, Teresa and Stephen Heath, eds. The Cine-
        matic Apparatus. New York: St. Martin's Press,
        1980. (213p)

1368.   Doob, Anthony N. and Robert J. Climie. "Delay of
        measurement and the effects of film violence."
        Journal of Experimental and Social Psychology 8
        (March 1972): 136-142.

1369.   Durgnat, Raymond. Films and Feelings. Cambridge:
        MIT Press, 1967. (288p)

1370.   Dworkin, Martin S. "Violence on the screen." Queen's
        Quarterly 63 (Autumn 1956): 415-423.

1371.   Dysinger, Wendell S. and Christian A. Ruckmick. The
        Emotional Responses of Children to the Motion Pic-
        ture Situation. New York: Macmillan, 1933. (122p)

1372.   Emery, Frederick E. "Psychological effects of the
        Western film: a study in television viewing." Hu-
        man Relations 12, no. 3 (1959): 195-229.

1373.   Fearing, F. "Influence of the movies on attitudes
        and behavior." Annals of the American Academy of
        Political and Social Science 254 (1947): 70-79.

1374.   Henny, Leonard M. "The role of filmmakers in revolu-
        tionary social change." Praxis 1 (Winter 1976):
        157-175.

1375.   Holaday, Perry W. and George D. Stoddard. Getting
        Ideas from the Movies. New York: Macmillan, 1933.
        (102p)

1376.   Jarvie, Ian C. "Film and the communication of val-
        ues." Archives Europeines de Sociologie 10 (1969):
        205-219.

1377.   Madsen, Roy P. The Impact of Film. New York: Mac-
        millan, 1973. (571p)

1378.   May, Lary L. "Reforming leisure: the birth of mass
        culture and the motion picture industry, 1896-1920."
        Ph.D. dissertation, University of California—Los
        Angeles, 1977. (315p)

1379. Mercey, A. A. "Social uses of the motion picture." Annals of the American Academy of Political and Social Science 250 (March 1947): 98-104.

1380. Moskowitz, K. "Clockwork violence." Sight and Sound 46 (Winter 1976/1977): 22-24+.

1381. Peterson, Ruth and L. L. Thurstone. Motion Pictures and the Social Attitudes of Children. New York: Macmillan, 1933. (75p)

1382. Robinson, D. "Violence." Sight and Sound 46 (Spring 1977): 74-77.

1383. Rosen, Irwin C. "The effect of the motion picture 'Gentleman's Agreement' on attitudes towards Jews." Journal of Psychology 26 (1948): 525-536.

1384. Schlickel, Richard. "Violence in the movies." Review of Existential Psychology and Psychiatry 8 (1968): 169-178.

1385. Sebastian, Richard J., et al. "Film violence and verbal aggression: a naturalistic study." Journal of Communication 28 (Summer 1978): 164-171.

1386. Shi, David E. "Transatlantic visions: the impact of the American cinema upon the French avant-garde, 1918-1924." Journal of Popular Culture 14 (Spring 1981): 583-596.

1387. Shuttleworth, Frank K. and Mark A. May. The Social Conduct and Attitudes of Movie Fans. New York: Macmillan, 1933. (142p)

1388. Siegel, Alberta E. "The effect of film-mediated fantasy aggression on strength of aggressive drive in young children." Ph.D. dissertation, Stanford University, 1956. (149p)

1389. Sklar, Robert. Movie-Made America: A Social History of American Movies. New York: Random House, 1975. (340p)

1390. Strebel, E. G. "French social cinema and the Popular Front." Journal of Contemporary History 12 (July 1977): 499-519.

1391. Teahan, John E. and Edward C. Podany. "Some effects on films of successful blacks on racial self-concept." International Journal of Social Psychiatry 20 (Autumn/Winter 1974): 274-280.

1392. Thomson, David. America in the Dark: Hollywood and the Gift of Unreality. New York: Morrow, 1977. (288p)

1393. "I remember when it was cinema." Sight and Sound
       46 (Summer 1977): 134-138.

1394. True, M. "Memory of justice and Lovejoy's nuclear
       war." Cross Currents 26 (Winter 1977): 416-419.

1395. Tudor, Andrew. Image and Influence: Studies in the
       Sociology of Film. New York: St. Martin's Press,
       1975. (260p)

1396. Vogel, Amos. Film as a Subversive Art. London:
       Weidenfeld and Nicolson, 1974. (336p)

1397. Wright, Basil. The Long View. New York: Knopf,
       1974. (709p)

1398. Zajonc, Robert B. "Some effects of the 'space' seri-
       als." Public Opinion Quarterly 18 (Winter 1954/
       1955): 367-374.

D. RADIO

1399. Bartlett, Kenneth G. "Social impact of the radio."
       Annals of the American Academy of Political and So-
       cial Science 250 (March 1947): 89-97.

1400. Berlo, David K. and Hideya Kumata. "The investigator:
       the impact of a satirical radio drama." Journalism
       Quarterly 33 (Summer 1956): 287-298.

1401. Eisenberg, Azriel. Children and Radio Programs. New
       York: Columbia University Press, 1936. (240p)

1402. Forer, Raymond. "The impact of a radio program on
       adolescents." Public Opinion Quarterly 19 (Summer
       1955): 184-194.

1403. Gruenberg, Sidonie M. "Radio and the child." Annals
       of the American Academy of Political and Social
       Science 177 (January 1935): 123-134.

1404. Hansen, B. F. "A critical evaluation of a documentary
       series of radio programs on racial and religious
       prejudice." Ph.D. dissertation, University of Min-
       nesota, 1953. (910p)

1405. Liu, Alan P.L. "Growth and modernizing function of
       rural radio in Communist China." Journalism Quar-
       terly 41 (Autumn 1964): 573-577.

1406. _____. "Mass communication and media in China's
       Cultural Revolution." Journalism Quarterly 46
       (Summer 1969): 314-319.

1407. Riggs, Frank L. "The changing role of radio." Jour-
       nal of Broadcasting 8 (Fall 1964): 331-339.

1408. Rössel-Majdan, Karl. Rundfunk und Kulturpolitik;
       Ein Beitrag zur Kultursoziologie. Köln: West-
       deutscher Verlag, 1962. (157p)

1409. Scupham, John. Broadcasting and the Community. Lon-
       don: Watts, 1967. (264p)

1410. Singer, Benjamin D. and Lindsay Green. The Social
       Functions of Radio in a Community Emergency. Toron-
       to: Copp Clark, 1972. (49p)

1411. A Sourcebook on Radio's Role in Development. Washing-
       ton, D.C.: Clearinghouse on Development Communica-
       tion, 1976. (85p)

1412. Thakur, B. S., et al. Impact of Radio on Our Villages.
       Hyderabad, India: Department of Journalism, Osmania
       University, 1964. (50p)

E. TELEVISION

1413. Adler, Richard P., ed. Understanding Television:
       Essays on Television as a Social and Cultural Force.
       New York: Praeger, 1981. (438p)

1414. Albert, Robert S. and Harry G. Maline. "The influence
       of social status on the uses of television." Public
       Opinion Quarterly 22 (Summer 1958): 145-151.

1415. Alemanno, R. "'Life size,' causa o effetto della
       violenza sociale?" Cinema Nuovo 25 (January/Februen-
       ary 1976): 43-47.

1416. Ammassari, Elke K. "Television influence and cultural
       attitudinal innovativeness: a causal approach."
       Ph.D. dissertation, Michigan State University,
       1972. (124p)

1417. Anderson, C. C. and T. O. Maguire. "The effect of
       TV viewing on the educational performance of ele-
       mentary school children." Alberta Journal of Edu-
       cational Research 24 (September 1978): 156-163.

1418. Appell, Clara T. "Television's impact upon middle
       class family life." Teachers College Record 61
       (February 1960): 265-274.

1419. Arons, Leon and Mark A. May, ed. Television and Hu-
       man Behavior. New York: Appleton-Century-Crofts,
       1963. (307p)

1420.   Asher, James J. and Robert I. Evans. "An investigation of some aspects of the social psychological
impact of an educational television program." Journal of Applied Psychology 43 (June 1959): 166-169.

1421.   Atkin, Charles K., et al. "Selective exposure to
televised violence." Journal of Broadcasting 23
(Winter 1979): 5-13.

1422.   Baran, Stanley J. "Prosocial and antisocial television content and modeling by high and low self-
esteem children." Journal of Broadcasting 18 (Fall
1975): 481-495.

1423.   Barth, R. J. and T. Swiss. "Impact of television on
reading." Reading Teacher 30 (November 1976): 236-
239.

1424.   Beier, E. G. "Hidden TV messages create social dis-
content." Intellect 104 (February 1976): 350.

1425.   Belson, William A. The Impact of Television: Methods
and Findings in Program Research. Melbourne,
Australia: Cheshire, 1968. (400p)

1426.   _____. "Measuring the effects of television: a
description of method." Public Opinion Quarterly
22 (Spring 1958): 11-18.

1427.   Berger, Arthur A. Television as an Instrument of Terror: Essays on Media, Popular Culture and Everyday
Life. New Brunswick, NJ: Transaction Books, 1980.
(214p)

1428.   Berk, Lynn M. "Great Middle American dream machine."
Journal of Communication 27 (Summer 1977): 27-31.

1429.   Berlogea, O., et al. "Influenta sociala a televi-
zionii." Lupta de Clasa 47 (1967): 75-83.

1430.   Berrnau, David R. and John A. Stookey. "Adolescents,
television and support for government." Public
Opinion Quarterly 44 (Fall 1980): 330-340.

1431.   Bogart, Leo. The Age of Television: A Study of
Viewing Habits and the Impact of Television on
American Life. 3rd ed. New York: Ungar, 1972.
(515p)

1432.   Brody, Gene H., et al. "Effects of television viewing
on family interactions: an observational study."
Family Relations 29 (April 1980): 216-220.

1433.   Brown, Ray. Children and Television. Beverly Hills:
Sage, 1976. (368p)

1434.   Brown, William R.   "Prime-time television environment
        and emerging rhetorical visions."   Quarterly Journal
        of Speech 62 (December 1976): 389-399.

1435.   Cater, Douglass and Stephen Strickland.   TV Violence
        and the Child: The Evolution and Fate of the Sur-
        geon General's Report.   New York: Russell Sage
        Foundation, 1975.   (178p)

1436.   Churchill, Gilbert A., Jr. and George P. Moschis.
        "Television and interpersonal influences on ado-
        lescent consumer learning."   Journal of Consumer
        Research 6 (June 1979): 23-25.

1437.   Cline, Victor B., et al.   "Desensitization of chil-
        dren to television violence."   Journal of Person-
        ality and Social Psychology 27 (September 1973):
        360-365.

1438.   Clinton, S.   "TV as a behavior model."   American Edu-
        cation 11 (July 1975): 40.

1439.   Coates, B., et al.   "Influence of Sesame Street and
        Mister Roger's Neighborhood on children's social
        behavior in the preschool."   Child Development 47
        (March 1976): 138-144.

1440.   Coffin, Thomas E.   "Television's effects on leisure-
        time activities."   Journal of Applied Psychology 32
        (1948): 550-558.

1441.   _____.   "Television's impact on society."   American
        Psychologist 10 (October 1955): 630-641.

1442.   Collins, W. A. and S. K. Getz.   "Children's social
        responses following modeled reactions to provoca-
        tion: prosocial effects of a television drama."
        Journal of Personality 44 (September 1976): 488-500.

1443.   Comstock, George A.   "The impact of television on
        American institutions."   Journal of Communication
        28 (Spring 1978): 12-28.

1444.   _____.   The Impact of Television on American In-
        stitutions and the American Public.   Syracuse, NY:
        Syracuse University, Communications Research Center,
        1977.   (48p)

1445.   _____.   Priorities for Action-Oriented Psychologi-
        cal Studies of Television and Behavior.   Santa Moni-
        ca, CA: Rand, 1977.   (14p)

1446.   _____.   Television and Human Behavior: The Key
        Studies.   Santa Monica, CA: Rand, 1975.   (250p)

1447.   _____.   Television in America.   Beverly Hills:
        Sage, 1980.   (155p)

1448.   _____. "Types of portrayal and aggressive beha-
          vior." Journal of Communication 27 (Summer 1977):
          189-198.

1449.   Comstock, George A. and Eli A. Rubinstein, eds.
          Television and Social Behavior. 5 vols. Washing-
          ton, D.C.: GPO, 1971.

1450.   Comstock, George A. and Marilyn Fisher. Television
          and Human Behavior: A Guide to the Pertinent Sci-
          entific Literature. Santa Monica, CA: Rand, 1975.
          (344p)

1451.   Comstock, George A., et al. Television and Human Be-
          havior. New York: Columbia University Press, 1978.
          (581p)

1452.   Coppa, Frank J. Screen and Society: The Impact of
          Television Upon Aspects of Contemporary Civiliza-
          tion. Chicago: Nelson-Hall, 1979. (217p)

1453.   Crawford, P., et al. The Impact of Violence on Tele-
          vision on Children. Toronto: North York Board of
          Education Research Report, 1976. (NA)

1454.   Cripps, E. J. "Violence and children's TV." America
          135 (September 11, 1976): 116-118.

1455.   Culkin, J. "New literacy: from the alphabet to
          television." Media and Methods 14 (October 1977):
          64-67+.

1456.   Demant, V. A. "The unintentional influences of tele-
          vision." Cross Currents 5 (Summer 1955): 220-225.

1457.   Diamond, Edwin. Sign-Off: The Last Days of Tele-
          vision. Cambridge: MIT Press, 1982. (273p)

1458.   Dieterich, D. and L. Ladevich. "Medium and the mes-
          sage: effects of television on children." Language
          Arts 54 (February 1977): 196-204.

1459.   Dominick, Joseph R. "The influence of social class,
          the family, and exposure to television violence on
          the socialization of aggression." Ph.D. disserta-
          tion, Michigan State University, 1970. (101p)

1460.   Donohue, Thomas R. "Favorite TV characters as beha-
          vioral models for the emotionally disturbed." Jour-
          nal of Broadcasting 21 (Summer 1977): 333-345.

1461.   Doolittle, John C. "Immunizing children against the
          possible antisocial effects of viewing television
          violence: a curricular intervention." Ph.D. dis-
          sertation, University of Wisconsin—Madison, 1975.
          (126p)

1462. Drabman, Ronald S. and Margaret H. Thomas. "Chil-
       dren's imitation of aggressive and prosocial beha-
       vior when viewing alone and in pairs." Journal of
       Communication 27 (Summer 1977): 199-205.

1463. Edgar, Patricia and Donald E. Edgar. "Television
       violence and socialization theory." Public Opinion
       Quarterly 35 (Winter 1971/1972): 608-612.

1464. "Effects of television on children and adolescents;
       symposium." Journal of Communication 25 (Autumn
       1975): 13-101.

1465. Eisler, Riane T. and David Loye. "Childhood and the
       chosen future." Journal of Clinical Child Psy-
       chology 9 (Summer 1980): 102-106.

1466. Epstein, Edward J. "Peddling a drug scare." Columbia
       Journalism Review 16 (November 1977): 51-54+.

1467. Eron, Leonard D., et al. "Does television cause
       aggression?" American Psychologist 27 (April 1972):
       253-263.

1468. Eron, Leonard D. "Relationship of TV viewing habits
       and aggressive behavior in children." Journal of
       Abnormal and Social Psychology 67, no. 2 (1963):
       193-196.

1469. Esslin, Martin. The Age of Television. San Fran-
       cisco: W. H. Freeman, 1982. (138p)

1470. Ezratty, S. "Television and society." Impact of
       Science on Society 15 (1965): 149-172.

1471. Feshbach, Seymour and Robert D. Singer. Television
       and Aggression: An Experimental Field Study. San
       Francisco: Jossey-Bass, 1971. (186p)

1472. Fitzsimmons, Stephen J. and Hobart G. Osborn. "The
       impact of social issues and public affairs tele-
       vision documentaries." Public Opinion Quarterly 32
       (Fall 1968): 379-397.

1473. Fowles, Jib. "Television and Americans: electrons
       and atoms." Journal of American Culture 3 (Fall
       1980): 432-439.

1474. Frank, Robert E. and Marshall G. Greenberg. The
       Public's Use of Television; Who Watches and Why.
       Beverly Hills: Sage, 1980. (368p)

1475. Friedrich, Lynette K. and Aletha H. Stein. "Pro-
       social television and young children: the effects
       of verbal labelling and role playing on learning
       and behavior." Child Development 46 (March 1975):
       27-38.

1476. Gerbner, George. "Proliferating violence." Society 14 (September/October 1977): 8, 10-14.

1477. Gerbner, George and Larry Gross. "Living with television: the violence profile." Journal of Communication 26 (Spring 1976): 173-194.

1478. _____. Violence Profile No. 6: Trends in Network Television Drama and Viewer Conceptions of Social Reality, 1967-73. Philadelphia: Annenberg School of Communications, University of Pennsylvania, 1974. (NA)

1479. Gerbner, George, et al. "The demonstration of power: violence profile no. 10." Journal of Communication 29 (Summer 1979): 177-196.

1480. _____. Violence Profile No. 8: Trends in Network Television Drama and Viewer Conceptions of Social Reality, 1967-76. Philadelphia: Annenberg School of Communications, University of Pennsylvania, 1977. (41p)

1481. Goranson, Richard E. "The impact of television violence." Contemporary Psychology 20 (April 1975): 291-292.

1482. _____. "Television effects: issues and evidence." Report to the Royal Commission on Violence in the Communications Industry. Toronto: 1976. (NA)

1483. Gorn, Gerald J., et al. "Role of educational television in changing the intergroup attitudes of children." Child Development 47 (March 1976): 277-280.

1484. Greenberg, Bradley S. "British children and televised violence." Public Opinion Quarterly 38 (Winter 1975): 531-547.

1485. Greenberg, Bradley S. and C. Edward Wotring. "Television violence and its potential for aggressive driving behavior." Journal of Broadcasting 18 (Fall 1975): 473-480.

1486. Greenberg, Bradley S., et al. "The soaps: what's on and who cares?" Journal of Broadcasting 26 (Spring 1982): 519-535.

1487. Hall, Stuart. "Television and culture." Sight and Sound 45 (Autumn 1976): 246-252.

1488. Hartnagel, Timothy F., et al. "Television violence and violent behavior." Social Forces 54 (December 1975): 341-351.

1489.   Hawkins, Robert P. and Suzanne Pingree. "Using tele-
         vision to construct social reality." Journal of
         Broadcasting 25 (Fall 1981): 347-364.

1490.   Hess, Robert D. and Harriet Goldman. "Parents' views
         of the effect of television on their children."
         Child Development 33 (1962): 411-426.

1491.   Himmelweit, Hilde T. "A theoretical framework for
         the consideration of the effects of television: a
         British report." Journal of Social Issues 18, no.
         2 (1962): 16-28.

1492.   _____, et al. Television and the Child: An Em-
         pirical Study of the Effect of Television on the
         Young. London: Oxford University Press, 1958.
         (522p)

1493.   Hirsch, Paul M. "Public policy toward television:
         mass media and education in American society."
         School Review 85 (August 1977): 481-512.

1494.   Howe, Michael T. Television and Children. Hamden,
         CT: Linnet Books, 1977. (157p)

1495.   Hughes, Michael. "The fruits of cultivation analysis:
         a reexamination of some effects of television
         watching." Public Opinion Quarterly 44 (Fall 1980):
         287-302.

1496.   Hur, Kenneth K. and John P. Robinson. "The social
         impact of 'Roots.'" Journalism Quarterly 55 (Spring
         1978): 19-24, 83.

1497.   Huston-Stein, Aletha, et al. "The effects of TV ac-
         tion and violence on children's social behavior."
         Journal of Genetic Psychology 138 (June 1981): 183-
         191.

1498.   Ingelfinger, F. J. "One huge apologia for violence."
         Columbia Journalism Review 15 (March 1977): 52+.

1499.   Jackson-Beeck, Marilyn and Jeff Sobal. "The social
         world of heavy television viewers." Journal of
         Broadcasting 24 (Winter 1980): 5-11.

1500.   Jenkins, Gladys G. "Families, mass communications and
         the marketplace." Childhood Education 54 (November/
         December 1977): 67-70.

1501.   Johnson, L. L. The Social Effects of Cable Television.
         Rand Paper 5390. March 1975. (12p)

1502.   Korzenny, Felipe and Kimberly Neuendorf. "Television
         viewing and self-concept of the elderly." Journal
         of Communication 30 (Winter 1980): 71-80.

1503. Lake, Sara, comp. Television's Impact on Children and
       Adolescents. Phoenix: Oryx Press, 1981. (102p)

1504. Lang, Kurt and Gladys E. Lang. "The unique perspec-
       tive of television and its effects: a pilot study."
       American Sociological Review 18 (February 1953):
       3-12.

1505. Larsen, Otto N., et al. "Goals and goal-achievement
       in television content: models for anomie?" Socio-
       logical Inquiry 33 (1963): 180-196.

1506. Lazarfield, Paul F. "Why is so little known about the
       effects of television on children and what can be
       done." Public Opinion Quarterly 19 (Fall 1955):
       243-251.

1507. Leckenby, J. D. "Attribution of dogmatism to TV char-
       acters." Journalism Quarterly 54 (Spring 1977): 14-
       19.

1508. Liebert, Robert M. and Robert A. Baron. "Some immedi-
       ate effects of televised violence on children's be-
       havior." Developmental Psychology 6 (May 1972):
       469-475.

1509. Liebert, Robert M., et al. The Early Window: Effects
       of Television on Children and Youth. New York: Per-
       gamon, 1973. (193p)

1510. Littell, Joseph F. Coping with Television. Evanston,
       IL: McDougal, Little, 1973. (213p)

1511. Littner, Ner. "A psychiatrist looks at television and
       violence." Television Quarterly 8 (Fall 1969): 7-23.

1512. Lowenstein, N. F. "Television violence and its effect
       on the young mind." News and Views 3 (November 1978):
       25-27.

1513. Maccoby, Eleanor E. "Television: its impact on school
       children." Public Opinion Quarterly 15 (Fall 1951):
       421-444.

1514. McDonagh, Edward C. "Television and the family." So-
       ciology and Social Research 35 (November 1950): 113-
       122.

1515. Mankiewicz, Frank and Joel Swerdlow. Remote Control:
       Television and the Manipulation of American Life.
       New York: Times Books, 1977. (308p)

1516. Martinez, Tomas. "Gambling, goods, and games." Soci-
       ety 14 (September/October 1977): 79-81.

1517. Mercer, Charles. "Are we more amused?" New Society
         14 (11 August 1977): 280-282.

1518. Meyer, Timothy P. "Some effects of real newsfilm vio-
         lence on the behavior of viewers." Journal of Broad-
         casting 15 (Summer 1971): 285.

1519. Milgrim, Stanley and R. Lance Shotland. Television
         and Antisocial Behavior: Field Experiments. New
         York: Academic Press, 1973. (183p)

1520. Miller, Thomas W. "Impact of television programming
         for children on family life: issues for family
         therapy." International Journal of Family Counseling
         5 (Fall 1977): 40-47.

1521. Murray, John P. "Television and violence: implica-
         tions of the Surgeon General's research program."
         American Psychologist 28 (June 1973): 472-478.

1522. Murray, John P. and S. Klippax. "Children's social
         behavior in three towns with differing television
         experience." Journal of Communication 28 (Winter
         1978): 19-29.

1523. Newcomb, Horace. "Assessing the violence profile
         studies of Gerbner and Gross: a humanistic critique
         and suggestion." Communication Research 5 (July
         1978): 264-282.

1524. _____, ed. Television: The Critical View. 2nd ed.
         New York: Oxford University Press, 1979. (557p)

1525. Noble, G. "Some comments on the nature of delinquents:
         identification with television, heroes, fathers, and
         best friends." British Journal of Social and Clini-
         cal Psychology 10 (1971): 172-180.

1526. Nystrom, C. L. "Immediate man: the symbolic environ-
         ment of fanatiasm." ETC 34 (March 1977): 19-34.

1527. O'Keefe, M. Timothy. "The anti-smoking commercials:
         a study of television's impact on behavior." Public
         Opinion Quarterly 35 (Summer 1971): 242-248.

1528. Osborn, D. K. and R. C. Endsley. "Emotional reactions
         of young children to TV violence." Child Development
         42 (1971): 321-331.

1529. Ozersky, D. "Television: the isolating medium." ETC
         34 (March 1977): 100-103.

1530. Parker, Edwin B. "Television and the process of cul-
         tural change." Journalism Quarterly 38 (Autumn 1961):
         537-540.

1531. Pearlin, Leonard I. "Social and personal stress and escape television." Public Opinion Quarterly 23 (Summer 1959): 255-259.

1532. Piepe, Anthony, et al. "Violence and television." New Society 41 (15 September 1977): 536-538.

1533. Potter, Rosemary L. New Season: The Positive Use of Commercial Television with Children. Columbus, OH: Merrill, 1976. (126p)

1534. Reeves, Byron. "Perceived TV reality as a predictor of children's social behavior." Journalism Quarterly 55 (Winter 1978): 682-689, 695.

1535. Reid, Leonard N. and Charles F. Frazer. "Television at play." Journal of Communication 30 (Autumn 1980): 66-73.

1536. Riley, John W., et al. "Some observations of the social effects of television." Public Opinion Quarterly 13 (Summer 1949): 223-235.

1537. Roberts, Churchill. "Children's and parents' television viewing and perceptions of violence." Journalism Quarterly 58 (Winter 1981): 556-564, 581.

1538. Rosen, Jay. "Television and technology." ETC 38 (Summer 1981): 162-166.

1539. Rubin, Alan M. "Child and adolescent television use and political socialization." Journalism Quarterly 55 (Spring 1978): 125-129.

1540. _____. "Directions in television and aging research." Journal of Broadcasting 26 (Spring 1982): 537-551.

1541. Rubinstein, Eli A. "Television and the young viewer." American Scientist 66 (November/December 1978): 685-693.

1542. _____. "The television violence report: what's next?" Journal of Communication 24 (Winter 1974): 80-88.

1543. Rue, Vincent M. "Television and the family: the question of control." The Family Coordinator 23 (January 1974): 73-81.

1544. Rutstein, Nat. Go Watch TV!: What and How Much Should Children Really Watch? New York: Sheed and Ward, 1974. (213p)

1545. Schramm, Wilbur L., et al. Television in the Lives of Our Children. Stanford: Stanford University Press, 1961. (324p)

1546.   Sex and Violence on TV. (U.S. House Committee on
        Interstate and Foreign Commerce. Subcommittee on
        Communications.) Washington, D.C.: G.P.O., 1977.
        (378p)

1547.   Shaw, Irene S. and David S. Newell. Violence on Tele-
        vision. London: British Broadcasting Corp., 1972.
        (220p)

1548.   Shayon, Robert L. Television and Our Children. New
        York: Longmans, Green, 1951. (94p)

1549.   Singer, Dorothy G. "Television and imaginative play."
        Journal of Mental Imagery 2 (Spring 1978): 145-164.

1550.   Singer, Dorothy G. and Jerome L. Singer. "Family tele-
        vision viewing habits and the spontaneous play of
        pre-school children." American Journal of Ortho-
        psychiatry 46 (July 1976): 496-502.

1551.   Singer, Jerome L. and Dorothy G. Singer. Television,
        Imagination, and Aggression: A Study of Pre-
        schoolers. Hillsdale, NJ: Lawrence Erlbaum, 1981.
        (213p)

1552.   Sirota, David. "Electronic minstrel: towards a new
        folklore and hero." ETC 35 (September 1978): 302-
        309.

1553.   Skornia, Harry J. "Great American teaching machine of
        violence." Intellect 105 (April 1977): 347-348.

1554.   _____. Television and Society: An Inquest and
        Agenda for Improvement. New York: McGraw Hill,
        1965. (268p)

1555.   Slater, Dan and William R. Elliott. "Television's in-
        fluence on social reality." Quarterly Journal of
        Speech 68 (February 1982): 69-79.

1556.   Snow, Robert P. "How children interpret TV violence
        in play context." Journalism Quarterly 51 (Spring
        1974): 13-21.

1557.   Sprafkin, Joyce N., et al. "Effects of a prosocial
        televised example on children's helping." Journal
        of Experimental Child Psychology 20 (August 1975):
        119-126.

1558.   Stein, Aletha H. and Lynette K. Friedrich. Impact of
        Television on Children and Youth. Chicago: Univer-
        sity of Chicago, 1975. (72p)

1559.   Surgeon General's Report by the Scientific Advisory Com-
        mittee on Social Behavior. Appendix A. (U.S. Senate
        Committee on Commerce. Subcommittee on Communica-
        tions.) Washington, D.C.: G.P.O., 1972. (526p)

1560.   Sweetser, Frank L.   "Home television and behavior:
        some tentative conclusions." Public Opinion Quar-
        terly 19 (Spring 1955): 79-84.

1561.   Symposium on Television Violence: Colloque sur la
        violence a la television. Ottawa: Canadian Radio-
        Television and Telecommunications Commission, 1976.
        (252p)

1562.   Tadros, Samy S.   "An investigation of the impact of
        television upon the maturing process of the adult."
        Ph.D. dissertation, Indiana University, 1960. (174p)

1563.   Tan, Alexis S. and Gerdean Tan.   "Television use and
        self-esteem of blacks." Journal of Communication 29
        (Winter 1979): 129-143.

1564.   Television and Socialization Processes in the Family.
        A documentation of the Prix Jeunesse 1975. Special
        English Issue of Fersehen und Bildung. Munich:
        Verlag Dokumentation, 1976. (192p)

1565.   Television as a Social Force; New Approaches to TV
        Criticism. New York: Praeger, 1975. (171p)

1566.   "Television: expectations, effects and choices." A
        submission prepared for the Royal Commission on Vio-
        lence in the Communications Industry. Ottawa:
        Vanier Institute of the Family, 1976. (NA)

1567.   Thomas, Margaret H. and Ronald S. Drabman. "Tolera-
        tion of real life aggression as a function of expo-
        sure to televised violence and age of subject."
        Merrill-Palmer Quarterly 21 (July 1975): 227-232.

1568.   Tichenor, Phillip J., et al. "Community pluralism and
        perception of television content." Journalism Quar-
        terly 54 (Summer 1977): 254-261.

1569.   Towers, Irwin M., et al. "A method of measuring the
        effects of television through controlled field ex-
        periments." Studies in Public Communication 4 (Au-
        tumn 1962): 87-110.

1570.   "TV violence does affect children." New Scientist 86
        (17 April 1980): 139.

1571.   Violence on Television. (U.S. Senate Committee on
        Commerce. Subcommittee on Communications.) Wash-
        ington, D.C.: G.P.O., 1974. (194p)

1572.   Wagoner, G. "Trouble is in your set: the TV as
        homunculus." Phi Delta Kappan 57 (November 1975):
        179-184.

1573.   Wartella, Ellen, ed.   Children Communicating: Media
        and Development of Thought, Speech, Understanding.
        Beverly Hills: Sage, 1979.   (286p)

1574.   Watt, James H.   "Television viewing and aggression:
        an examination of the catharsis, facilitation, and
        arousal models."   Ph.D. dissertation, University of
        Wisconsin—Madison, 1973.   (162p)

1575.   Wells, Alan F.   Picture Tube Imperialism: The Impact
        of U.S. Television on Latin America.   Maryknoll, NY:
        Orbis Books, 1972.   (127p)

1576.   Wiley, Richard E.   "Violence, the media, and the
        school."   NASSP Bulletin 60 (May 1976): 19-25.

1577.   Winick, Mariann P. and Charles Winick.   The Television
        Experience: What Children See.   Beverly Hills:
        Sage, 1979.   (215p)

1578.   Winn, Marie.   The Plug-In Drug: Television, Children,
        and the Family.   New York: Viking, 1977.   (231p)

1579.   Withey, Stephen B. and Ronald P. Abeles, eds.   Tele-
        vision and Social Behavior: Beyond Violence and
        Children.   Hillsdale, NJ: Lawrence Erlbaum, 1980.
        (356p)

1580.   Zuckerman, Diana M., et al.   "Children's television
        viewing, racial and sex-role attitudes."   Journal of
        Applied Social Psychology 10 (July/August 1980):
        281-294.

5
The Mass Media As Creators and Reflectors of Public Opinion

A. MASS MEDIA (GENERAL)

1581. Alexander, Yonah. "Terrorism, the media and the police." Police Studies 1 (June 1978): 45-52.

1582. Altheide, David L. and Robert P. Snow. Media Logic. Beverly Hills: Sage, 1979. (254p)

1583. Baehr, Helen, ed. Women and Media. New York: Pergamon Press, 1980. (137p)

1584. Becker, Lee B., et al. "Newspaper and television dependencies: effects on evaluations of public officials." Journal of Broadcasting 23 (Fall 1979): 465-475.

1585. Berelson, Bernard and Morris Janowitz, eds. Reader in Public Opinion and Communication. 2nd ed. New York: Free Press, 1966. (788p)

1586. Brasch, Walter M. Black English and the Mass Media. Amherst: University of Massachusetts Press, 1981. (345p)

1587. Broman, Barry M. "Tatzepao: medium of conflict in China's 'Cultural Revolution.'" Journalism Quarterly 46 (Spring 1969): 100-104, 127.

1588. Buchstein, Frederick D. "The role of the news media in the 'death of God' controversy." Journalism Quarterly 49 (Spring 1972): 79-85.

1589. Butler, David E. and Ewe Kitziner, eds. The 1975 Referendum. London: Macmillan, 1976. (315p)

1590.   Butler, Matilda and William Paisley.   Women and the
        Mass Media: Sourcebook for Research and Action.
        New York: Human Sciences Press, 1980.   (432p)

1591.   Cancian, Francesca M. and Bonnie L. Ross.   "Mass media
        and the women's movement: 1900-1977."   Journal of
        Applied Behavioral Science 17 (January/March 1981):
        9-26.

1592.   Cantril, Albert H.   "The press and the pollster."   An-
        nals of the American Academy of Political and Social
        Science 427 (September 1976): 45-52.

1593.   _____, ed.   Polling on the Issues: Twenty-one
        Perspectives on the Role of Opinion Polls in the
        Making of Public Policy.   Cabin John, MD: Seven
        Locks Press, 1980.   (210p)

1594.   Carlson, Robert O., ed.   Communications and Public
        Opinion: A Public Opinion Quarterly Reader.   New
        York: Praeger, 1975.   (642p)

1595.   Changing Public Attitudes Toward Television and Other
        Media, 1959-1976.   New York: Television Information
        Office, 1977.   (24p)

1596.   Coffin, Tristram P.   The Female Hero in Folklore and
        Legend.   New York: Seabury, 1975.   (223p)

1597.   Cossio, Carlos.   La Opinion publica: essencia, el
        periodismo, el cine, la radio y la television.   4 ed.
        corr. y ampliada.   Buenos Aires: Editorial Paidos,
        1973.   (246p)

1598.   Dalton, Pen.   "Feminist art practice and the mass me-
        dia: a 'personal' account."   Women's Studies Inter-
        national Quarterly 3, no. 1 (1980): 55-57.

1599.   Davison, Walter P.   Mass Communication and Conflict
        Resolution; The Role of the Information Media in the
        Advancement of International Understanding.   New
        York: Praeger, 1974.   (155p)

1600.   Dennis, Everette E., et al., eds.   Enduring Issues in
        Mass Communication.   St. Paul: West, 1978.   (380p)

1601.   Deza, Alfonso B.   "Mass communication media: exten-
        sions of man."   Impact 13 (July 1978): 228-231.

1602.   Doob, Leonard W.   Public Opinion and Propaganda.   2nd
        ed.   Hamden, CT: Archon, 1966.   (612p)

1603.   Dordick, H. S., et al.   Telecommunications in Urban
        Development.   Rand Memorandum 6069-RC.   July 1969.
        (182p)

1604.   Dröge, Franz W., et al. Wirkungen der Massenkommuni-
        kation. Münster: Regensberg, 1969. (219p)

1605.   Farr, Leonard, et al. Public Communications to Support
        Crisis Relocation Planning. 18 September 1975.
        (158p) NTIS-AD-A022 465/9GA.

1606.   Fine, Seymour H. The Marketing of Ideas and Social
        Issues. New York: Praeger, 1981. (227p)

1607.   Fisher, Heinz-Dietrich and Stefan R. Melnik, eds.
        Entertainment: A Cross-Cultural Examination. New
        York: Hastings House, 1979. (338p)

1608.   Flowerman, S. H. "Mass propaganda in the war against
        bigotry." Journal of Abnormal and Social Psychology
        42 (1947): 429-439.

1609.   Friedman, Leslie J. Sex Role Stereotyping in the Mass
        Media: An Annotated Bibliography. New York: Gar-
        land, 1977. (324p)

1610.   Funkhouser, G. Ray. "The issue of the sixties: an
        exploratory study in the dynamics of public opinion."
        Public Opinion Quarterly 37 (Spring 1973): 62-75.

1611.   Gardner, James M. and Michael S. Radel. "Portrait of
        the disabled in the media." Journal of Community
        Psychology 6 (July 1978): 269-274.

1612.   Gartrell, J. W. and N. M. Mendenhall. Attitudes
        Towards Changes in Communications Technology: The
        Introduction of Teleconferencing. October, 1975.
        (42p) NTIS-N76-14347/8GA.

1613.   Geiger, Louis G. "Muckrakers—then and now." Jour-
        nalism Quarterly 43 (Autumn 1966): 469-476.

1614.   Gerbner, George. "Death in prime time: notes on the
        symbolic functions of dying in the mass media." An-
        nals of the American Academy of Political and Social
        Science 447 (January 1980): 64-70.

1615.   Graber, Doris A. Crime News and the Public. New York:
        Praeger, 1980. (239p)

1616.   Halliwell, Betty M. "A method for the content analysis
        of cartoons: the case of attitudes toward contra-
        ception and population growth." Ph.D. dissertation,
        University of California at Los Angeles, 1972. (265p)

1617.   Halloran, James D. "Mass communication: symptom or
        cause of violence?" International Social Science
        Journal 30, no. 4 (1978): 816-833.

1618. Hardin, Thomas L. "American press and public opinion
       in the first Sino-Japanese war." Journalism Quar-
       terly 50 (Spring 1973): 54-59.

1619. Hulteng, John L. and Roy P. Nelson. The Fourth Estate;
       An Informal Appraisal of the News and Opinion Media.
       New York: Harper and Row, 1971. (356p)

1620. Janowitz, Morris and Paul M. Hirsch. Reader in Public
       Opinion and Mass Communication. 3rd ed. New York:
       Free Press, 1981. (440p)

1621. Jerome, F. "Prime time science and newsstand techno-
       logy; is it all just hoopla?" PE—Professional En-
       gineer 51 (September 1981): 12-14.

1622. Kenrick, Douglas T. and Sara E. Gutierres. "Contrast
       effects and judgments of physical attractiveness:
       when beauty becomes a social problem." Journal of
       Personality and Social Psychology 38 (January 1980):
       131-140.

1623. Kepplinger, Hans M. and Herbert Roth. "Creating a
       crisis: German mass media and oil supply, 1973-74."
       Public Opinion Quarterly 43 (Fall 1979): 285-296.

1624. King, Josephine and Mary Stott. Is This Your Life?
       Images of Women in the Media. London: Virago, 1977.
       (199p)

1625. Kliman, Bernice W. "'The Biscuit Eater': racial
       stereotypes, 1939-1972." Phylon 39 (March 1978):
       87-96.

1626. Laing, Robert B. "Public opinion perspectives on mass
       communication and agenda-setting." Ph.D. disserta-
       tion, University of Washington, 1975. (89p)

1627. Lalande, Marc. The Media Mirage: An Address by the
       Honourable Marc Lalande, Minister Responsible for
       the Status of Women to the Ottawa Women's Canadian
       Club. Ottawa: Health and Welfare Canada, 1975.
       (17p)

1628. Lefever, Ernest W. "The prestige press, foreign poli-
       cy, and American survival." Orbis 20 (Spring 1976):
       207-225.

1629. Lenes, M. S. and E. J. Hart. "Influence of pornography
       and violence on attitudes and guilt." Journal of
       School Health 45 (October 1975): 447-451.

1630. McGinnies, E. "A cross-cultural comparison of printed
       communication versus spoken communication in per-
       suasion." Journal of Psychology 60 (1965): 1-8.

1631. MacKuen, Michael B. and Steven L. Coombs. More Than
       News: Media Power in Public Affairs. Beverly
       Hills: Sage, 1981. (231p)

1632. Mass Media: The Image, Role, and Social Conditions of
       Women: A Collection and Analysis of Research Ma-
       terials. Paris: UNESCO, 1979. (78p)

1633. Maugh, Thomas H. "The media: the image of the sci-
       entist is bad." Science 200 (7 April 1978): 37.

1634. Media and Non-Media Effects on the Formation of Public
       Opinion. (American Institute for Political Communi-
       cation.) Washington, D.C.: American Institute for
       Political Communication, 1969. (47p)

1635. Mendelsohn, Harold A. "Socio-psychological perspec-
       tives on the mass media and public anxiety." Jour-
       nalism Quarterly 40 (1963): 511-516.

1636. Mickiewicz, Ellen P. Media and the Russian Public.
       New York: Praeger, 1981. (156p)

1637. Miller, Susan H. "The content of news photos: women's
       and men's roles." Journalism Quarterly 52 (Spring
       1975): 70-75.

1638. Monaco, James. Celebrity: The Media as Image Makers.
       New York: Dell, 1978. (258p)

1639. Nelson, John W. Your God is Alive and Well and Ap-
       pearing in Popular Culture. Philadelphia: Westmin-
       ster, 1977. (217p)

1640. Noelle-Neumann, E. "Mass communication media and
       public opinion." Journalism Quarterly 36 (1959):
       401-409.

1641. Nordenstreng, Kaarle. "Who determines public opinion?"
       E.B.U. Review 24 (September 1973): 22-24.

1642. Novic, Kenneth and Peter M. Sandman. "How use of mass
       media affects views on solutions to environmental
       problems." Journalism Quarterly 51 (Autumn 1974):
       448-452.

1643. Ogden, Rollo. "Journalism and public opinion." Ameri-
       can Political Science Review 7 (February 1913): 194-
       200.

1644. Olien, C. N., et al. "Community structure and media
       use." Journalism Quarterly 55 (Autumn 1978): 445-455.

1645. Petryszak, Nicholas. "The Frankfurt School's theory
       of manipulation." Journal of Communication 27 (Sum-
       mer 1977): 32-40.

1646. Powell, David E.   Anti-Religious Propaganda in the
       Soviet Union: A Study in Mass Persuasion.   Cam-
       bridge: MIT Press, 1975.   (206p)

1647. Price, Thomas J.   "An element of international image
       construction: a twenty-year American printed media
       image of the Soviet Union, 1947-1967."   Ph.D. dis-
       sertation, Florida State University, 1970.   (166p)

1648. Roberts, Norman P.   "The changing images of Africa in
       some selected American media from 1930 to 1969."
       Ph.D. dissertation, American University, 1971.
       (298p)

1649. Robertson, Leon S.   "The great seat belt campaign
       flop."   Journal of Communication 26 (Autumn 1976):
       41-45.

1650. Rollings, Harry E. and Jim Blascovich.   "The case of
       Patricia Hearst: pretrial publicity and opinion."
       Journal of Communication 27 (Spring 1977): 58-65.

1651. Rose, A. M.   "The study of the influence of the mass
       media on public opinion."   Kyklos 15 (1962): 465-482.

1652. Rossell, Christine H.   "The effect of community leader-
       ship and media on public behavior."   Theory into
       Practice 17 (April 1978): 131-139.

1653. Saenger, G.   "Male and female relations in the American
       comic strip."   Public Opinion Quarterly 19 (1955/
       1956): 195-205.

1654. Schultz, John H.   "Liberalism and conservatism: a
       study of mass-media foreign policy attitudes."   Ph.D.
       dissertation, University of Southern California,
       1968.   (407p)

1655. Simon, Armando.   "A quantitative, nonreactive study
       of mass behavior with emphasis on the cinema as be-
       havioral catalyst."   Psychological Reports 48 (June
       1981): 775-785.

1656. Smythe, Dallas W.   Dependency Road: Communications,
       Capitalism, Consciousness, and Canada.   Norwood:
       Ablex, 1981.   (347p)

1657. _____.   Space Satellite Communications and Public
       Opinion.   Urbana: Institute of Communications Re-
       search, University of Illinois, 1960.   (39p)

1658. Stamps, Charles H.   The Concept of the Mass Audience
       in American Broadcasting: An Historical Descriptive
       Study.   New York: Arno Press, 1979.   (401p)

1659. Steinberg, Charles S. The Mass Communicators: Public
       Relations, Public Opinion and Mass Media. New York:
       Harper, 1958. (470p)

1660. Sternthal, Brian. "Persuasion and the mass communica-
       tion process." Ph.D. dissertation, Ohio State Uni-
       versity, 1972. (234p)

1661. Strouse, James C. The Mass Media, Public Opinion, and
       Public Policy Analysis: Linkage Explorations. Co-
       lumbus, Ohio: Merrill, 1975. (279p)

1662. Supadhiloke, Boonlert. "Mass communication and know-
       ledge and attitude gaps about population and family
       planning in a developing urban society." Ph.D. dis-
       sertation, University of Wisconsin—Madison, 1976.
       (318p)

1663. Tan, Alexis S. "Evaluation of newspapers and televi-
       sion by blacks and Mexican-Americans." Journalism
       Quarterly 55 (Winter 1978): 673-681.

1664. Tichenor, Phillip J. and Daniel B. Wackman. "Mass media
       and community public opinion." American Behavioral
       Scientist 16 (March/April 1973): 593-606.

1665. Tuchman, Gaye. "Women's depiction by the mass media."
       Signs 4 (Spring 1979): 528-542.

1666. Tunstall, Jeremy and David Walker. Media Made in Cali-
       fornia: Hollywood, Politics, and the News. New
       York: Oxford University Press, 1981. (204p)

1667. Turk, Herman. "Imageries of social control: on the
       publicized birth and early life of Proposition 13."
       Urban Life 8 (October 1979): 335-358.

1668. Volper, Ronald J. "Feminist goals as depicted in the
       behavior of the husband versus the wife in selected
       American family comic strips from 1960-1974—a con-
       tent analysis." Ph.D. dissertation, New York Univer-
       sity, 1975. (242p)

1669. Ward, Jean. "Attacking the King's English: implica-
       tion for journalism in the feminist critique." Jour-
       nalism Quarterly 52 (Winter 1975): 699-705.

B. PRINT MEDIA

1. BOOKS

1670. Allen, Mary. The Necessary Blankness: Women in Major
       American Fiction of the Sixties. Urbana: University
       of Illinois Press, c 1976. (226p)

1671. Basch, Francoise. Relative Creatures, Victorian Women
       in Society and the Novel. Trans. by Anthony Rudolf.
       New York: Schocken, 1974. (360p)

1672. Berg, Karin W. "Looking at women in literature."
       Scandinavian Review 63 (June 1975): 48-55.

1673. Broderick, Dorothy M. Image of the Black in Children's
       Fiction. New York: Bowker, 1973. (219p)

1674. Butcher, Margaret. The Negro in American Culture.
       New York: Knopf, 1956. (294p)

1675. Calder, Jenni. Women and Marriage in Victorian Fic-
       tion. New York: Oxford University Press, 1976.
       (223p)

1676. Cohn, Jan. "Women as superfluous characters in Ameri-
       can realism and naturalism." Studies in American
       Fiction 1 (Autumn 1973): 154-162.

1677. Colby, Vineta. Yesterday's Woman: Domestic Realism
       in the English Novel. Princeton, NJ: Princeton
       University Press, 1974. (269p)

1678. Cornillon, Susan, comp. Images of Women in Fiction;
       Feminist Perspectives. Bowling Green, OH: Bowling
       Green University Popular Press, c 1972. (396p)

1679. Dabbs, James M., Jr. Civil Rights in Recent Southern
       Fiction. Atlanta: Southern Regional Council, c
       1969. (153p)

1680. Dusinberre, Juliet. Shakespeare and the Nature of
       Women. London: Macmillan, 1975. (329p)

1681. Earnest, Ernest P. The American Eve in Fact and Fic-
       tion, 1775-1914. Urbana: University of Illinois
       Press, c 1974. (280p)

1682. Friedman, Leonard M. "The nature and role of women as
       conceived by representative authors of eighteenth
       century France." Ph.D. dissertation, New York Uni-
       versity, 1970. (273p)

1683. Friend, Beverly. "Virgin territory: women and sex in
       science fiction." Extrapolation 14 (December 1972):
       49-59.

1684. Gasiorowska, Xenia. Women in Soviet Fiction, 1917-
       1964. Madison: University of Wisconsin Press, 1968.
       (288p)

1685. Gorsky, Susan. "Old maids and new women: alternatives
       to marriage in Englishwomen's novels, 1847-1915."
       Journal of Popular Culture 7 (Summer 1973): 68-85.

1686.   Gross, Seymour L. and John E. Hardy, ed.   Images of
        the Negro in American Literature.   Chicago: Uni-
        versity of Chicago Press, 1966.   (321p)

1687.   Hardwick, Elizabeth.   Seduction and Betrayal; Women
        in Literature.   New York: Random House, 1974.
        (208p)

1688.   Harless, James D.   "An experimental investigation into
        the impact of adventure-mystery novels on attitudes
        of readers."   Ph.D. dissertation, University of Iowa,
        1967.   (266p)

1689.   _____.   "The impact of adventure fiction on readers:
        the nice-guy type."   Journalism Quarterly 49 (Summer
        1972): 306-315.

1690.   _____.   "The impact of adventure fiction on readers:
        the tough-guy type."   Journalism Quarterly 49 (Spring
        1972): 65-73.

1691.   Heikkinen, H.   "Sex bias in chemistry texts: where is
        woman's place?"   Science Teacher 45 (January 1978):
        16-21.

1692.   Hillman, Judith Z.   "An analysis of male and female
        roles in two periods of children's literature."
        Ph.D. dissertation, University of Nebraska—Lincoln,
        1973.   (170p)

1693.   Ifkovic, Edward J.   "God's country and the woman: the
        development of an American identity in the popular
        novel, 1893-1913."   Ph.D. dissertation, University
        of Massachusetts, 1972.   (496p)

1694.   Johnson, Lemuel A.   The Devil, the Gargoyle, and the
        Buffoon: The Negro as Metaphor in Western Litera-
        ture.   Port Washington, NY: Kennikat, 1971.   (185p)

1695.   Jones, James P.   "Nancy Drew, WASP super girl of the
        1930's."   Journal of Popular Culture 6 (Spring 1973):
        707-717.

1696.   Kane, Michael B.   Minorities in Textbooks; A Study of
        Their Treatment in Social Studies Texts.   Chicago:
        published in cooperation with the Anti-Defamation
        League of B'nai B'rith by Quadrangle Books, 1970.
        (148p)

1697.   Kaplan, Sydney J.   Feminine Consciousness in the Modern
        British Novel.   Urbana: University of Illinois Press,
        c 1975.   (182p)

1698.   Kedesdy, Deirdre A.   "Images of women in the American
        best seller: 1870-1900."   Ph.D. dissertation, Tufts
        University, 1976.   (219p)

1699. Klotman, Phyllis R. "The white bitch archetype in
       contemporary black fiction." Bulletin of the Midwest
       Modern Language Association 6 (Spring 1973): 96-110.

1700. Lippert, Anne. "The changing role of women as viewed
       in the literature of English- and French-speaking
       West Africa." Ph.D. dissertation, Indiana Univer-
       sity, 1972. (290p)

1701. Lyle, Jack, ed. The Black American and the Press; A
       Symposium. Los Angeles: Ward Ritchie Press, 1968.
       (86p)

1702. Lyons, Anne W. "Myth and agony: the Southern woman
       as belle." Ph.D. dissertation, Bowling Green State
       University, 1974.

1703. McCullough, Norman V. The Negro in English Literature,
       A Critical Introduction. Ilfracombe, England:
       Stockwell, 1962. (176p)

1704. McGinnis, Janice D. "Sexism in the New Encyclopaedia
       Britannica." Dalhousie Review 59 (1979): 250-264.

1705. McKendrick, Melveena. Woman and Society in the Spanish
       Drama of the Golden Age; A Study of the Mujer Varonil.
       London and New York: Cambridge University Press,
       1974. (346p)

1706. McLean, G. N. "Sexism in general business texts."
       Journal of Business Education 53 (February 1978):
       215-217.

1707. Mews, Hazel. Frail Vessels: Woman's Role in Women's
       Novels from Fanny Burney to George Eliot. London:
       Athlone, 1969. (209p)

1708. Miles, Rosalind. The Fiction of Sex: Themes and
       Functions of Sex Difference in the Modern Novel.
       New York: Barnes and Noble, 1974. (208p)

1709. Nelson, Gayle. "The double standard in adolescent
       novels." English Journal 64 (February 1975): 56-58.

1710. Pfeiffer, K. Ludwig. "The novel and society: reflec-
       tions on the interaction of literary and cultural
       paradigms." PTL: A Journal for Descriptive Poetics
       and Theory 3 (1978): 45-69.

1711. Pratt, Annis. "Women and nature in modern fiction."
       Contemporary Literature 13 (Autumn 1972): 476-490.

1712. Rogers, Katharine M. The Troublesome Helpmate; A His-
       tory of Misogyny in Literature. Seattle: University
       of Washington Press, 1966. (288p)

1713. Snow, Kimberly. "Image of woman in the American novel."
Aphra 2 (Winter 1970): 56-68.

1714. Starke, Catherine J. Black Portraiture in American
Fiction; Stock Characters, Archetypes, and Individu-
als. New York: Basic Books, 1971. (280p)

1715. Stegeman, Beatrice. "The divorce dilemma: the new
woman in contemporary African novels." Critique 15,
no. 3 (1973): 81-93.

1716. Steins, Martin. Das Bild des Schwarzen in der
Europäischen Kolonialliteratur 1870-1918; Ein Beitrag
zur Literarischen Imagologie. Frankfurt a.M.:
Thesen, 1972. (249p)

1717. Stone, Donald D. "Victorian feminism in the nineteenth
century novel." Women's Studies 1 (1972): 65-92.

1718. Thomson, Patricia. The Victorian Heroine; A Changing
Ideal, 1837-1873. London and New York: Oxford University Press, 1956. (178p)

1719. Showalter, Elaine, comp. Women's Liberation and Literature. New York: Harcourt, Brace, Jovanovich,
1971. (338p)

1720. Wells, Nancy. "Women in American literature." English
Journal 62 (November 1973): 1159-1162.

1721. Winthrop, Henry. "Sexuality in literature." Colorado
Quarterly 21 (Winter 1973): 337-358.

1722. Wolff, Cynthia G. "A mirror for men: stereotypes of
women in literature." Massachusetts Review 13
(Winter/Spring 1972): 205-218.

1723. Woodward, Helen. The Lady Persuaders. New York: Ob-
olensky, 1960. (189p)

1724. Yellin, Jean F. The Intricate Knot: Black Figures in
American Literature, 1776-1863. New York: New York
University Press, 1972. (260p)

1725. Zerbe, Evelyn A. "Veil of shame: role of women in the
modern fiction of North Africa and the Arab world."
Ph.D. dissertation, Indiana University, 1974. (204p)

B. PRINT MEDIA

2. MAGAZINES

1726. Adburgham, Alison. Women in Print: Writing Women and
        Women's Magazines from the Restoration to the Acces-
        sion of Victoria. London: Allen and Unwin, 1972.
        (302p)

1727. Atwater, Tony. "Editorial policy of Ebony before and
        after the Civil Rights Act of 1964." Journalism
        Quarterly 59 (Spring 1982): 87-91.

1728. Bailey, Margaret. "The women's magazine short-story
        heroine in 1957 and 1967." Journalism Quarterly 46
        (Summer 1969): 364-366.

1729. Baron, Harold. "The magazine Vanity Fair and its
        ability to interpret and reflect the literary trends
        of its times: some interrelations of literature,
        the magazine, and mass communications in a commer-
        cial society." Ph.D. dissertation, New York Univer-
        sity, 1970. (286p)

1730. Bennison, Sherilyn C. "Reform agitation in the Ameri-
        can periodical press, 1920-29." Journalism Quarterly
        48 (Winter 1971): 652-659, 713.

1731. Berelson, Bernard and Patricia J. Salter. "Majority
        and minority Americans: an analysis of magazine
        fiction." Public Opinion Quarterly 10 (1946): 168-
        190.

1732. Brown, Richard M. "The gatekeeper reassessed: a re-
        turn to Lewin." Journalism Quarterly 56 (Autumn
        1979): 595-601, 679.

1733. Clark, Rebecca L. "How women's magazines cover living
        alone." Journalism Quarterly 58 (Summer 1981): 291-
        294.

1734. Clarke, Peter and Virginia Esposito. "A study of oc-
        cupational advice for women in magazines." Journalism
        Quarterly 43 (Autumn 1966): 477-485.

1735. Cooper, Nancy. "Feminist periodicals." Mass Communi-
        cations Review 3 (Summer 1977): 15-22.

1736. Customs, Costumes, Habits, and the National Magazine.
        New York: Crowell, 1928. (30p)

1737. DiBacco, Thomas V. "The business press and Vietnam:
        ecstasy or agony?" Journalism Quarterly 45 (Autumn
        1968): 426-435.

1738. Durocher, Aurele A. "Verbal opposition to industri-
       alism in American magazines, 1830-1860." Ph.D. dis-
       sertation, University of Minnesota, 1955. (357p)

1739. Fedler, Fred, et al. "'Time' magazine revisited:
       presidential stereotypes persist." Journalism Quar-
       terly 56 (Summer 1979): 353-359.

1740. Fishwick, Marshall W. "Easy vehicles: magazines in
       American culture." Magazine Studies Quarterly 1
       (Winter 1976/1977): 4-14.

1741. Flora, Cornelia B. "Changes in women's status in wo-
       men's magazine fiction: differences by social
       class." Social Problems 26 (June 1979): 558-569.

1742. _____. "Passive female: her comparative image by
       class and culture in women's magazine fiction."
       Marriage and Family 33 (August 1971): 435-444.

1743. Fowler, Bridget. "'True to me always': an analysis
       of women's magazine fiction." British Journal of
       Sociology 30 (March 1979): 91-119.

1744. Garcia, Hazel. "Of punctilios among the fairer sex:
       colonial American magazines, 1741-1776." Journalism
       History 3 (Summer 1976): 48-55+.

1745. Gottlieb, Robert and Irene Wolt. Thinking Big: The
       Story of Los Angeles Times, Its Publishers, and Their
       Influence on Southern California. New York: Putnam,
       1977. (603p)

1746. Greenberg, Bradley S. and Sandra Kahn. "Blacks in
       Playboy cartoons." Journalism Quarterly 47 (Autumn
       1970): 557-560.

1747. Hart, Roderick P., et al. "Religion and the rhetoric
       of the mass media." Review of Religious Research 21
       (Summer 1980): 256-275.

1748. Hausdorff, Don M. "Magazine humor and popular morali-
       ty, 1929-34." Journalism Quarterly 41 (Autumn 1964):
       509-516.

1749. Hirsch, Paul M. "An analysis of Ebony: the magazine
       and its readers." Journalism Quarterly 45 (Summer
       1968): 261-270.

1750. Johns-Heine, P. and H. H. Gerth. "Values in mass
       periodical fiction, 1921-1940." Public Opinion
       Quarterly 13 (1949): 105-113.

1751. Kaiser, Kathy. "The new women's magazines: it's the
       same old story." Frontiers 4 (Spring 1979): 14-17.

1752. Lamplugh, G. R. "Image of the Negro in popular maga-
      zine fiction, 1875-1900." Journal of Negro History
      57 (April 1972): 177-189.

1753. McBride, Sarah E. "Woman in the popular magazines for
      women in America, 1830-1956." Ph.D. dissertation,
      University of Minnesota, 1966. (888p)

1754. Malamuth, Neil M. and Barry Spinner. "A longitudinal
      content analysis of sexual violence in the best-
      selling erotic magazines." Journal of Sex Research
      16 (August 1980): 226-237.

1755. Masel-Walters, Lynne. "A burning cloud by day: the
      history and content of the 'Woman's Journal.'"
      Journalism History 3 (Winter 1976): 103-110.

1756. Middleton, Russell. "Fertility values in American
      magazine fiction." Public Opinion Quarterly 24
      (Spring 1960): 139-143.

1757. Miller, Susan H. "Changes in women's/lifestyle sec-
      tions." Journalism Quarterly 53 (Winter 1976): 641-
      647.

1758. Nasir, S. J. "The portrayal of the Arab world in men's
      popular magazines." Journal of Human Relations 12
      (1964): 424-435.

1759. Oates, William R. "Social and ethical content in sci-
      ence coverage by newsmagazines." Journalism Quar-
      terly 50 (Winter 1973): 680-684.

1760. Peter, Jon. "Women's magazines: a survey of the
      field." Folio 6 (April 1977): 74-79.

1761. Quebral, Nora C. "'Farm Journal' and American agri-
      culture, 1877-1965." Ph.D. dissertation, University
      of Illinois, 1966. (239p)

1762. Reed, Sandra K. and Marilyn Coleman. "Female sex-role
      models in adolescent fiction: changing over time?"
      Adolescence 16 (Fall 1981): 581-586.

1763. Reuss, Carol. "The Ladies' Home Journal and Hoover's
      food program." Journalism Quarterly 49 (Winter
      1972): 740-742.

1764. Roberts, Donald F., et al. "Letters in mass magazines
      as 'outcroppings' of public concern." Journalism
      Quarterly 46 (Winter 1969): 743-752.

1765. Ryant, Carl G. "From isolation to intervention: the
      Saturday Evening Post, 1939-42." Journalism Quar-
      terly 48 (Winter 1971): 679-687.

1766.   Schoof, Jack F. "A study of didactic attitudes on the
        fine arts in America as expressed in popular maga-
        zines during the period 1786-1800." Ph.D. disserta-
        tion, Ohio University, 1967. (147p)

1767.   Showalter, Stuart W. "Coverage of conscientious ob-
        jectors to the Vietnam War: an analysis of the edi-
        torial content of American magazines, 1964-1972."
        Ph.D. dissertation, University of Texas—Austin,
        1975. (173p)

1768.   Shuey, A. M., et al. "Stereotyping of Negroes and
        whites: an analysis of magazine pictures." Public
        Opinion Quarterly 17 (1953): 281-287.

1769.   Silver, Sheila. "The magazine for suburban women:
        role models in McCall's, 1964 and 1974." Magazine
        Studies Quarterly 1 (Spring 1977): 4-23.

1770.   Smith, James S. "America's magazine missionaries of
        culture." Journalism Quarterly 43 (Autumn 1966):
        449-458.

1771.   Smith, M. Dwayne and Marc Matre. "Social norms and
        sex roles in romance and adventure magazines." Jour-
        nalism Quarterly 52 (Summer 1975): 309-315.

1772.   Sorenson, J. S. and D. D. Sorenson. "Comparison of
        science content in magazines in 1964-65 and 1969-70."
        Journalism Quarterly 50 (Spring 1973): 97-101.

1773.   Stewart, Janice S. "Content and readership of teen
        magazines." Journalism Quarterly 41 (Autumn 1964):
        580-583.

1774.   Taylor, M. "Employed women in recent periodical short
        fiction: the fictionalized portrait of employed
        women projected against a background of factual
        data." Ed.D. dissertation, Indiana University, 1955.
        (196p)

1775.   White, Cynthia L. Women's Magazines, 1693-1968. Lon-
        don: Joseph, 1971, c 1970.

1776.   Zook, Mervin D. "How U.S. magazines covered objectors
        in World War II." Journalism Quarterly 48 (Autumn
        1971): 550-554.

B.   PRINT MEDIA

3.   NEWSPAPERS

1777.   Allen, Richard L. and William T. Bielby.   "Blacks' re-
          lationship with the print media."   Journalism Quar-
          terly 56 (Autumn 1979): 488-496, 545.

1778.   Ayalew, Kanno.   "Evaluative encoding by 'The New York
          Times' and 'The Times' of London during selected
          African crises."   Ph.D. dissertation, Indiana Uni-
          versity, 1968.   (193p)

1779.   Baran, Stanley J.   "Dying black/dying white: coverage
          in six newspapers."   Journalism Quarterly 50 (Winter
          1973): 761-763.

1780.   Barcus, Francis E.   "A content analysis of trends in
          Sunday comics, 1900-1959."   Journalism Quarterly 38
          (Spring 1961): 171-180.

1781.   Barger, Harold M.   "Images of political authority in
          four types of black newspapers."   Journalism Quar-
          terly 50 (Winter 1973): 645-651, 672.

1782.   Barnhart, Thomas F.   "Newspaper leadership in times of
          depression."   Journalism Quarterly 10 (March 1933):
          1-13.

1783.   Berg, Meredith W. and David M. Berg.   "The rhetoric
          of war preparation: the New York press in 1898."
          Journalism Quarterly 45 (Winter 1968): 653-660.

1784.   Blankenburg, William B.   "The role of the press in an
          Indian massacre, 1871."   Journalism Quarterly 45
          (Spring 1968): 61-70.

1785.   Brandner, Lowell and Joan Sistrunk.   "The newspaper:
          molder or mirror of community values?"   Journalism
          Quarterly 43 (Autumn 1966): 497-504.

1786.   Brinkman, Del.   "Do editorial cartoons and editorials
          change opinions?"   Journalism Quarterly 45 (Winter
          1968): 724-726.

1787.   Carl, LeRoy M.   "Editorial cartoons fail to reach many
          readers."   Journalism Quarterly 45 (Autumn 1968):
          533-535.

1788.   Chaudhary, Anju G.   "Press portrayal of black offi-
          cials."   Journalism Quarterly 57 (Winter 1980): 636-
          641.

1789. Clapper, Raymond. "Are our newspapers reflecting pub-
       lic sentiment?" Journalism Quarterly 13 (March
       1936): 17-23.

1790. Combs, Barbara and Paul Slovic. "Newspaper coverage
       of causes of death." Journalism Quarterly 56 (Win-
       ter 1979): 837-843.

1791. Drew, Dan G. and Susan H. Miller. "Sex stereotyping
       and reporting." Journalism Quarterly 54 (Spring
       1977): 142-146.

1792. Finkle, Lee. Forum for Protest: The Black Press
       During World War II. Rutherford, NJ: Fairleigh
       Dickinson University Press, 1975. (249p)

1793. Fought, John P. "News and editorial treatment of
       alleged reds and radicals by selected newspapers and
       periodicals during 1918-21." Ph.D. dissertation,
       Southern Illinois University, 1970. (248p)

1794. Gannon, Franklin R. The British Press and Germany,
       1936-1939. Oxford: Clarendon Press, 1971. (314p)

1795. Gosnell, Cullen B. and Raymond B. Nixon, ed. Public
       Opinion and the Press. Atlanta: Emory University,
       1933. (177p)

1796. Gower, Calvin W. "Kansas 'border town' newspapers
       and the Pike's gold rush." Journalism Quarterly 44
       (Summer 1967): 281-288.

1797. Grey, David L. and Trevor R. Brown. "Letters to the
       editor: hazy reflections of public opinion." Jour-
       nalism Quarterly 47 (Autumn 1970): 450-456, 471.

1798. Gross, Harriet E. and Sharyne Merritt. "Effect of
       social/organizational context on gatekeeping in
       lifestyle pages." Journalism Quarterly 58 (Autumn
       1981): 420-427.

1799. Halaas, David F. Boom Town Newspapers; Journalism on
       the Rocky Mountain Mining Frontier, 1859-1881. Al-
       buquerque: University of New Mexico Press, 1981.
       (146p)

1800. Harris, H. and P. M. Lewis. "The press, public beha-
       vior, and public opinion." Public Opinion Quarterly
       12 (1948): 220-226.

1801. Hartgen, Stephen A. "The interpretation of the Chinese
       Communist Revolution, 1945-1949: by four American
       daily newspapers." Ph.D. dissertation, University of
       Minnesota, 1976. (437p)

1802.   Hines, Neal O. "Atomic energy and the press: two
         years after Hiroshima." Journalism Quarterly 24
         (December 1947): 315-322.

1803.   Huxford, Gary. "The English libertarian tradition in
         the colonial newspaper." Journalism Quarterly 45
         (Winter 1968): 677-686.

1804.   Jones, Marjorie. Justice and Journalism; A Study of
         the Influence of Newspaper Reporting Upon the Admin-
         istration of Justice by Magistrates. London: Barry
         Rose, 1974. (180p)

1805.   Kelly, Thomas J. "White press/black man. An analysis
         of the editorial opinion of the four Chicago daily
         newspapers toward the race problem: 1954-1968."
         Ph.D. dissertation, University of Illinois, 1971.
         (451p)

1806.   Kobre, Sidney. "The first American newspaper: a
         product of environment." Journalism Quarterly 17
         (December 1940): 335-345.

1807.   Kreiling, Albert L. "The making of racial identities
         in the black press: a cultural analysis of race
         journalism in Chicago, 1878-1929." Ph.D. disserta-
         tion, University of Illinois, 1973. (507p)

1808.   Lippmann, Walter. "The press and public opinion."
         Political Science Quarterly 46 (June 1931): 161-170.

1809.   Lundberg, George A. "The newspaper and public opin-
         ion." Journal of Social Forces 4 (1926): 709-715.

1810.   MacDougall, C. D. "The American press's influence on
         public opinion." International Journal of Opinion
         and Attitude Research 3 (1949): 251-262.

1811.   Martin, Kingsley. "Public opinion; rationalization of
         the press and democracy." Political Quarterly 1
         (July/September 1930): 428-435.

1812.   Merritt, Richard L. "Public opinion in colonial Amer-
         ica: content analyzing the colonial press." Public
         Opinion Quarterly 27 (1963): 356-371.

1813.   Merritt, Sharyne and Harriet Gross. "Women's page/
         lifestyle editors: does sex make a difference?"
         Journalism Quarterly 55 (Autumn 1978): 508-514.

1814.   Mobius, J. Mark. "The Korean press and public opinion
         about Japan." Journalism Quarterly 42 (Autumn 1965):
         623-631.

1815.   Morris, Monica. "Newspapers and the new feminists:
         black out as social control?" Journalism Quarterly
         50 (Spring 1973): 37-42.

1816.   Okonkwor, Raphael C.   "The press and Nigerian nation-
        alism, 1859-1960."   Ph.D. dissertation, University
        of Minnesota, 1976.   (282p)

1817.   Olson, Kenneth E.   "The newspaper in times of social
        change."   Journalism Quarterly 12 (March 1935): 9-19.

1818.   Pierce, Robert N.   "Public opinion and press opinion
        in four Latin American cities."   Journalism Quarterly
        46 (Spring 1969): 53-60.

1819.   Pool, Ithiel de Sola, et al.   The Prestige Press: A
        Comparative Study of Political Symbols.   Cambridge:
        MIT Press, 1970.   (359p)

1820.   Schillinger, Elisabeth H.   "British and U.S. newspaper
        coverage of the Bolshevik Revolution."   Journalism
        Quarterly 43 (Spring 1966): 10-16.

1821.   Simmons, George E.   "The 'Cold War' in large-city
        dailies of the United States."   Journalism Quarterly
        25 (December 1948): 354-359, 400.

1822.   Skidmore, Joe.   "The Copperhead Press and the Civil
        War."   Journalism Quarterly 16 (December 1939):
        345-355.

1823.   Spilka, Bernard, et al.   "Sex discrimination after
        death: a replication, extension, and a difference."
        Omega: Journal of Death and Dying 10, no. 3 (1979/
        1980): 227-233.

1824.   Stevens, John D.   "Conflict-cooperation content in 14
        black newspapers."   Journalism Quarterly 47 (Autumn
        1970): 566-568.

1825.   Thackrey, Russell I.   "What some newspapers are doing
        to combat war hysteria."   Journalism Quarterly 19
        (June 1942): 179-184.

1826.   Watson, Elmo S.   "The Indian Wars and the press, 1866-
        1867."   Journalism Quarterly 17 (December 1940):
        301-310.

1827.   Wax, Darold D.   "The image of the Negro in the Maryland
        Gazette, 1745-75."   Journalism Quarterly 46 (Spring
        1969): 73-80, 86.

1828.   Waymack, W. W.   "Editorial pages in wartime—their
        techniques and ideology."   Journalism Quarterly 19
        (March 1942): 34-39.

1829.   Wilkerson, Marcus M.   "The press and the Spanish-
        American War."   Journalism Quarterly 9 (June 1932):
        129-148.

1830. Wolfe, Mansell W. "Images of the United States in the
       Hispanic American press: a content analysis of news
       and opinions of this country appearing in daily
       newspapers from nineteen Latin American republics."
       Ph.D. dissertation, Indiana University, 1963. (553p)

1831. Woodward, Julian L. "Foreign news in American morning
       newspapers; a study in public opinion." Ph.D. dis-
       sertation, Columbia University, 1930. (118p)

1832. Zaremba, Alan J. "An exploratory analysis of national
       perceptions of the Arab-Israeli conflict as repre-
       sented through world newspapers: an international
       communication study." Ph.D. dissertation, State
       University of New York—Buffalo, 1977. (298p)

C. FILM

1833. Bogle, Donald. Toms, Coons, Mulattoes, Mammies, and
       Bucks: An Interpretive History of Blacks in Ameri-
       can Films. New York: Viking, 1973. (260p)

1834. Callahan, Michael A. "A critical study of the image
       of marriage in the contemporary American cinema."
       Ph.D. dissertation, University of Southern Cali-
       fornia, 1971. (319p)

1835. Cripps, Thomas. Slow Fade to Black: The Negro in
       American Film, 1900-1942. New York: Oxford Univer-
       sity Press, 1977. (447p)

1836. Dick, Bernard F. "Celluloid woman." Southern Quar-
       terly 16 (July 1978): 345-357.

1837. Donnerstein, Edward and Leonard Berkowitz. "Victim
       reactions in aggressive erotic films as a factor in
       violence against women." Journal of Personality and
       Social Psychology 41 (October 1981): 710-724.

1838. Durgnat, Raymond. A Mirror for England; British Movies
       from Austerity to Affluence. New York: Praeger,
       1971. (336p)

1839. Dyer, Peter J. "The face of the goddess." Films and
       Filming 5 (June 1959): 13-15+.

1840. Ebel, Henry. "The new theology: Star Trek, Star Wars,
       Close Encounters, and the crisis of pseudo-rational-
       ity." Journal of Psychohistory 5 (Spring 1978):
       487-498.

1841. Elliott, William R. and William J. Schenck-Hamlin.
       "Film, politics, and the press: the influence of
       'All the President's Men.'" Journalism Quarterly 56
       (Autumn 1979): 546-553.

1842.   Fenigstein, Allan. "Does aggression cause a preference
        for viewing media violence?" Journal of Personality
        and Social Psychology 37 (December 1979): 2307-2317.

1843.   French, Brandon. On the Verge of Revolt: Women in
        American Films of the Fifties. New York: Ungar,
        1978. (165p)

1844.   French, Philip. Westerns: Aspects of a Movie Genre.
        2nd ed. New York: Oxford University Press, 1978.
        (208p)

1845.   Goldberg, A. "The effects of two types of sound mo-
        tion pictures on attitudes of adults toward minority
        groups." Ph.D. dissertation, Indiana University,
        1956. (142p)

1846.   Greadington, Barbara A. "The effect of black films on
        the self-esteem of black adolescents." Ph.D. disser-
        tation, University of Miami, 1977. (172p)

1847.   Haskell, Molly. From Reverence to Rape: The Treatment
        of Women in the Movies. New York: Holt, Rinehart
        and Winston, 1974. (388p)

1848.   Heininger, Janet E. "Not so liberated leading ladies:
        images of women in films of the 1930s." Film Li-
        brary Quarterly 14, no. 1-2 (1981): 29-39.

1849.   Holmlund, Christine. "Tots to tanks: Walt Disney
        presents feminism for the family." Social Text 2
        (Summer 1979): 122-132.

1850.   Hulett, H. E. "Estimating the net effect of a commer-
        cial motion picture upon the trend of local public
        opinion." American Sociological Review 14 (1949):
        263-275.

1851.   Hurley, Neil P. The Reel Revolution; A Film Primer
        on Liberation. Maryknoll, NY: Orbis Books, 1978.
        (175p)

1852.   Jackson, Donald G. "The changing myth of Franken-
        stein: a historical analysis of the interactions
        of a myth, technology, and society." Ph.D. disser-
        tation, University of Texas—Austin, 1976. (257p)

1853.   Kay, Karyn and Gerald Peary, eds. Women and the Cin-
        ema. New York: Dutton, 1977. (464p)

1854.   Kirby, Jack T. "D. W. Griffith's racial portraiture."
        Phylon 39 (June 1978): 118-127.

1855.   Leab, Daniel J. From Sambo to Superspade: The Black
        Experience in Motion Pictures. Boston: Houghton
        Mifflin, 1975. (301p)

1856. Leaming, Barbara D. "Engineers of human souls—the transition to socialist realism in the Soviet cinema of the 1930's." Ph.D. dissertation, New York University, 1976. (301p)

1857. Linton, James. "But it's only a movie." Jump Cut 17 (April 1978): 16-19.

1858. Mapp, Edward. Blacks in American Films: Today and Yesterday. Metuchen, NJ: Scarecrow Press, 1972, c 1971. (278p)

1859. _____. "The portrayal of the Negro in American motion pictures, 1962-1968." Ph.D. dissertation, New York University, 1970. (188p)

1860. Mason, John L. "The identity crisis theme in American feature films, 1960-1969." Ph.D. dissertation, Ohio State University, 1973. (396p)

1861. May, Mary. Screening Out the Past; The Birth of Mass Culture and the Motion Picture Industry. New York: Oxford University Press, 1980. (304p)

1862. Mellen, Joan. Big Bad Wolves: Masculinity in the American Film. New York: Pantheon, 1977. (365p)

1863. _____. Women and their Sexuality in the New Film. New York: Horizon, c 1973. (255p)

1864. Movshovitz, Howard. "The delusion of Hollywood's 'women's films.'" Frontiers 4 (Spring 1979): 9-13.

1865. Murray, James P. To Find an Image: Black Films from Uncle Tom to Super Fly. Indianapolis: Bobbs-Merrill, c 1973. (205p)

1866. Noble, Peter. The Negro in Films. London: Robinson, 1948. (288p)

1867. Rosen, Marjorie. Popcorn Venus; Women, Movies and the American Dream. New York: Coward, McCann and Geoghegan, c 1973. (416p)

1868. Schechter, Harold and Charles Molesworth. "'It's not nice to fool Mother Nature': the disaster movie and technological guilt." Journal of American Culture 1 (Spring 1978): 44-50.

1869. Schwartz, Jack. "The portrayal of education in American motion pictures." Ph.D. dissertation, University of Illinois, 1963. (178p)

1870. Shain, Russell E. "An analysis of motion pictures about war released by the American film industry, 1939-1970." Ph.D. dissertation, University of Illinois, 1972. (455p)

1871. Shale, Richard A. "Donald Duck joins up: the Walt
       Disney studio during World War II."   Ph.D. disserta-
       tion, University of Michigan, 1976. (325p)

1872. Silet, Charles and Gretchen M. Bataille. "The Indian
       in film: a critical survey." Quarterly Review of
       Film Studies 2 (February 1977): 56-78.

1873. Sloan, Kay. "Sexual warfare in the silent cinema:
       comedies and melodramas of woman suffragism." Amer-
       ican Quarterly 33 (Fall 1981): 412-436.

1874. Thomson, David. America in the Dark: Hollywood and
       the Gift of Unreality. New York: Morrow, 1977.
       (288p)

1875. Williams, Carol T. The Dream Beside Me: The Movies
       and the Children of the Forties. Rutherford: Fair-
       leigh Dickinson University Press, 1980. (304p)

1876. "Women and film: a discussion of feminist aesthetics."
       New German Critique 13 (Winter 1978): 83-107.

                        D.   RADIO

1877. Cutter, Charles H. "Nation-building in Mali: art,
       radio, and leadership in a preliterate society."
       Ph.D. dissertation, University of California—Los
       Angeles, 1971. (381p)

1878. Garnett, Bernard E. How Soulful is 'Soul' Radio?
       Nashville: Race Relations Information Center, 1970.
       (41p)

1879. Karpf, Anne. "Women and radio." Women's Studies In-
       ternational Quarterly 3, no. 1 (1980): 41-54.

1880. Wilcox, Dennis L. "Radio: its nation building role
       in New Guinea." Gazette 19, no. 2 (1973): 107-116.

                     E.   TELEVISION

1881. Age Stereotyping and Television. (Hearings before
       the U.S. House of Representatives, Select Committee
       on Aging.) Washington, D.C.: G.P.O., 1977. (236p)

1882. Alley, Robert S. Television: Ethics for Hire? Nash-
       ville: Abington, 1977. (192p)

1883. Ammassari, Elke K. "Television influence and cultural
       attitudinal innovativeness: a causal approach."
       Ph.D. dissertation, Michigan State University, 1972.
       (124p)

1884. "Anti-gay group's TV spot turned tide of Florida vote."
       Advertising Age 48 (13 June 1977): 2.

1885. Banks, C. A. "Content analysis of the treatment of
       black Americans on television." Social Education 41
       (April 1977): 336-339+.

1886. Berk, Lynn M. "The great middle American dream ma-
       chine." Journal of Communication 27 (Summer 1977):
       27-31.

1887. Browne, Don R. "The American image as presented abroad
       by U.S. television." Journalism Quarterly 45 (Sum-
       mer 1968): 307-316.

1888. Buhle, Paul. "The pinking of American TV." Libera-
       tion 20 (June 1977): 4-8, 32.

1889. Dates, Jannette. "Race, racial attitudes and adoles-
       cent perceptions of black television characters."
       Journal of Broadcasting 24 (Fall 1980): 549-560.

1890. DeFleur, Melvin L. "Occupational roles as portrayed
       on television." Public Opinion Quarterly 28 (1964):
       57-74.

1891. Dominick, Joseph R. "The portrayal of women in prime
       time, 1953-1977." Sex Roles 5 (August 1979): 405-
       411.

1892. _____. "Children's viewing of crime shows and at-
       titudes on law enforcement." Journalism Quarterly
       51 (Spring 1974): 5-12.

1893. Donaldson, Joy. "The visibility and image of handi-
       capped people on television." Exceptional Children
       47 (March 1981): 413-416.

1894. Downing, Mildred. "Heroine of the daytime serial."
       Journal of Communication 24 (March 1974): 130-137.

1895. Downs, A. Chris. "Sex-role stereotyping on prime-time
       television." Journal of Genetic Psychology 138
       (June 1981): 253-258.

1896. Fehr, Lawrence A. "Media violence and catharsis in
       college females." Journal of Social Psychology 109
       (December 1979): 307-308.

1897. Filoso, Karen L. "Female adolescents' perceptions of
       self, of their television fictional role models, and
       of their real world role models: an exploratory
       study." Ph.D. dissertation, Ohio State University,
       1974. (280p)

1898.   Frommer, Harvey. "A description of how professional
        football employed the medium of television to in-
        crease the sport's economic growth and cultural im-
        pact, 1960-1970." Ph.D. dissertation, New York
        University, 1974. (208p)

1899.   Fuller, Claude C. "Attitudes toward television com-
        mercials in five major urban cities." Ph.D. disser-
        tation, Louisiana State University and Agricultural
        and Mechanical College, 1972. (192p)

1900.   Gerbner, George, et al. "Aging with television:
        images on television drama and conceptions of social
        reality." Journal of Communication 30 (Winter 1980):
        37-47.

1901.   _____. "Cultural indicators: violence profile no.
        9." Journal of Communication 28 (Summer 1978): 176-
        207.

1902.   Gitlin, Todd. "Prime time ideology: the hegemonic
        process in television entertainment." Social Prob-
        lems 26 (February 1979): 251-266.

1903.   Goethals, Gregor T. The TV Ritual: Worship at the
        Video Altar. Boston: Beacon Press, 1981. (64p)

1904.   Goldsen, Rose K. The Show and Tell Machine: How
        Television Works and Works You Over. New York:
        Dial, 1977. (427p)

1905.   Gould, Christopher, et al. "TV's distorted vision of
        poverty." Communication Quarterly 29 (Fall 1981):
        309-315.

1906.   Greenfield, Jeff. Television: The First Fifty Years.
        New York: Abrams, 1977. (280p)

1907.   Hadden, Jeffrey K. and Charles E. Swann. Prime Time
        Preachers: The Rising Powers of Televangelism.
        Reading, MA: Addison-Wesley, 1981. (217p)

1908.   Harris, Mary B. and Sara D. Voorhees. "Sex-role
        stereotypes and televised models of emotion." Psy-
        chological Reports 48 (June 1981): 826.

1909.   Harvey, Susan E., et al. "Prime time television: a
        profile of aggressive and prosocial behaviors."
        Journal of Broadcasting 23 (Spring 1979): 179-189.

1910.   Haskell, Deborah. "The depiction of women in leading
        roles in prime time television." Journal of Broad-
        casting 23 (Spring 1979): 191-196.

1911.   Hofeldt, Roger L. "Cultural bias in M*A*S*H." Society
        15 (July/August 1978): 96-99.

1912. Kellner, Douglas. "Network television and American society: introduction to a critical theory of television." Theory and Society 10 (January 1981): 31-62.

1913. Kelly, Hope and Howard Gardner, eds. Viewing Children Through Television. San Francisco: Jossey-Bass, 1981. (107p)

1914. Larson, Robert F. "The effects of a sex-education television series on the attitudes and family sex communication patterns of senior high school students." Ph.D. dissertation, University of Michigan, 1969. (366p)

1915. Lemon, Judith. "Women and blacks on prime-time television." Journal of Communication 27 (Autumn 1977): 70-79.

1916. Long, Michael L. and Rita J. Simon. "The roles and statuses of women on children and family TV programs." Journalism Quarterly 51 (Spring 1974): 107-110.

1917. Lopate, Carol. "Daytime television: you'll never want to leave home." Feminist Studies 3 (Spring/ Summer 1976): 69-82.

1918. Lowry, Dennis T. "Alcohol consumption patterns and consequences on prime time network TV." Journalism Quarterly 58 (Spring 1981): 3-?

1919. McGhee, Paul E. and Terry Frueh. "Television viewing and the learning of sex-role stereotypes." Sex Roles 6 (April 1980): 179-188.

1920. McNeil, Jean C. "Feminism, femininity and the television series: a content analysis." Journal of Broadcasting 19 (Summer 1975): 259-271.

1921. McNulty, Thomas M. "Network television documentary treatment of the Vietnam War, 1965 to 1969." Ph.D. dissertation, Indiana University, 1974. (264p)

1922. Mayes, Sandra L. and K. B. Valentine. "Sex role stereotyping in Saturday morning cartoon shows." Journal of Broadcasting 23 (Winter 1979): 41-50.

1923. Meister, J.W. Gregg. "Mass media ministry: understanding television." Theology Today 37 (October 1980): 351-356.

1924. Mendelsohn, Gilbert and Morrissa Young. Network Children's Programming: A Content Analysis of Black and Minority Treatment on Children's Television. Washington: Black Efforts for Soul in Television, 1972. (10p)

1925. Miles, Betty, et al. Channeling Children: Sex Stereo-
        typing in Prime Time TV. Princeton: Women on Words
        and Images, 1975. (80p)

1926. Mowitt, John. "Of mice 'and kids." Social Text 2
        (Summer 1979): 53-61.

1927. O'Bryant, Shirley L. and Charles R. Corder-Bolz. "The
        effects of television on children's stereotyping of
        women's work roles." Journal of Vocational Behavior
        12 (1978): 233-244.

1928. Peevers, Barbara H. "Androgyny on the TV screen? An
        analysis of sex-role portrayal." Sex Roles 5 (De-
        cember 1979): 797-809.

1929. Petersen, Marilyn. "The visibility and image of old
        people on television." Journalism Quarterly 50
        (Autumn 1973): 569-573.

1930. Poindexter, Paula M. and Carolyn A. Stroman. "Blacks
        and television: a review of the research litera-
        ture." Journal of Broadcasting 25 (Spring 1981):
        103-122.

1931. Pride, Richard A. and Daniel H. Clarke. "Race rela-
        tions in television news: a content analysis of the
        networks." Journalism Quarterly 50 (Summer 1973):
        319-328.

1932. Rainville, Raymond E. "Recognition of covert racial
        prejudice." Journalism Quarterly 55 (Summer 1978):
        256-259.

1933. Schreiber, E. M. "Education and change in American
        opinions on a woman for President." Public Opinion
        Quarterly 42 (Summer 1978): 171-182.

1934. Seasonwein, Roger and Leonard Sussman. "Can extremists
        using TV move an audience?" Journalism Quarterly 49
        (Spring 1972): 61-64, 78.

1935. Seggar, John F. "Imagery of women in television drama:
        1974." Journal of Broadcasting 19 (Summer 1975):
        273-282.

1936. Seggar, John F. and P. Wheeler. "World of work on TV:
        ethnic and sex representation in TV drama." Journal
        of Broadcasting 17 (Spring 1973): 201-214.

1937. Shafer, Byron and Richard Larson. "Did TV create the
        social issue?" Columbia Journalism Review 12 (Sep-
        tember/October 1973): 10-17.

1938. Signorielli, Nancy. "Marital status in television dra-
        ma: a case of reduced options." Journal of Broad-
        casting 26 (Spring 1982): 585-597.

1939. Stein, Ben. "Fantasy and culture on television." So-
       ciety 16 (March/April 1979): 89-94.

1940. Stephens, Lenora C. "Telecommunications and the urban
       black community: an interdisciplinary study of pub-
       lic television, 1952-1975." Ph.D. dissertation,
       Emory University, 1976. (244p)

1941. Tan, Alexis S. and Gerdean Tan. "Television use and
       self-esteem of blacks." Journal of Communication 29
       (Winter 1979): 129-135.

1942. Theberge, Leonard J., ed. Crooks, Con Men, and Clowns:
       Businessmen in TV Entertainment. Washington, D.C.:
       Media Institute, 1981. (38p)

1943. Wahl, Otto F. and Rachel Roth. "Television images of
       mental illness: results of a metropolitan Washing-
       ton media watch." Journal of Broadcasting 26 (Spring
       1982): 599-605.

1944. Weiner, Jonathan. "Prime time science." The Sciences
       20 (September 1980): 6-11.

1945. Wilhoit, G. Cleveland and Harold DeBock. "'All in the
       Family': racial attitudes." Journal of Communica-
       tion 26 (Autumn 1976): 69-74.

1946. Window Dressing on the Set: Women and Minorities in
       Television. (U.S. Commission on Civil Rights.)
       Washington, D.C.: Commission on Civil Rights, 1977.
       (181p)

1947. Wober, J. M. "Televised violence and paranoid per-
       ception: the view from Great Britain." Public Opin-
       ion Quarterly 42 (Fall 1978): 315-321.

6
Politics and the Mass Media

A. MASS MEDIA (GENERAL)

1948. Adler, Kenneth P. "Mass media responsibility to political elites." Journal of Communication 8 (Summer 1958): 51-55.

1949. Alexander, Herbert E. "Communications and politics: the media and the message." Law and Contemporary Problems 34 (Spring 1969): 255-277.

1950. Atkin, Charles K. "How imbalanced campaign coverage affects audience exposure patterns." Journalism Quarterly 48 (Summer 1971): 235-244.

1951. Atkin, Charles K. and Gary Heald. "The effects of political advertising." Public Opinion Quarterly 40 (Summer 1976): 216-228.

1952. Atkin, Charles K., et al. "News media exposure, political knowledge and campaign interest." Journalism Quarterly 53 (Summer 1976): 231-237.

1953. Balfour, Michael. Propaganda in War, 1939-1945: Organisations, Policies, and Publics in Britain and Germany. London: Routledge and Kegan Paul, 1979. (520p)

1954. Berman, Paul J. and Anthony G. Oettinger. The Medium and the Telephone: The Politics of Information Resources. June, 1976. (174p) NTIS - PB-257 479/6GA.

1955. Bethell, Leslie. "Brazil—the last 15 years." Index on Censorship 8 (July/August 1979): 3-7.

1956. Brownstein, Charles N. "The effect of media, message, and interpersonal influence on the perception of political figures." Ph.D. dissertation, Florida State University, 1971. (130p)

1957. Bybee, Carl R., et al. "Mass communication and voter volatility." Public Opinion Quarterly 45 (Spring 1981): 69-90.

1958. Byrne, G. C. "Mass media and political socialization of children and pre-adults." Journalism Quarterly 46 (1969): 140-142.

1959. Carey, James W. The Politics of the Electronic Revolution: Further Notes on Marshall McLuhan. Urbana: Institute of Communication Research, University of Illinois, 1972 (?). (41p)

1960. Carey, John. "How media shape campaigns." Journal of Communication 26 (Spring 1976): 50-57.

1961. Chafee, Zechariah. "Propaganda and conscription of public opinion." Journalism Bulletin 2, no. 2 (June 1926): 7-8.

1962. Chaffee, Steven H. Political Communication: Issues and Strategies for Research. Beverly Hills, CA: Sage, 1975. (319p)

1963. Chase, Edward T. "Politics and technology." Yale Review 52 (March 1963): 321-339.

1964. Chester, Edward W. Radio, Television, and American Politics. New York: Sheed and Ward, 1969. (342p)

1965. Chimutengwende, Chenhamo C. "The media and the state in South African politics." Black Scholar 10 (September 1978): 44-57.

1966. Christensen, Reo M. and Robert O. McWilliams. Voice of the People: Readings in Public Opinion and Propaganda. New York: McGraw-Hill, 1967. (632p)

1967. Clarke, Peter and Eric Fredin. "Newspapers, television and political reasoning." Public Opinion Quarterly 42 (Summer 1978): 143-160.

1968. Cohen, Akiba A. "Radio vs. TV: the effect of the medium." Journal of Communication 26 (Spring 1976): 29-35.

1969. Cranson, Pat. "Political convention broadcasts: their history and influence." Journalism Quarterly 37 (Spring 1960): 186-194.

1970. Davison, W. Phillips. "Political significance of recognition via mass media—an illustration from the Berlin Blockade." Public Opinion Quarterly 20 (1956/1957): 327-333.

1971. Dovring, Karin. Frontiers of Communication; The Americas in Search of Political Culture. Boston: Christopher Publishing House, 1975. (172p)

1972. _____. Road of Propaganda: The Semantics of Biased Communication. New York: Philosophical Library, 1959. (158p)

1973. Dreyer, Edward C. "Media use and electoral choices: some political consequences of information exposure." Public Opinion Quarterly 35 (Winter 1971/1972): 544-553.

1974. Edom, C. C. "Photo-propaganda: the history of its development." Journalism Quarterly 24 (1947): 221-238.

1975. Eger, John M. "The telecommunications revolution: better inauguration of policies by nations of the world." Computers and People 26 (May 1977): 13-15, 24.

1976. Emery, Edwin. "Changing role of the mass media in American politics." Annals of the American Academy of Political and Social Science 427 (September 1976): 84-94.

1977. Evolution of Public Attitudes Toward the Mass Media During an Election Year. (American Institute for Political Communication.) Washington, D.C.: 1969. (81p)

1978. Fagen, R. R. Politics and Communication: An Analytic Study. Boston: Little, Brown, 1966. (162p)

1979. Feigert, Frank B. "Political competence and mass media use." Public Opinion Quarterly 40 (Summer 1976): 234-238.

1980. Galloway, Jonathan F. The Politics and Technology of Satellite Communication. Lexington, MA: Heath, 1972. (247p)

1981. Gold, Vic. PR as in President: A Pro Looks at Press Agents, Media, and the 1976 Candidates. New York: Doubleday, 1977. (251p)

1982. Grossman, Michael B. and Francis E. Rourke. "The media and the Presidency: an exchange analysis." Political Science Quarterly 91 (Fall 1976): 455-470.

1983. Hazen, Baruch A. Soviet Propaganda: A Case Study
       of the Middle East Conflict. New Brunswick, NJ:
       Transaction Books, 1976. (239p)

1984. Herzstein, Robert E. The War that Hitler Won; The
       Most Infamous Propaganda Campaign in History. New
       York: Putnam, 1978. (491p)

1985. Hollander, Gayle D. Soviet Political Indoctrination;
       Developments in Mass Media and Propaganda Since
       Stalin. New York: Praeger, 1972. (244p)

1986. Jackson-Beeck, Marilyn. "Interpersonal and mass com-
       munication in children's political socialization."
       Journalism Quarterly 56 (Spring 1979): 48-53.

1987. Jacobson, Gary C. "The impact of radio and television
       on American election campaigns." Ph.D. disserta-
       tion, Yale University, 1972. (165p)

1988. Kelley, Stanley. "Elections and the mass media."
       Law and Contemporary Problems 27 (1962): 307-362.

1989. Kinsley, Michael. Outer Space and Inner Sanctums:
       Government, Business and Satellite Communication.
       New York: Wiley, 1976. (280p)

1990. Kraus, Sidney and Dennis Davis. The Effects of Mass
       Communication on Political Behavior. University
       Park: Pennsylvania State University Press, c 1976.
       (308p)

1991. Lang, Gladys E. and Kurt Lang. "The inferential
       structure of political communications: a study in
       unwitting bias." Public Opinion Quarterly 19 (Sum-
       mer 1955): 168-183.

1992. Lasswell, Harold D., et al. Propaganda and Communica-
       tion in World History, Vol. II: Emergence of Public
       Opinion in the West. Honolulu: University of Ha-
       waii Press, 1979. (700p)

1993. Lawrence, Gary C. "Media effects in congressional
       election." Ph.D. dissertation, Stanford University,
       1972. (220p)

1994. Lee, John, ed. Diplomatic Persuaders: New Role of
       the Mass Media in International Relations. New
       York: Wiley, 1968. (205p)

1995. Leith, James A. The Idea of Art as Propaganda in
       France, 1750-1799. A Study in the History of Ideas.
       Toronto: University of Toronto Press, 1965. (184p)

1996. Levy, Steven A. "INTELSAT: technology, politics and
       the transformation of a regime." International Or-
       ganization 29 (Summer 1975): 655-680.

1997.   Locher, Jack S.   "Changing media and Presidential
        campaigns: 1900, 1948, 1956."   Ph.D. dissertation,
        University of Pennsylvania, 1970.   (116p)

1998.   Lubell, Samuel.   "The new technology of election re-
        porting."   Columbia Journalism Review 3 (Summer
        1964): 4-8.

1999.   McCombs, Maxwell E.   "Negro use of television and
        newspapers for political information."   Journal of
        Broadcasting 12 (Summer 1968): 261-266.

2000.   McLuhan, Marshall.   "New media as political forms."
        Explorations 3 (1954): 6-13.

2001.   _____.   "Technology and political change."   Inter-
        national Journal 7 (Summer 1952): 189-195.

2002.   Martin, L. John.   "Recent theory on mass media poten-
        tial in political campaigns."   Annals of the Ameri-
        can Academy of Political and Social Science 427
        (September 1976): 125-133.

2003.   Mayo, Charles G.   "The mass media and campaign strategy
        in a mayoralty election."   Journalism Quarterly 41
        (1964): 353-359.

2004.   Meadow, Robert G.   "Issue emphasis and public opinion:
        the media during the 1972 Presidential campaign."
        American Politics Quarterly 4 (April 1976): 177-192.

2005.   Moriarity, James.   "Campaigns and the new technology."
        Science News 98 (12 September 1970): 229-230.

2006.   Morris, Roger.   "Henry Kissinger and the media: a
        separate peace."   Columbia Journalism Review 8
        (May/June 1974): 14-25.

2007.   Morrison, Bruce J. and Richard C. Sherman.   "Who re-
        sponds to sex in advertising?"   Journal of Adver-
        tising Research 12 (April 1972): 15-19.

2008.   Nimmo, Dan.   "Political image makers and the mass me-
        dia."   Annals of the American Academy of Political
        and Social Science 427 (September 1976): 33-44.

2009.   The 1972 Presidential Campaign: Nixon Administration
        -Mass Media Relationships.   Washington: American
        Institute for Political Communication, 1974.   (425p)

2010.   Paletz, David L. and Robert M. Entman.   Media, Power,
        Politics.   New York: Free Press, 1981.   (308p)

2011.   Patterson, Thomas E.   The Mass Media Election: How
        Americans Choose Their President.   New York: Prae-
        ger, 1980.   (203p)

2012.   Phillips, Glen D. "The use of radio and television
        by Presidents of the United States." Ph.D. disser-
        tation, University of Michigan, 1968. (337p)

2013.   Phillips, Kevin. Mediacracy: American Politics and
        the Politics of the Communications Age. New York:
        Doubleday, 1975. (246p)

2014.   Political Power and Communications in Indonesia.
        Edited by Karl D. Jackson and Lucian W. Pye. Berke-
        ley: University of California Press, 1978. (424p)

2015.   Pool, Ithiel de Sola and Arthur B. Corte. "The impli-
        cations for American foreign policy of low-cost
        non-voice communications. A report to the Depart-
        ment of State." October, 1975. (209p) NTIS-PB
        256 064/7GA.

2016.   Porter, Gregory S. "Mass media and the political so-
        cialization of children and adolescents." Ph.D.
        dissertation, University of Iowa, 1977. (184p)

2017.   Read, William H. Foreign Policy: The High and Low
        Politics of Telecommunications. February, 1976.
        (64p) NTIS-PB-252 316/5GA.

2018.   Rhodes, Anthony. Propaganda, The Art of Persuasion:
        World War II. New York: Chelsea House, 1976.
        (319p)

2019.   Riegel, O. W. "Communications by satellite: the po-
        litical barriers." Quarterly Review of Economics
        and Business 11, no. 4 (1971): 23-35.

2020.   _____. Organizing for Chaos: The Story of the New
        Propaganda. New Haven: Yale University Press,
        1934. (231p)

2021.   Robinson, Gertrude J. Tito's Maverick Media: The
        Politics of Mass Communication in Yugoslavia. Uni-
        versity of Illinois Press, 1977. (263p)

2022.   Robinson, John P. "Perceived media bias and the 1968
        vote: can the media affect behavior after all?"
        Journalism Quarterly 49 (Summer 1972): 239-246.

2023.   Rocca Torres, Luis. El Gobierno militar y las com-
        mucaciones en el Peru. Lima: Ediciones Populares
        Los Andes, 1975. (127p)

2024.   Rosenbloom, Henry. Politics and the Media. Rev. ed.
        Fitznoy, Australia: Scribe, 1978. (160p)

2025.   Rothschild, Michael L. "The effects of political ad-
        vertising on the voting behavior of a low involve-
        ment electorate." Ph.D. dissertation, Stanford Uni-
        versity, 1975. (305p)

2026. Rubin, Richard L. Press, Party, and Presidency. New York: Norton, 1981. (246p)

2027. Rugh, William. The Arab Press; News Media and Political Process in the Arab World. Syracuse: Syracuse University Press, 1979. (205p)

2028. Rupp, Leila J. Mobilizing Women for War; German and American Propaganda, 1939-1945. Princeton, NJ: Princeton University Press, 1978. (243p)

2029. Schatz-Bergfeld, Marianne. Massenkommunikation und Herrschaft: Zur Rolle von Massenkommunikation als Steuerungselement Moderner Demokrat. Meisenheine a Glan: Hain, 1974. (276p)

2030. Schütte, Manfred. Politische Werbung und Totalitare Propaganda. Dusseldorf und Wien: Econ-Verlag, 1968. (237p)

2031. Seymour-Ure, Colin. The Political Impact of Mass Media. Beverly Hills, CA: Sage, 1974. (296p)

2032. Spragens, William C. The Presidency and the Mass Media in the Age of Television. Washington: University Press of America, 1979. (425p)

2033. Tarantino, Anthony G. "Chinese media of communication: their history and political impact in respect to Western developments." Ph.D. dissertation, University of California—Irvine, 1975. (202p)

2034. Taylor, Charles L. "Communications development and political stability." Comparative Political Studies 1 (January 1969): 557-564.

2035. Taylor, Philip M. The Projection of Britain: British Overseas Publicity and Propaganda, 1913-1939. Cambridge: Cambridge University Press, 1981. (363p)

2036. Thomson, Oliver. Mass Persuasion in History: An Historical Analysis of the Development of Propaganda Techniques. Edinburgh: Paul Harris, 1977. (142p)

2037. Weaver, David H., et al. Media Agenda-Setting in a Presidential Election: Issues, Images, and Interest. New York: Praeger, 1981. (227p)

2038. Wilson, Charles, ed. Parliaments, Peoples and Mass Media. (Symposium on Parliament and Its Contacts with Public Opinion Through Press, Radio, and Television.) London: Cassell, 1970. (144p)

2039. Wimmer, Roger D. "A multivariate analysis of the use and effects of the mass media in the 1968 Presidential election." Ph.D. dissertation, Bowling Green State University, 1976. (162p)

2040. Winkler, Allan M.   The Politics of Propaganda; The
       Office of War Information, 1942-1945. New Haven:
       Yale University Press, 1978. (230p)

                   B.   PRINT MEDIA

2041. Allport, Floyd and Milton Lepkin. "Building war
       morale with news headlines." Public Opinion Quar-
       terly 7 (Summer 1943): 211-221.

2042. Anderson, Fenwick. "Hail to the editor-in-chief:
       Cox vs. Harding 1920." Journalism History 1 (Sum-
       mer 1974): 46-49.

2043. Balutis, Alan P. "Congress, the President and the
       press." Journalism Quarterly 53 (Autumn 1976):
       509-515.

2044. Beaverbrook, William M.A., Baron. Politicians and
       the Press. London: Hutchinson, 1925. (127p)

2045. Bernstein, M. H. "Political ideas of selected Ameri-
       can business journals." Public Opinion Quarterly
       17 (1953/1954): 258-267.

2046. Bowers, Thomas A. "The coverage of political adver-
       tising by the Prestige Press in 1972." Mass Com-
       munications Review 2 (July 1975): 19-24.

2047. _____. "Newspaper political advertising and the
       agenda-setting function." Journalism Quarterly 50
       (Autumn 1973): 552-556.

2048. Carr, Barbara C.L. "Variations on the anarchist:
       politics reflected in fiction." Ph.D. dissertation,
       Indiana University, 1976. (190p)

2049. Christoph, James B. "The press and politics in Bri-
       tain and America." Political Quarterly 34 (April-
       June 1963): 137-150.

2050. Copeland, Fayette. "Civil War editors called it
       propaganda." Journalism Quarterly 14 (June 1937):
       144-145.

2051. Dasbach, Anita M. "U.S.-Soviet magazine propaganda:
       America Illustrated and USSR." Journalism Quarterly
       43 (Spring 1966): 73-84.

2052. Eksteins, Modris. The Limits of Reason: The German
       Democratic Press and the Collapse of Weimar Demo-
       cracy, An Allied and Axis Visual Record, 1933-1945.
       London: Oxford University Press, 1975. (337p)

2053.   Ferguson, LeRoy and Ralph Smuckler. Politics in the
        Press. East Lansing: Michigan State University
        Press, c 1954. (100p)

2054.   Gregg, James E. "Newspaper editorial endorsements
        and California elections, 1948-62." Journalism
        Quarterly 42 (Autumn 1965): 532-538.

2055.   Hamburger, Ernest. "German Labor Front Press: a
        Nazi propaganda experiment." Journalism Quarterly
        21 (September 1944): 243-255.

2056.   Humke, Ronald G., et al. "Candidates, issues and
        party in newspaper political advertisements." Jour-
        nalism Quarterly 52 (Autumn 1975): 499-504.

2057.   Marbut, F. B. "The United States Senate and the
        press, 1838-41." Journalism Quarterly 28 (1951):
        342-350.

2058.   Mott, Frank L. "Newspapers in Presidential campaigns."
        Public Opinion Quarterly 8 (1944): 348-367.

2059.   Mullen, James J. "How candidates for the Senate use
        newspaper advertising." Journalism Quarterly 40
        (1963): 532-538.

2060.   _____. "Newspaper advertising in the Johnson-
        Goldwater campaign." Journalism Quarterly 45 (Sum-
        mer 1968): 219-225.

2061.   Rarick, Galen R. "Political persuasion: the news-
        paper and the sexes." Journalism Quarterly 47 (Sum-
        mer 1970): 360-364.

2062.   Robinson, John P. "The press and the voter." Annals
        of the American Academy of Political and Social
        Science 427 (September 1976): 95-103.

2063.   _____. "The press as kingmaker: what surveys from
        last five campaigns show." Journalism Quarterly 51
        (Winter 1974): 587-594.

2064.   Rosentraub, M. S. and B. A. Burke. "Mass communica-
        tion and decision-making; a case study of the geo-
        graphy of newspaper information and local govern-
        ment." Journal of Environmental Systems 8, no. 3
        (1978/1979): 267-281, 289-291.

2065.   Ruud, Charles A. "The printing press as an agent of
        political change in early twentieth-century Russia."
        Russian Review 40 (October 1981): 378-395.

2066.   Shaw, Donald L. "News bias and the telegraph: a
        study of historical change." Journalism Quarterly
        44 (Spring 1967): 3-12.

2067. Shaw, Donald L. and Maxwell E. McCombs.   The Emergence
       of American Political Issues: The Agenda-Setting
       Function of the Press.   St. Paul: West, 1977.
       (211p)

2068. Smith, Culver H.   The Press, Politics, and Patronage;
       The American Government's Use of Newspapers, 1789-
       1875.   Athens: University of Georgia Press, 1977.
       (351p)

2069. Vinyard, Dale and Roberta S. Sigel.   "Newspapers and
       urban voters."   Journalism Quarterly 48 (1971):
       486-493.

2070. Weaver, David H. and G. Cleveland Wilhoit.   "News
       magazine visibility of Senators."   Journalism Quar-
       terly 51 (Spring 1974): 67-72.

2071. Wilhoit, G. Cleveland and Taik Sup Auh.   "Newspaper
       endorsement and coverage of public opinion polls in
       1970."   Journalism Quarterly 51 (Winter 1974): 654-
       658.

C.   FILM

2072. Chappetta, Robert.   "The meaning is not the message."
       Film Quarterly 25 (Summer 1972): 10-18.

2073. Cinema and the State.   Strasbourg: Council of Europe,
       1979.   (228p)

2074. Davis, John.   "Notes on Warner Brothers foreign poli-
       cy: 1918-1948."   Velvet Light Trap 4 (Spring 1972):
       23-33.

2075. Esnault, Philippe.   "Cinema and politics."   Cineaste
       3 (Winter 1969/1970): 4-11.

2076. Franklin, John H.   "Birth of a Nation—propaganda as
       history."   Massachusetts Review 20 (Autumn 1979):
       417-434.

2077. Furhammer, Leif and F. Isaksson.   Politics and Film.
       New York: Praeger, 1971.   (257p)

2078. Goodwin, Michael and Greil Marcus.   Double Feature;
       Movies and Politics.   New York: Outerbridge and
       Lazard, 1972.   (127p)

2079. Hollins, T. J.   "The Conservative Party and film
       propaganda between the wars."   English Historical
       Review 96 (April 1981): 359-369.

2080.   Houn, Franklin W. "Motion pictures and propaganda
        in Communist China." Journalism Quarterly 34 (Fall
        1957): 481-492.

2081.   Johnston, Winifred. Memos on the Movies: War Propa-
        ganda, 1914-1939. Norman: Cooperative Books,
        1939. (68p)

2082.   Katz, Robert. "Projecting America through films."
        Hollywood Quarterly 4 (Spring 1950): 298-308.

2083.   Kustow, Michael. "Without and within: thoughts on
        politics, society, and self in some recent films."
        Sight and Sound 36 (Summer 1967): 113-117.

2084.   Lewis, Jonathan. "Before hindsight." Sight and
        Sound 46 (Spring 1977): 68-73.

2085.   Lyons, Timothy J. "Hollywood and World War I, 1914-
        1918." Journal of Popular Film 1 (Winter 1972):
        15-30.

2086.   McConnell, Frank. "Film and writing: the political
        dimension." Massachusetts Review 13 (Autumn 1972):
        543-562.

2087.   McConnell, Robert L. "Hollywood and political issues:
        three films of the Depression Era." Ph.D. disser-
        tation, University of Iowa, 1977. (286p)

2088.   Manvell, Roger. Films and the Second World War.
        South Brunswick, NJ: Barnes, 1974. (388p)

2089.   Michelson, Annette. "Film and the radical aspiration."
        Film Culture 42 (Fall 1966): 34-42+.

2090.   Peavy, Dannis. "Political attitudes in American sci-
        ence fiction films." Velvet Light Trap 4 (Spring
        1972): 13-18.

2091.   "Propaganda films about the War in Vietnam." Film
        Comment 4 (Fall 1966): 4-23.

2092.   Rosten, L. C. "Movies and propaganda." Annals of
        the American Academy of Political and Social Sci-
        ence 254 (1947): 116-124.

2093.   Roth, William D. "Technology, film, and the body
        politic." Ph.D. dissertation, University of Cali-
        fornia—Berkeley, 1970. (321p)

2094.   Sarris, Andrew. Politics and Cinema. New York: Co-
        lumbia University Press, 1978. (215p)

2095.   Strebel, E. G. "Primitive propaganda; the Boer War
        films." Sight and Sound 46 (Winter 1976/1977): 45-
        47.

2096.   "Struggle on two fronts: a conversation with Jean-Luc
        Godard." Film Quarterly 22 (Winter 1968/1969): 20-
        35.

2097.   Vas, Robert. "Sorcerers or apprentices: some as-
        pects of propaganda films." Sight and Sound 32
        (Autumn 1963): 199-204.

                        D.   RADIO

2098.   Bryson, L. and D. Rowden.   "Radio as an agency of
        national unity." Annals of the American Academy of
        Political and Social Science 244 (1946): 137-143.

2099.   Cusack, Mary A.   "The emergence of political editori-
        alizing in broadcasting." Journal of Broadcasting
        8 (1963): 53-62.

2100.   Delfiner, Henry. Vienna Broadcasts to Slovakia,
        1938-1939:   A Case Study in Subversion.   Boulder:
        East European Quarterly; New York: distributed by
        Columbia University Press, 1974.   (142p)

2101.   Grandin, Thomas. The Political Use of Radio.   Geneva:
        Geneva Research Centre, 1939.   (116p)

2102.   Hale, Julian A.   Radio Power: Propaganda and Inter-
        national Broadcasting.   Philadelphia: Temple Uni-
        versity Press, 1975.   (196p)

2103.   Houn, Franklin W.   "Radio broadcasting and propaganda
        in Communist China." Journalism Quarterly 34 (Sum-
        mer 1957): 366-377.

2104.   Kaltenborn, Rolf.   "Radio and politics." Ph.D. dis-
        sertation, Yale University, 1944.   (346p)

2105.   Kris, Ernst and Hans Speier.   German Radio Propaganda;
        Report on Home Broadcasts During the War.   London:
        Oxford University Press, 1944.   (529p)

2106.   Kushner, James M.   "African Liberation Broadcasting."
        Journal of Broadcasting 18 (Summer 1974): 299-309.

2107.   Lean, Edward T.   Voices in the Darkness; The Story of
        the European Radio War.   London: Secker and War-
        burg, 1943.   (243p)

2108.   Lisann, Maury.   Broadcasting to the Soviet Union:
        International Politics and Radio.   New York: Prae-
        ger, 1975.   (199p)

2109.   Pohle, Heinz.   Der Rundfunk als Instrument der Politik;
        zur Geschichte des Deutschen Rundfunks von 1923-38.
        Hamburg: Verlag Hans Bredow-Institut, 1955.   (480p)

2110. Radio Stations of the Cold War. Moscow: Novasti,
       1973. (55p)

2111. Schnabel, Reimund, comp. Missbrauchte Mikrofone.
       Deutsche Rundfunkpropaganda in Zweiten Weltkrieg.
       Wien: Europa-Verlag, 1967. (506p)

2112. Willis, Edgar E. "Radio and Presidential campaigning."
       Central States Speech Journal 20 (1969): 187-193.

2113. Wolfe, G. Joseph. "Some reactions to the advent of
       campaigning by radio." Journal of Broadcasting 13
       (Summer 1969): 305-314.

                    E. TELEVISION

2114. Bagdikian, Ben H. "TV, the President's medium." Co-
       lumbia Journalism Review 1 (1962): 34-38.

2115. Blumer, Jay G. and Denis McQuail. Television in Poli-
       tics; Its Uses and Influence. Chicago: University
       of Chicago Press, 1969. (379p)

2116. Bowman, Kwame N. "Black television and domestic co-
       lonialism." Ph.D. dissertation, Stanford Univer-
       sity, 1977. (189p)

2117. Brown, William R. "Television and the Democratic
       National Convention in 1968." Quarterly Journal of
       Speech 55 (1969): 237-246.

2118. Campbell, Angus. "Has television reshaped politics?"
       Columbia Journalism Review 1 (Fall 1962): 10-13.

2119. Combs, James E. "Political advertising as a popular
       mythmaking form." Journal of American Culture 2
       (Summer 1979): 331-340.

2120. Diamond, Edwin. The Tin Kazoo: Television, Politics,
       and the News. Cambridge: MIT Press, 1975. (269p)

2121. Dizard, Wilson P. "The political impact of televi-
       sion abroad." Journal of Broadcasting 9 (Summer
       1965): 195-214.

2122. Doig, I. "Kefauver versus crime: television boasts
       a Senator." Journalism Quarterly 39 (1962): 483-490.

2123. Dominick, Joseph R. "Television and political so-
       cialization." Educational Broadcasting Review 6
       (1972): 48-55.

2124. Driberg, Tom. "The first TV election." New Statesman
       61 (10 March 1961): 374-376.

2125. Forbes, Jim. "Television/France/socialism." Sight
       and Sound 51 (Spring 1982): 103-105.

2126. Frank, Robert S. Message Dimensions of Television
       News. Lexington, MA: Lexington Books, 1973.
       (120p)

2127. Friel, Charlotte. "The influence of television in
       the political career of Richard M. Nixon, 1946-
       1962." Ph.D. dissertation, New York University,
       1968. (386p)

2128. Fuchs, Douglas A. "Does TV election news influence
       voters?" Columbia Journalism Review 4 (Fall 1965):
       39-41.

2129. Gilbert, Robert E. Television and Presidential Poli-
       tics. North Quincy, MA: Christopher, 1972. (335p)

2130. Glaser, William A. "Television and voting turnout."
       Public Opinion Quarterly 29 (1965): 71-86.

2131. Goldie, Grace W. Facing the Nation: Television and
       Politics, 1936-76. London: Bodley Head, 1977.
       (367p)

2132. Goldstein, W. "Network television and political
       change: two issues in democratic theory." Western
       Political Quarterly 20 (1967): 875-887.

2133. Graber, Doris A. "Press and TV as opinion resources
       in Presidential campaigns." Public Opinion Quar-
       terly 40 (Fall 1976): 285-303.

2134. Hahn, Dan. "The effects of television on Presidential
       campaigns." Today's Speech 18 (1970): 4-17.

2135. Hale, Katherine D. "Measuring the impact of a tele-
       vised political program: combining three research
       perspectives." Ph.D. dissertation, University of
       Oklahoma, 1977. (119p)

2136. Hofstetter, C. Richard. Bias in the News: Network
       Television Coverage of the 1972 Election Campaign.
       Columbus: Ohio State University Press, c 1976.
       (213p)

2137. Hurley, Neil P. "Chilean television: a case study of
       political communication." Journalism Quarterly 51
       (Winter 1974): 683-698, 725.

2138. Joslyn, Richard A. "The content of political spot
       ads." Journalism Quarterly 57 (Spring 1980): 92-98.

2139. Just, M. R. "Political polling and political televi-
       sion." Current History 67 (August 1974): 79-86.

2140. Kellerman, Richard. "Political impact of TV." Na-
       tion 200 (11 January 1965): 24-26.

2141. Kraus, Sidney. "The political use of television."
       Journal of Broadcasting 8 (Summer 1964): 219-228.

2142. Kumar, Krishan. "The political consequences of tele-
       vision." Listener 82 (3 July 1969): 1-3.

2143. Lang, Gladys E. and Kurt Lang. "Political participa-
       tion and the television perspective." Social Prob-
       lems 4 (October 1956): 107-116.

2144. _____. Politics and Television. Chicago: Quad-
       rangle, 1968. (315p)

2145. McKnaught, Kenneth W. "The failure of television in
       politics." Canadian Forum 38 (August 1958): 104-
       105.

2146. MacNeil, Robert. The People Machine; The Influence
       of Television in American Politics. New York:
       Harper and Row, 1968. (362p)

2147. Mendelsohn, Harold A. "TV and youth: a new style
       for politics." Nation 202 (6 June 1966): 669-673.

2148. Mendelsohn, Harold A. and I. Crespi. Polls, Televi-
       sion, and the New Politics. San Francisco: Chand-
       ler, 1970. (329p)

2149. Merelman, Richard M. "Mass culture and political
       ideology: the television Western." Ph.D. disser-
       tation, Yale University, 1965. (248p)

2150. Mickelson, Sig. The Electronic Mirror: Politics in
       an Age of Television. New York: Dodd, Mead, c
       1972. (304p)

2151. Patterson, Thomas E. and Robert D. McClure. The Un-
       seeing Eye: The Myth of Television Power in National
       Politics. New York: Putnam, c 1976. (218p)

2152. Pickles, W. "Political attitudes in the television
       age." Political Quarterly 30 (January/March 1959):
       54-66.

2153. Pool, Ithiel de Sola and Herbert E. Alexander. Poli-
       tics in a Wired Nation. N.P., 1971. (75p)

2154. Prisuta, Robert H. "Televised sports and political
       values." Journal of Communication 29 (Winter 1979):
       94-102.

2155. Raucek, Joseph S. "The influence of television on
       American politics." Politics 28 (1963): 124-134.

2156. Remond, R. and C. Neuschwander. "Television et com-
       portement politique." Revue Francaise de Science
       Politique 13 (1963): 325-347.

2157. Robinson, Michael J. "Public affairs television and
       the growth of political malaise: the case of 'The
       Selling of the Pentagon.'" American Political Sci-
       ence Review 70 (June 1976): 409-432.

2158. Rubin, Bernard. Political Television. Belmont, CA:
       Wadsworth, 1967. (200p)

2159. Saldich, Anne R. Electronic Democracy; Television's
       Impact on the American Political Process. New York:
       Praeger, 1979. (122p)

2160. Seabury, Paul. "Television, a new campaign weapon."
       New Republic 127 (1 December 1952): 12-14.

2161. Smith, Anthony, ed. Television and Political Life:
       Studies in Six European Countries. New York: St.
       Martin's Press, 1979. (261p)

2162. Spero, Robert. The Duping of the American Voter:
       Dishonesty and Deception in Presidential TV Adver-
       tising. New York: Lippincott and Crowell, 1980.
       (232p)

2163. Tan, Alexis S. "Mass media use, issue knowledge and
       political involvement." Public Opinion Quarterly
       44 (Summer 1980): 241-248.

2164. Thomson, Charles A.H. Television and Presidential
       Politics. Washington, D.C.: Brookings Institution,
       1956. (173p)

2165. _____. "Television, politics and public policy."
       Public Policy 8 (1958): 368-406.

2166. Wangermee, Robert. "Television et politique." Etudes
       de Radio-Television 10 (1965): 2-19.

2167. Washburn, Frank. "The television panel as a vehicle
       of political persuasion." Western Speech 16 (1952):
       245-253.

2168. Whale, J. The Half-Shut Eye: Television and Politics
       in Britain and America. New York: St. Martin's
       Press, 1969. (219p)

2169. Wilhelmsen, Frederick D. and Jane Bret. Telepolitics;
       The Politics of Neuronic Man. Plattsburgh, NY:
       Tundra, 1972. (254p)

2170. Willis, Edgar E. "McLuhanism, television, and poli-
       tics." Quarterly Journal of Speech 54 (1968): 404-
       409.

2171.   Windlesham, Lord.   "Television as an influence on po-
        litical opinion."   Political Quarterly 35 (1964):
        375-385.

2172.   Wyckoff, Gene.   The Image Candidates; American Poli-
        tics in the Age of Television.   New York: Macmillan,
        1968.   (274p)

7

Buyer Beware: Advertising
and the Mass Media

A. MASS MEDIA (GENERAL)

2173. Abromeit, Heidrun. Das Politische in der Werbung;
Wahlwerbung und Wirtschaftswerbung in der Bundes-
republik. Opladen: Westdeutscher Verlag, 1972.
(230p)

2174. Advertising and Advertising Agencies: Summary of a
Report on a Postal Survey of Advertisers' Opinions.
London: Institute of Practicioners in Advertising,
1972. (18p)

2175. Advertising and Small Business. Hearings before the
U.S. House of Representatives Subcommittee on Acti-
vities of Regulatory Agencies Relating to Small
Business, June 7, 11, 14, 18, 1971. (666+ A350p)

2176. Advertising and Women: A Report on Advertising Por-
traying or Directed to Women. New York: National
Advertising Review Board, 1975. (21p)

2177. Agnew, Hugh E. and Warren B. Dygert. Advertising Media. New York and London: McGraw-Hill, 1938.
(465p)

2178. Albion, Mark S. and Paul W. Farris. The Advertising
Controversy: Evidence on the Economic Effects of
Advertising. Boston: Auburn House, 1981. (226p)

2179. Armour, Robert A. and J. Carol Williams. "Image
making and advertising in the funeral industry."
Journal of Popular Culture 14 (Spring 1981): 701-710.

2180.   Attracting and Holding Customers; How Publicity Can
        Bring Customers—Finding and Holding Your Trade—
        What to Sell Your Customers. Chicago: Shaw, c
        1919. (230p)

2181.   Baker, Samm S. The Permissable Lie; The Inside Truth
        About Advertising. Cleveland: World, 1968. (236p)

2182.   Barker, Paul, ed. Arts in Society. London: Fontana/
        Collins, 1977. (285p)

2183.   Barmash, Isadore. The World Is Full of It; How We
        Are Oversold, Overinfluenced, and Overwhelmed by
        the Communications Manipulators. New York: Dela-
        corte, 1974. (269p)

2184.   Barnes, Michael, ed. The Three Faces of Advertising.
        London: Advertising Association, 1975. (277p)

2185.   Becker, Lee B. "Media advertising credibility."
        Journalism Quarterly 53 (Summer 1976): 216-222.

2186.   Bogart, Leo. "Mass advertising: the message, not
        the measure." Harvard Business Review 54 (September
        1976): 107-116.

2187.   Borden, Neil H. The Economic Effects of Advertising.
        Chicago: Irwin, 1942. (988p)

2188.   Bowen, Lawrence. "Advertising and the poor: a com-
        parative study of patterns of response to televi-
        sion and magazine advertising between middle-income
        and low-income groups." Ph.D. dissertation, Uni-
        versity of Wisconsin, 1974. (208p)

2189.   Boyenton, William H. "Enter the ladies—86 proof: a
        study in advertising ethics." Journalism Quarterly
        44 (Autumn 1967): 445-453.

2190.   Brown, Bruce W. Images of Family Life in Magazine
        Advertising, 1920-1978. New York: Praeger, 1981.
        (131p)

2191.   Brozen, Yale, ed. Advertising and Society. New York:
        University Press, 1974. (189p)

2192.   Burke, John G. "Wood pulp, water pollution, and ad-
        vertising." Technology and Culture 20 (January
        1979): 175-195.

2193.   Buzzi, Giancarlo. Advertising; Its Cultural and Po-
        litical Effects. Trans. by B. David Garmize. Min-
        neapolis: University of Minnesota Press, 1968.
        (147p)

2194.   Carrell, Bob. The Mass Media as Gatekeepers in Re-
          spect to Advertising. Ph.D. dissertation, Univer-
          sity of Illinois, 1969. (245p)

2195.   Cherington, Paul T. The Consumer Looks at Adver-
          tising. New York and London: Harper, 1928. (196p)

2196.   Chu, James. "Advertising in China: its policy,
          practice and evolution." Journalism Quarterly 59
          (Spring 1982): 40-45, 91.

2197.   Clark, Thomas B. The Advertising Smoke Screen. New
          York and London: Harper, 1944. (228p)

2198.   Clement, Wendell E. "A study of the advertising
          process and its influence on consumer behavior."
          Ph.D. dissertation, American University, 1967.
          (268p)

2199.   Colldeweih, Jack H. "The effects of mass media con-
          sumption on accuracy of beliefs about the candidates
          in a local Congressional election." Ph.D. disser-
          tation, University of Illinois, 1968. (115p)

2200.   "Corporate advertising: a further look at how some
          companies use an ad series." Industrial Marketing
          62 (September 1977): 90+.

2201.   Courtney, Alice E. and Thomas W. Whipple. Sex Stereo-
          typing in Advertising: An Annotated Bibliography.
          Cambridge, MA: Marketing Science Institute, 1980.
          (96p)

2202.   Crane, Edgar G. Marketing Communications; A Beha-
          vioral Approach to Men, Messages and Media. New
          York: Wiley, 1965. (569p)

2203.   Cranston, Pat. "Political convention broadcasts:
          their history and influence." Journalism Quarterly
          37 (Spring 1960): 186-194.

2204.   DeBakey, Lois. "Happiness is only a pill away: Madi-
          son Avenue rhetoric without reason." Addictive
          Diseases 3, no. 2 (1977): 273-286.

2205.   Decker, Ronald L. "Advertising as a threat to atti-
          tudinal freedom." Ph.D. dissertation, University
          of Iowa, 1973. (141p)

2206.   Dench, Ernest A. Advertising by Motion Picture. Cin-
          cinnati: Standard Publishing, 1916. (255p)

2207.   "Directory of top 200 advertised brands including me-
          dia strategy for each." Media Decisions 11 (July
          1976): 121-204+.

2208. Dispenza, Joseph E. Advertising the American Woman.
      Dayton: Pflaum, c 1975. (181p)

2209. Divita, S. F. Advertising and the Public Interest.
      (Selected papers from the Conference on Advertising
      and the Public Interest, Washington, D.C., May,
      1973.) Chicago: American Marketing Association,
      1974. (264p)

2210. Durand, Richard M., et al. "Racial differences in
      perceptions of media advertising credibility."
      Journalism Quarterly 56 (Autumn 1979): 562-566.

2211. Elkin, Frederick. Rebels and Colleagues; Advertising
      and Social Change in French Canada. Montreal:
      McGill-Queen's University Press, 1973. (227p)

2212. Elliott, Blanche B. A History of English Advertising.
      London: Business Publications, 1962. (231p)

2213. Ewen, Stuart. Captains of Consciousness; Advertising
      and the Social Roots of the Consumer Culture. New
      York: McGraw-Hill, c 1976. (261p)

2214. Foster, G. Allen. Advertising: Ancient Market Place
      to Television. New York: Criterion, 1967. (224p)

2215. Fowles, Jib. "An atomized society in the 1980s?"
      Futurist 11 (December 1977): 377-379.

2216. _____. Mass Advertising as Social Forecast: A
      Method for Futures Research. Westport, CT: Green-
      wood, 1976. (153p)

2217. Fox, Frank W. Madison Avenue Goes to War; The Strange
      Military Career of American Advertising, 1941-45.
      Provo: Brigham Young University Press, c 1975.
      (98p)

2218. Fox, H. W. and S. R. Renas. "Stereotypes of women in
      the media and their impact on women's careers."
      Human Resource Management 16 (Spring 1977): 28-31.

2219. Frostick, Michael. Advertising and the Motor Car.
      London: Lund Humphries, 1970. (159p)

2220. Gardner, D. M. "Deception in advertising: a receiver
      oriented approach to advertising." Journal of Ad-
      vertising 5, no. 4 (1976): 5-11+.

2221. Garrett, Thomas M. An Introduction to Some Ethical
      Problems of Modern American Advertising. Rome:
      Gregorian University Press, 1961. (209p)

2222. Gentry, Curt. The Vulnerable Americans. Garden City,
      NY: Doubleday, 1966. (333p)

2223.   Glatzer, Robert. The New Advertising; The Great Cam-
        paigns from Avis to Volkswagen. New York: Citadel
        Press, 1970. (191p)

2224.   Gluck, Felix, comp. World Graphic Design; Fifty
        Years of Advertising Art. New York: Watson Gup-
        till, 1968. (175p)

2225.   Goffman, Erving. Gender Advertisements. Cambridge,
        MA: Harvard University Press, 1979. (84p)

2226.   Grass, R. C. and W. H. Wallace. "Advertising com-
        munication: print vs. TV." Journal of Advertising
        Research 14, no. 5 (1974): 19-23.

2227.   Hammell, William, comp. The Popular Arts in America:
        A Reader. 2nd ed. New York: Harcourt Brace Jo-
        vanovich, 1977. (501p)

2228.   Hanson, Philip. The Development of Advertising in
        Eastern Europe. London: Advertising Association,
        1973 (?). (140p)

2229.   Harder, Virgil E. "A history of direct mail adver-
        tising." Ph.D. dissertation, University of Illi-
        nois, 1958. (266p)

2230.   Harding, Thomas W. The Popular Practice of Fraud.
        London and New York: Longmans, Green, 1935. (376p)

2231.   Heighton, Elizabeth J. and Don R. Cunningham. Adver-
        tising in the Broadcasting Media. Belmont, CA:
        Wadsworth, 1976. (439p)

2232.   Hermanns, Arnold. Sozialisation Durch Werbung;
        Sozialisationswirkung von Werbeaussagen in Massen-
        medien. Düsseldorf: Bertelsmann Universitätsver-
        lag, c 1972. (140p)

2233.   Hileman, Donald G. "Changes in the buying and selec-
        tion of advertising media." Journalism Quarterly
        45 (Summer 1968): 279-285.

2234.   Hobson, John W. The Selection of Advertising Media.
        5th ed. London: Published on behalf of the Insti-
        tute of Practitioners in Advertising by Business
        Books, 1968. (217p)

2235.   Hornung, Clarence P. and Fridolf Johnson. 200 Years
        of American Graphic Art: A Retrospective Survey of
        the Printing Arts and Advertising Since the Colo-
        nial Period. New York: Braziller, 1976. (211p)

2236.   How It Was in Advertising: 1776-1976. Compiled by
        the editors of Advertising Age. Chicago: Crain,
        1976. (110p)

2237. "How PR executives shape corporate advertising." Public Relations Journal 32 (November 1976): 32-33.

2238. Howard, John A. and James Hulbert. Advertising and the Public Interest; A Staff Report to the Federal Trade Commission. Chicago: Crain, 1973. (96p)

2239. Hutchinson, Ray. The Gospel According to Madison Avenue. New York: Bruce, 1969. (161p)

2240. Ignasias, C. Dennis. "Propaganda and public opinion in Harding's foreign affairs: the case for Mexican recognition." Journalism Quarterly 48 (Spring 1971): 41-52.

2241. Inglis, Fred. The Imagery of Power: A Critique of Advertising. London: Heinemann, 1972. (139p)

2242. James, Don L. Youth, Media, and Advertising. Austin: Bureau of Business Research, Graduate School of Business, University of Texas, 1971. (137p)

2243. Jellinek, J. Stephan. The Inner Editor: Offense and Defense of Communication. New York: Stein and Day, 1977. (198p)

2244. Johnson, Myron. American Advertising, 1800-1900. Scotia, NY: Americana Review, 1960. (unpaged)

2245. Key, Wilson B. Subliminal Seduction; Ad Media's Manipulation of a Not So Innocent America. Englewood Cliffs, NJ: Prentice-Hall, 1973. (206p)

2246. Kottman, E. John. "Toward an understanding of truth in advertising." Journalism Quarterly 47 (Spring 1970): 81-86.

2247. Kuhns, William. Waysteps to Eden; Ads and Commercials. New York: Herder and Herder, 1970. (32p)

2248. Langholz Leymore, Varda. Hidden Myth: Structure and Symbolism in Advertising. New York: Basic Books, 1975. (208p)

2249. Littlefield, James E., comp. Readings in Advertising: Current Viewpoints on Selected Topics. St. Paul: West, 1975. (450p)

2250. McClure, Leslie W. and Paul C. Fulton. Advertising in the Printed Media. New York: Macmillan, 1964. (338p)

2251. McLuhan, Marshall. The Mechanical Bride: Folklore of Industrial Man. New York: Vanguard Press, 1951. (157p)

2252.   Maloney, J. C. "Advertising research and an emerging
        science of mass persuasion." Journalism Quarterly
        41 (1964): 517-528.

2253.   Marquez, F. T. "Advertising content: persuasion,
        information, or intimidation?" Journalism Quarterly
        54 (Autumn 1977): 482-491.

2254.   Napolitan, J. "Media costs and effects in political
        campaigns." Annals of the American Academy of Po-
        litical and Social Science 427 (September 1976):
        114-124.

2255.   Nowak, Kjell, et al. Mass Communication and Adver-
        tising. Stockholm: Economic Research Institute at
        the Stockholm School of Economics and AB Svenska
        Telegrambyran, 1967. (118p)

2256.   Pease, Otis A. The Responsibilities of American Ad-
        vertising; Private Control and Public Influence,
        1920-1940. New Haven: Yale University Press, 1958.
        (232p)

2257.   Presbrey, Frank. The History and Development of Ad-
        vertising. Garden City, NY: Doubleday, Doran,
        1929. (642p)

2258.   Preston, I. L. "Comment on defining misleading adver-
        tising and deception in advertising." Journal of
        Marketing 40 (July 1976): 54-59.

2259.   Printers' Ink. Advertising: Today, Yesterday, To-
        morrow; An Omnibus of Advertising. New York:
        McGraw-Hill, 1963. (472p)

2260.   Robertson, Thomas S. and John R. Rossiter. "Children
        and commercial persuasion: an attribution theory
        analysis." Journal of Consumer Research 1 (June
        1974): 13-20.

2261.   Rotzoll, Kim B., et al. Advertising in Contemporary
        Society: Perspectives Toward Understanding. Co-
        lumbus, OH: Grid, c 1976. (151p)

2262.   Sampson, Henry. A History of Advertising from the
        Earliest Times. London: Chatto and Windus, 1874.
        (616p)

2263.   Schultze, Quentin J. Walter Dill Scott and Scientific
        Advertising. Urbana: Department of Advertising,
        College of Communications, University of Illinois,
        1977. (28p)

2264.   Schwartz, Tony. Media, the Second God. New York:
        Random House, 1981. (206p)

2265.   _____. The Responsive Chord. Garden City, NY: Anchor Press, 1973. (173p)

2266. Seldin, Joseph J. The Golden Fleece; Selling the Good Life to Americans. New York: Macmillan, 1963. (305p)

2267. Sethi, S. Prakash. Advocacy Advertising and Large Corporations: Social Conflict, Big Business Image, The News Media, and Public Policy. Lexington, MA: Lexington Books, 1977. (355p)

2268. Shukle, Terrance. Giraffe Raps: A Tale of Advertising in America. Ann Arbor: Giraffe, distributed in the U.S. by Street Fiction Press, c 1976. (112p)

2269. Significations de la publicite. Liege: Commission Art et Societe, Universite de Liege, 1974. (149p)

2270. Simon, Richard. "Advertising as literature: the utopian fiction of the American marketplace." Texas Studies in Literature and Language 22 (Summer 1980): 154-174.

2271. Sissors, Jack Z. and E. R. Petray. Advertising Media Planning. Chicago: Crain, 1976. (341p)

2272. Skelly, F. R. "Changing attitudes of public opinion." Public Relations Journal 32 (November 1976): 15-17.

2273. Storer, Louise K. "Military and nationalistic themes in war-time American consumer advertising." Ph.D. dissertation, New York University, 1971. (190p)

2274. Stridsberg, Albert. Controversy Advertising: How Advertisers Present Points of View of Public Affairs. New York: Hastings House, 1977. (189p)

2275. Surlin, Stuart H. The Social Effects of Advertising as Perceived by Advertising Executives, Businessmen, and the General Public. Athens: School of Journalism, University of Georgia, 1974. (69p)

2276. Sutherland, Max and John Galloway. "Role of advertising: persuasion or agenda setting." Journal of Advertising Research 21 (October 1981): 25-29.

2277. Sutnar, Ladislav. Visual Design in Action: Principles, Purposes. New York: Hastings House, 1961. (Unpaged)

2278. Teixeira, Antonio. Music to Sell By: The Craft of Jingle Writing. Boston: Berklee Press, 1974. (96p)

2279.   Thompson, M. J. "Government regulation of advertising:
        killing the consumer in order to save him." Anti-
        trust Law and Economics Review 8, no. 1 (1976): 81-
        92.

2280.   Tijmstra, L. F. "The challenge of TV to the press:
        the impact of television on advertising revenues
        and circulations of newspapers." Gazette; Inter-
        national Journal of the Science of the Press 5
        (1959): 293-315.

2281.   Todd, Judith. The Big Sell; Structure and Strategy
        of the Mass Media: Radio and Television, Press,
        Cinema, Advertising. London: Lawrence and Wishart,
        1961. (109p)

2282.   Trump, Fred. Buyer Beware! New York: Abingdon
        Press, 1965. (207p)

2283.   Turner, Ernest S. The Shocking History of Adver-
        tising. London: Joseph, 1953. (303p)

2284.   Turner, Ronny F. and Charles Edgley. "Subliminal se-
        duction: popular vocabularies of motive and the
        myth of mental masseuse." Free Inquiry in Creative
        Sociology 7 (May 1979): 14-17, 22.

2285.   Udry, J. R., et al. "Can mass media advertising in-
        crease contraceptive use?" Family Planning Per-
        spectives 4, no. 3 (1972): 37-44.

2286.   Unwin, Stephen J.F. "How culture, age and sex affect
        advertising response." Journalism Quarterly 50
        (Winter 1973): 735-743.

2287.   Van Dam, A. "Can advertising change lifestyles?"
        Business Quarterly 41 (Winter 1976): 35-38.

2288.   Van Til, Roy G. "The content of U.S. automobile ad-
        vertising, 1949-73: impact on the shaping of wants
        and product development." Ph.D. dissertation, Bos-
        ton College, 1975. (418p)

2289.   Vries, Leonard de and Ilonka Van Amstel. The Wonder-
        ful World of American Advertisements, 1865-1900.
        Chicago: Follett, 1972. (142p)

2290.   Warren, Denise. "Commercial liberation." Journal of
        Communication 28 (Winter 1979): 169-173.

2291.   Wedding, Nugent. "Advertising as a method of mass
        communication of ideas and information." Journal
        of Advertising 4 (Summer 1975): 6-10.

2292.   Weir, Walter. Truth in Advertising and Other Here-
        sies. New York: McGraw-Hill, 1963. (224p)

2293. Wight, Robin. The Day the Pigs Refused to be Driven
       to the Market; Advertising and the Consumer Revolu-
       tion. New York: Random House, c 1974. (230p)

2294. Williamson, Judith. Decoding Advertisements: Ide-
       ology and Meaning in Advertising. London: Marion
       Boyars, 1978. (180p)

2295. Wilson, Alexander, ed. Advertising and the Community.
       Manchester: Manchester University Press, 1968.
       (231p)

2296. Wood, James P. Advertising and the Soul's Belly;
       Repetition and Memory in Advertising. Athens: Uni-
       versity of Georgia Press, 1961. (116p)

2297. _____. The Story of Advertising. New York: Ron-
       ald Press, 1958. (512p)

2298. Wright, John, ed. The Commercial Connection: Adver-
       tising and the American Mass Media. New York:
       Dell, 1979. (347p)

2299. Wright, John S. and John E. Mertes, comp. Adver-
       tising's Role in Society. St. Paul: West, 1974.
       (501p)

2300. Wright, Peter L. "Analyzing media effects on adver-
       tising responses." Public Opinion Quarterly 28
       (Summer 1974): 192-205.

B. PRINT MEDIA

2301. Belkaoui, A. and J. M. Belkaoui. "Comparative analy-
       sis of the roles portrayed by women in print adver-
       tisements: 1958, 1970, 1972." Journal of Marketing
       Research 13 (May 1976): 168-172.

2302. Berkman, Dave. "Advertising in Ebony and Life: Ne-
       gro aspirations vs. reality." Journalism Quarterly
       40 (Winter 1963): 53-64.

2303. Bowers, Thomas A. "Issue personality information in
       newspaper political advertising." Journalism Quar-
       terly 49 (Autumn 1972): 446-452.

2304. Brandsberg, George. The Free Papers, A Comprehensive
       Study of America's Shopping Guide and Free Circula-
       tion Newspaper Industry. Ames, Iowa: Wordsmith,
       1969. (153p)

2305. Carter, David E. "The changing face of Life's adver-
       tisements." Journalism Quarterly 46 (Spring 1969):
       87-93.

2306. Costello, Ellen M. "The impact of language in job
       advertising on fair practices in hiring: a research
       note." Journal of Applied Social Psychology 9 (Ju-
       ly/August 1979): 323-325.

2307. Coughlin, Robert E. and Karen A. Goldstein. The Pub-
       lic's View of the Outdoor Environment as Interpreted
       by Magazine Ad-Makers. Philadelphia: Regional
       Science Research Institute, 1968. (38p)

2308. Courtney, Alice E. and S. W. Lockertez. "Woman's
       place: an analysis of the roles portrayed by women
       in magazine advertisements." Journal of Marketing
       Research 8 (February 1971): 92-95.

2309. Crane, Burton. A Century of Financial Advertising in
       the New York Times. New York: New York Times,
       1957. (128p)

2310. Darwin, Bernard R.M., ed. The Dickens Advertiser, A
       Collection of the Advertisements in the Original
       Parts of Novels by Charles Dickens. New York: Mac-
       millan, 1930. (208p)

2311. Drepperd, Carl W., comp. Early American Advertising
       Art, A Collection of Wood Cut and Stereotype Illu-
       strations Used in American Newspaper, Almanac and
       Magazine Advertising, 1750 to 1850. New York:
       Youth Group of Magazines, 1943. (48p)

2312. Forte, Frances L. "Effect of sex of subject on re-
       call of gender-stereotyped magazine advertisements."
       Psychological Reports 49 (October 1981): 619-622.

2313. Gantz, Walter, et al. "Approaching invisibility:
       the portrayal of the elderly in magazine advertise-
       ments." Journal of Communication 30 (Winter 1980):
       56-60.

2314. Gaw, Walter A. "Some important trends in the develop-
       ment of magazines in the United States as an adver-
       tising medium." Ph.D. dissertation, New York Uni-
       versity, 1942. (237p)

2315. Geizer, Ronald. "Advertising in Ebony: 1960 and
       1969." Journalism Quarterly 48 (Spring 1971): 131-
       134.

2316. Gitter, A. George, et al. "Trends in appearance of
       models in Ebony ads over 17 years." Journalism
       Quarterly 49 (Autumn 1972): 547-550.

2317. Gunderson, Gilbert N. The Story of Classified Ads
       and Their Relation to Human Progress. New York:
       New York Telegram and Evening Mail, c 1924. (59p)

2318. Hood, Peter. Ourselves and the Press; A Social Study
       of News, Advertising and Propaganda. London: John
       Lane, 1939. (287p)

2319. Jorgenson, Dale O. "Agency and communication trends
       in consumer goods advertising." Personality and
       Social Psychology Bulletin 7 (September 1981): 410-
       414.

2320. King, Ellie. "Sex bias in psychoactive drug adver-
       tisements." Psychiatry 43 (May 1980): 129-137.

2321. Kingsbury, Susan M. "Measuring the ethics of American
       newspapers, V: an index of pernicious medical ad-
       vertising." Journalism Quarterly 11 (September
       1934): 276-284.

2322. Knight, Oliver. "Scripps and his adless newspaper."
       Journalism Quarterly 41 (Winter 1964): 51-64.

2323. Landes, J. D. "An analysis of classified advertising
       in newspapers." Ph.D. dissertation, University of
       North Carolina, 1960. (182p)

2324. Larson, Cedric. "Patent medicine advertising and the
       Early American press." Journalism Quarterly 14 (De-
       cember 1937): 333-341.

2325. Lorimor, E. S. "Classified advertising: a neglected
       medium." Journal of Advertising 6 (Winter 1976):
       17-25.

2326. Lumby, Malcolm E. "Men who advertise for sex." Jour-
       nal of Homosexuality 4 (Fall 1978): 63-72.

2327. Millum, Trevor. Images of Woman; Advertising in Wo-
       men's Magazines. Totowa, NJ: Rowman and Little-
       field, 1975. (206p)

2328. Mullen, James J. "Newspaper advertising in the Ken-
       nedy-Nixon campaign." Journalism Quarterly 40
       (Winter 1963): 3-11.

2329. "New technology will increase classified revenues/
       profits." Editor and Publisher 110 (8 January 1977):
       38.

2330. The Newspaper as an Advertising Medium; A Handbook of
       the Newspaper in North America: Its Beginnings, Its
       Development, Its Services to the Public, and Its
       Usefulness to Buyers of Advertising. New York:
       Bureau of Advertising, American Newspaper Publishers
       Association, c 1940. (170p)

2331. Nichols, John E. "Publishers and drug advertising:
       1933-38." Journalism Quarterly 49 (Spring 1972):
       144-147.

2332. O'Keefe, M. Timothy. "A study of advertising in the
       Moscow news." Journalism Quarterly 44 (Winter
       1967): 724-726.

2333. Schafer, Judith K. "New Orleans slavery in 1850 as
       seen in advertisements." Journal of Southern His-
       tory 47 (February 1981): 33-56.

2334. Stockburger, David W. and James O. Davis. "Selling
       the female image as mental patient." Sex Roles 4
       (February 1978): 131-134.

2335. Thomson, William A. Making Millions Read and Buy;
       The Influence and Use of the Newspaper in Adver-
       tising. New York: Drey, c 1934. (248p)

2336. Watkins, Julian L. The Best Advertisements from
       Reader's Digest, 1955-1961, and the Qualities That
       Made Them Effective. New York: Random House, 1962.
       (141p)

C.   RADIO

2337. Dunlap, Orrin E. Radio in Advertising. New York
       and London: Harpers, 1931. (383p)

2338. Hettinger, Herman S. A Decade of Radio Advertising.
       Chicago: University of Chicago Press, 1933. (354p)

2339. Morell, Peter. Poisons, Potions, and Profits; The
       Antidote to Radio Advertising. New York: Knight,
       1937. (327p)

2340. O'Neill, Neville, ed. The Advertising Agency Looks
       at Radio. New York and London: Appleton, 1932.
       (232p)

D.   TELEVISION

2341. Aaker, David A. and Donald E. Bruzzone. "Viewer per-
       ceptions of prime-time television advertising."
       Journal of Advertising Research 21 (October 1981):
       15-23.

2342. Adler, Richard P., et al. The Effects of Television
       Advertising on Children. Lexington, MA: Lexington
       Books, 1980. (371p)

2343. "Advertiser says TV commercials capture attention
       print can miss." Broadcasting 92 (21 March 1977):
       55-56.

2344. Atkin, Charles K. "Effects of drug commercials on young viewers." Journal of Communication 28 (Autumn 1978): 71-79.

2345. Baldwin, Thomas F. and Stuart H. Surlin. "The contribution of the visual element in television commercials." Journalism Quarterly 46 (Autumn 1969): 607-610.

2346. Barcus, Francis E. Pre-Christmas Advertising to Children: A Comparison of the Advertising Content of Children's Programs in April and November of 1975. Newtonville, MA: Action for Children's Television, 1976. (41 leaves)

2347. Barcus, Francis E. and Lucille McLaughlin. Food Advertising on Children's Television: An Analysis of Appeals and Nutritional Content. Newtonville, MA: Action for Children's Television, 1978. (145p)

2348. Bardwick, J. M. and S. I. Schumann. "Portrait of American men and women in TV commercials." Psychology 4, no. 4 (1967): 18-23.

2349. Barry, T. E. and A. A. Sheikh. "Race as a dimension in children's TV advertising: the need for more research." Journal of Advertising 6, no. 3 (1977): 5-10.

2350. Blechman, Robert K. "Savage mind on Madison Avenue: a structural analysis of television advertising." ETC 37 (Spring 1980): 38-52.

2351. Broadcast Advertising and Children. Hearings before the U.S. House of Representatives, Subcommittee on Communications, July 14-17, 1975. Washington: G.P.O., 1976. (495p)

2352. Bush, R. F. "There are more blacks in TV commercials." Journal of Advertising Research 17 (February 1977): 21-25.

2353. Courtney, Alice E. and Thomas W. Whipple. "Women in TV commercials." Journal of Communication 24, no. 1 (1974): 110-118.

2354. Coyle, D. W. "International TV advertising in the 1970's." International Advertiser 10, no. 3 (1969): 5-8.

2355. Critchley, R. A. Television and Media Effect: A Review of the Relevant Research. London: British Bureau of Television Advertising, c 1974. (134p)

2356. Diamant, Lincoln. Television's Classic Commercials; The Golden Years, 1948-1958. New York: Hastings House, 1971. (305p)

2357.   _____, ed. The Anatomy of a Television Commercial;
         The Story of Eastman Kodak's "Yesterdays," Winner of
         13 International Awards. New York: Hastings House,
         1970. (191p)

2358.   Dominick, Joseph R. and G. E. Rauch. "The image of
         women in network TV commercials." Journal of Broad-
         casting 16 (Summer 1972): 259-265.

2359.   Donohue, Thomas R., et al. "Do kids know what TV
         commercials intend?" Journal of Advertising Re-
         search 20 (October 1980): 51-57.

2360.   Edible TV: Your Child and Food Commercials. (U.S.
         Senate Select Committee on Nutrition and Human
         Needs; committee print.) September, 1977. (89p)

2361.   Feldman, Shel and Abraham Wolf. "What's wrong with
         children's commercials?" Journal of Advertising
         Research 14 (February 1974): 39-43.

2362.   Ferguson, Clara P. Preadolescent Children's Atti-
         tudes Toward Television Commercials. Austin:
         Bureau of Business Research, Graduate School of
         Business, University of Texas, 1975. (74p)

2363.   Francher, J. "It's the Pepsi generation . . .: ac-
         celerated aging and the television commercial." In-
         ternational Journal of Aging and Human Development
         4 (1973): 245-255.

2364.   FTC Staff Report on Television Advertising to Chil-
         dren. Washington, D.C.: Federal Trade Commission,
         1978. (346p)

2365.   Goldberg, Marvin E. and Gerald J. Gorn. "Some unin-
         tended consequences of TV advertising to children."
         Journal of Consumer Research 5 (June 1978): 22-29.

2366.   Golasen, Rose K. "Why television advertising is de-
         ceptive and unfair." ETC 35 (Winter 1978): 354-375.

2367.   Gorn, Gerald J. and Marvin E. Goldberg. "Children's
         responses to repetitive television commercials."
         Journal of Consumer Research 6 (March 1980): 421-
         424.

2368.   Haefner, James E. and Steven E. Permut. "An approach
         to the evaluation of deception in television adver-
         tising." Journal of Advertising 3 (Fall 1974): 40-
         45.

2369.   Hefzallah, I. M. and W. P. Maloney. "Content analysis
         of TV commercials." International Journal of In-
         structional Media 5, no. 1 (1977/1978): 9-25.

2370. "How TV sells children; symposium." Journal of Com-
       munication 27 (Winter 1977): 100-157.

2371. Jennings-Walstedt, Joyce, et al. "Influence of tele-
       vision commercials on women's self-confidence and
       independent judgment." Journal of Personality and
       Social Psychology 38 (February 1980): 203-210.

2372. Krugman, Herbert E. "The impact of television adver-
       tising: learning without involvement." Public
       Opinion Quarterly 29 (Fall 1965): 349-356.

2373. Lull, James T., et al. "Recognition of female stereo-
       types in TV commercials." Journalism Quarterly 54
       (Spring 1977): 153-157.

2374. Nutrition Education—1973. Parts 3-5: TV Advertising
       of Food to Children. Hearings before the U.S. Sen-
       ate Select Committee on Nutrition and Human Needs,
       March 5, 6, 12, 1973. (255-546p)

2375. Nutrition Education—1973. Part 8: Broadcast Indus-
       try's Response to TV Ads. Hearings before the U.S.
       Senate Select Committee on Nutrition and Human
       Needs, June 11, 1973. (663-712p)

2376. O'Donnell, William J. and Karen J. O'Donnell. "Up-
       date: sex-role messages in TV commercials." Jour-
       nal of Communication 28 (Winter 1978): 156-158.

2377. O'Keefe, M. Timothy. "The anti-smoking commercials:
       a study of television's impact on behavior." Public
       Opinion Quarterly 35 (Summer 1971): 242-248.

2378. Paletz, David L., et al. Politics in Public Service
       Advertising on Television. New York: Praeger,
       1977. (123p)

2379. Paulson, Steven K. "Printed advertisements as indi-
       cators of Christian institutional secularization."
       Review of Religious Research 19 (Fall 1977): 78-83.

2380. Pearce, Alan. The Economics of Children's Television:
       An Assessment of the Impact of a Reduction in the
       Amount of Advertising. Washington, D.C.: Office
       of Plans and Policy, Federal Communications Commis-
       sion, 1974. (49p)

2381. Pingree, Suzanne. "The effects of nonsexist televi-
       sion commercials and perceptions of reality on chil-
       dren's attitudes about women." Psychology of Women
       Quarterly 2 (Spring 1978): 262-277.

2382. Pollay, Richard W., et al. "Regulation hasn't changed
       TV ads much." Journalism Quarterly 57 (Autumn 1980):
       438-446.

2383.   Ray, Michael L. and Peter Webb.   Experimental Research
         on the Effects of TV Clutter: Dealing With a Diffi-
         cult Media Environment.   Cambridge, MA: Marketing
         Science Institute, 1976.   (51p)

2384.   Robertson, Thomas S.   "Parental mediation of televi-
         sion advertising effects."   Journal of Communication
         29 (Winter 1979): 12-25.

2385.   _____, et al.   Televised Medicine Advertising and
         Children.   New York: Praeger, 1979.   (175p)

2386.   Ross, Rhonda P., et al.   "Nutritional misinformation
         of children: a developmental and experimental anal-
         ysis of the effects of televised food commercials."
         Journal of Applied Developmental Psychology 1 (Win-
         ter 1981): 329-347.

2387.   Rossiter, John R.   "Children's susceptibility to
         television advertising: a behavioral test of cog-
         nition and attitude."   Ph.D. dissertation, Univer-
         sity of Pennsylvania, 1974.   (135p)

2388.   Rossiter, John R. and Thomas S. Robertson.   "Children's
         dispositions toward proprietary drugs and the role
         of television advertising."   Public Opinion Quar-
         terly 44 (Fall 1980): 316-329.

2389.   _____.   "Children's TV commercials: testing the
         defenses."   Journal of Communication 24, no. 4
         (1974): 137-144.

2390.   Scheibe, Cyndy.   "Sex roles in TV commercials."   Jour-
         nal of Advertising Research 19 (February 1979): 23-
         27.

2391.   Schuetz, Stephen and Joyce N. Sprafkin.   "Portrayal of
         prosocial and aggressive behaviors in children's
         TV commercials."   Journal of Broadcasting 23 (Winter
         1979): 33-40.

2392.   Stevens, Paul.   I Can Sell You Anything; How I Made
         Your Favorite TV Commercials with Minimum Truth and
         Maximum Consequences.   New York: Wyden, 1972.
         (245p)

2393.   Tan, Alexis S.   "TV beauty ads and role expectations
         of adolescent female viewers."   Journalism Quarterly
         56 (Summer 1979): 283-288.

2394.   Winick, Charles, et al.   Children's Television Com-
         mercials; A Content Analysis.   New York: Praeger,
         1973.   (156p)

2395.   Witek, John.   Response Television: Combat Advertising
         of the 1980s.   Chicago: Crain, 1981.   (208p)

8
Glimpses Beyond: The Future of Mass Communications

2396. Abramson, Norman. Satellite Trends and Defense Communications. June, 1976. (29p) NTIS-AD-AO 32 288/3GA.

2397. Allan, R. "Coming: the era of telemedicine." IEEE Spectrum 13 (December 1976): 30-35.

2398. Anderson, L. "At Future Directions Forum, Arthur D. Little predicts world wide telecom boom from now to 1985." Telephony 193 (4 July 1977): 28-29.

2399. Asimov, Isaac. "Advertising in the year 2000." Advertising Age 48 (9 May 1977): 47-48.

2400. _____. "Ultimate library can free us all for a new kind of life." Science Digest 88 (September 1980): 30-35.

2401. Baer, Walter S. Intelligent Terminals for New Communication Services. August, 1975. (15p) NTIS-AD-A022 269/5GA.

2402. _____. Interactive Television—Prospects for Two-Way Services on Cable. Rand Report 888-MF. November 1971. (105p)

2403. _____. Telecommunications Technology in the 1980s. Santa Monica, CA: Rand, 1978. (63p)

2404. Bagdikian, Ben H. The Information Machines: Their Impact on Men and the Media. New York: Harper and Row, 1971. (395p)

2405. Baran, Paul. The Future of Newsprint, 1970-2000. Menlo Park, CA: Institute for the Future, 1971. (49p)

2406. _____. Some Changes in Information Technology
Affecting Marketing in the Year 2000. Rand Paper
3717. July, 1968. (34p)

2407. Baran, Paul and Andrew J. Lipinski. The Future of
the Telephone Industry. Menlo Park, CA: Institute
for the Future, 1971. (171p)

2408. Benjow, P. "Advertising's stake in the communications
future." Broadcasting 93 (18 July 1977): 10.

2409. Block, Martin P. "The potential impact of broadband
communication network technology on consumer marketing communication: a computer simulation experi-
ment." Ph.D. dissertation, Michigan State University, 1975. (315p)

2410. Bourn, Derek and N. Howard. The Future of Tele-
Communications. London: Fabian Society, 1970.
(32p)

2411. Cater, Douglass and Michael J. Nyhan, ed. The Future
of Public Broadcasting. New York: Praeger, 1976.
(372p)

2412. Chittock, J. "Future playback: the new technologies."
Sight and Sound 45 (Spring 1976): 116-117+.

2413. Communication '85; Symposium on the State of the Art
in Communication. (Society for Technical Communication.) San Diego: UNIVELT, 1975. (80p)

2414. Compaine, Benjamin M. The Newspaper Industry in the
1980s: An Assessment of Economics and Technology.
White Plains, NY: Knowledge Industry Publications,
1980. (290p)

2415. Comstock, George A. The Long-Range Impact of Television. Rand Paper 5750. October, 1976. (11p)

2416. _____. Television and Human Behavior: The Research Horizon, Future and Present. Santa Monica,
CA: Rand, 1975. (120p)

2417. Curran, Charles. The BBC in the Eighties. London:
British Broadcasting Corporation, 1973. (22p)

2418. Davidson, Mark. "Satellite technology is catching up
with fantasy visions of tomorrow." Science Digest
85 (January 1979): 42-45.

2419. DeLuca, Stuart M. Television's Transformation: The
Next 25 Years. San Diego: A. S. Barnes, 1980.
(287p)

2420.   Dickson, Edward W. and Raymond Bowers. The Video
        Telephone: A New Era in Telecommunications—A Pre-
        liminary Technological Assessment. New York:
        Praeger, 1974. (241p)

2421.   Dineh, Moghdam. Computers in Newspaper Publishing:
        User-Oriented Systems. New York: Marcel Dekker,
        1978. (207p)

2422.   "Direct-broadcast satellites seen within range by TV
        technologists." Broadcasting 92 (20 June 1977): 62.

2423.   Disch, Robert, comp. The Future of Literacy. Engle-
        wood Cliffs, NJ: Prentice-Hall, 1973. (177p)

2424.   Dordick, H. S. The New Communication Technology and
        For What? Rand Paper 3847. May, 1968. (26p)

2425.   Feldman, L. "Home electronics; what the future will
        bring." Radio-Electronics 52 (September 1981):
        49-52.

2426.   Flato, L. "U.S. data communications revolution is
        about to explode worldwide." Datamation 23 (June
        1977): 194-197.

2427.   Fleisig, R. and J. Bernstein. "See $10 wrist trans-
        ceivers within 10 years." Communications News 14
        (July 1977): 22-23.

2428.   Fleming, M. "Pictorial communication: an essay on
        its plight." Audio-Visual Communication Review 10
        (1962): 223-237.

2429.   Fletcher, James C. "Communications satellites: past
        and future." Computers and People 26 (April 1977):
        21-23.

2430.   "For radio there will be an even brighter tomorrow."
        Broadcasting 92 (4 April 1977): 45+.

2431.   "Future communications to bring many new uses." Com-
        munications News 13 (September 1976): 39.

2432.   The Future of Communications Technology. Ottawa:
        Department of Communications, 1971. (233p)

2433.   "Future of news media: a long range look at . . . ."
        Public Relations Journal 23 (January 1967): 15-21.

2434.   The Future of Satellite Communications. (Twentieth
        Century Fund. Task Force on International Satellite
        Communications.) New York: Twentieth Century Fund,
        1970. (80p)

2435.   Golomb, S. W. "Some scenarios on communications by
        the year 2000." Astronautics and Aeronautics 14
        (January 1976): 66-69.

2436.   Grosswirth, Marvin. "Hold the line; even more
        startling telephone tricks are on the way." Sci-
        ence Digest 85 (January 1979): 47-51.

2437.   Gundlach, R. "Technology update: communications;
        digital takeover is underway." Electronics 48 (16
        October 1975): 82-86.

2438.   Haigh, Robert W., et al., eds. Communications in the
        Twenty-First Century. New York: Wiley, 1981.
        (240p)

2439.   Herschbein, Irving and Bert Paolucci. "The future of
        magazine printing." Folio 5 (June 1976): 18-20.

2440.   Hester, Albert L. Newspaper and the Future. Athens:
        Henry W. Grady School of Journalism and Mass Com-
        munication, University of Georgia, 1980. (97p)

2441.   Hills, Philip, ed. The Future of the Printed Word:
        The Impact of the Implications of the New Communi-
        cations Technology. Westport, CT: Greenwood Press,
        1980. (172p)

2442.   Hoggart, Richard and Janet Morgan, eds. The Future
        of Broadcasting: Essays on Authority, Style and
        Choice. London: Macmillan, 1982. (166p)

2443.   Hupe, H. H. "Broadcast satellite moving closer to
        reality." Astronautics and Aeronautics 15 (January
        1977): 27-28.

2444.   Jugenheimer, Donald W. "Future communications tech-
        nological advances and their principal implications
        for advertising." Ph.D. dissertation, University
        of Illinois, 1972. (317p)

2445.   Lemelshtrich, Noam. Two-Way Communication: Political
        and Design Analysis of a Home Terminal. Beverly
        Hills: Sage, 1974. (40p)

2446.   Lewin, Leonard, ed. Telecommunications in the U.S.:
        Trends and Policies. Dedham, MA: Artech, 1981.
        (449p)

2447.   Lindsay, Robert. "Earth satellite communications:
        issues and portents." Ph.D. dissertation, Univer-
        sity of Minnesota, 1965. (228p)

2448.   Lopez, D. A. and P. Gray. "Substitution of communi-
        cation for transportation—a case study." Manage-
        ment Science 23 (July 1977): 1149-1160.

2449.   MacFadden, Gary. "The press in Utopia." Montana
         Journalism Review 19 (1976): 2-10.

2450.   McHale, John. "The future of art and mass culture."
         Futures 10 (June 1978): 178-190.

2451.   McPhail, Thomas L. Electronic Colonialism: The Fu-
         ture of International Broadcasting and Communica-
         tion. Beverly Hills: Sage, 1981. (260p)

2452.   Maritime Communications for the 1980's. Workshop
         Proceedings. 6 November 1975. (183p) NTIS-PB-
         251 088/1GA.

2453.   Martin, James T. The Telematic Society: A Challenge
         for Tomorrow. Englewood Cliffs, NJ: Prentice-Hall,
         1981. (244p)

2454.   _____. Future Developments in Telecommunications.
         Englewood Cliffs, NJ: Prentice-Hall, 1971. (413p)

2455.   The Media Today and Tomorrow. (International Organi-
         sation of Journalists.) Prague, 1974. (131p)

2456.   Meier, A. R. "Another side to future shock that isn't
         so bad." Telephony 191 (4 October 1976): 52-54+.

2457.   Meredith, Dennis. "Future world of television;
         another revolution coming." Science Digest 88
         (September 1980): 16-21.

2458.   Merriman, J.H.H. "Telecommunication in the future."
         Electronics and Power 22 (March 1976): 180-185.

2459.   The Mind Stretchers: An Exploration into the Future
         of Mass Communications in the United States, Febru-
         ary, 1976. Washington: National Association of
         Broadcasters, 1976. (46p)

2460.   Mott, Frank L. "Magazines and books, 1975: a merging
         of two fields." Journalism Quarterly 32 (1955):
         21-26.

2461.   "A new fiber may be the key to future paper needs."
         Inland Printer/American Lithographer 180 (January
         1978): 48-50.

2462.   Papay, James P. and Kenneth A. Polcyn. "The educa-
         tional potential of broadcast satellite technology:
         an overview of some present and future activities."
         Educational Technology 13, no. 4 (1973): 39-43.

2463.   Park, Rolla E. Future Growth of Cable Television.
         Rand Paper 4527. December, 1970. (18p)

2464. _____, et al. Projecting the Growth of Television
       Broadcasting: Implications for Spectrum Use. San-
       ta Monica: Rand, 1976. (308p)

2465. Pawley, Edward. "Through a glass darkly; some
       glimpses of technical trends and their effect on
       broadcasting." E.B.U. Review 24 (May 1973): 14-20.

2466. Peterson, Theodore. "The bright, bleak future of
       American magazines." In Serial Publications in
       Large Libraries, pp. 1-10. Edited by Walter Allen.
       Urbana: University of Illinois, Graduate School of
       Library Science, 1970.

2467. _____. "Magazines: today and tomorrow." Gazette;
       International Journal of the Science of the Press 10
       (1964): 215-229.

2468. Polon, Martin. "Future of home entertainment and the
       four horsemen of technology." Sight and Sound 49
       (Autumn 1980): 224-229.

2469. Pool, Ithiel de Sola, et al. Communications, Com-
       puters and Automation for Development. New York:
       UN Institute for Training and Research, 1975. (61p)

2470. Porter, W. "Journalism, communications and the fu-
       ture of the discipline." Gazette; International
       Journal of the Science of the Press 40 (1963): 580-
       593.

2471. A Preliminary Review of Current Practices and Trends
       in Rural Telecommunications Development and Recom-
       mendations for Future Development. (Booker T.
       Washington Foundation/Cablecommunications Resource
       Center, Washington, D.C.) August, 1975. NTIS-PB-
       254 366/86A. (131p)

2472. Report on the Committee on the Future of Broadcasting.
       (Home Department. Committee on the Future of Broad-
       casting.) London: HMSO, 1977. (522p)

2473. Rhodes, J. "Future telephone networks." Telecommuni-
       cations 10 (November 1976): 25-28.

2474. Rosenberger, Gary. "Tomorrowvision." Science Digest
       90 (March 1982): 38-39.

2475. Russell, Nick. "The impact of facsimile transmission."
       Journalism Quarterly 58 (Autumn 1981): 406-410.

2476. Sandbank, C. P. "Communications in the 21st century."
       Proceedings of the Institution of Electrical En-
       gineers 127A (January 1980): 12-20.

2477. Schmidbauer, M. "Kommunikation-satelliten und bil-
       dung. Ein blick in die zukunft." Fernsehen und
       Bildung 4, no. 1-2 (1970): 1-22.

2478. Scrivener, R. C. "Decade of decision as computer
       and voice communications move together." Communi-
       cations News 14 (June 1977): 44-45.

2479. Sigel, Efrem, et al., ed. Videotext: The Coming
       Revolution in Home/Office Information Retrieval.
       New York: Harmony Books, 1980. (153p)

2480. Sitterley, E. F. "About the automated, in-line pic-
       ture—is it fact, futurism, or gobbledy-gook?" In-
       land Printer/American Lithographer 178 (February
       1977): 54-55.

2481. _____. "Narrow-web rotogravure is here: where is
       it going? where?" Inland Printer/American Litho-
       grapher 179 (April 1977): 54-55.

2482. Smith, Ralph L. The Wired Nation; Cable TV: The
       Electronic Communications Highway. New York:
       Harper and Row, 1972. (128p)

2483. Taylor, John P. "The future of equipment: what
       could happen is not necessarily what will be al-
       lowed to happen." Television/Radio Age 21 (19 Au-
       gust 1974): 22+.

2484. Telecommunications and Society, 1976-1991. Report to
       the Office of Telecommunications Policy, Executive
       Office of the President. 22 June 1976. (153p)
       NTIS-PB-256 829/3GA.

2485. Telecommunications: Trends and Directions. Washing-
       ton, D.C.: Electronic Industries, 1981. (98p)

2486. Tressel, George W., et al. The Future of Educational
       Telecommunication. Lexington, MA: Lexington Books,
       1975. (126p)

2487. "TV in the 1980's." Media Decisions 10 (July 1975):
       55-57+.

2488. Unwin, Stephen J.F. "Where advertising will fit in
       the future society." Advertising Age 45 (8 July
       1974): 29-34.

2489. "Visions of a communications revolution." New Sci-
       entist 94 (8 April 1982): 66.

2490. Waller, L. "Lasercom gliding toward 1980's test."
       Electronics 50 (7 July 1977): 74-75.

2491. Whye, J. S. "Telecommunication; the way ahead."
       Electronics and Power 26 (September 1980): 719-726.

2492. Wiley, Richard E. "Data communications: policies
       developing in the United States." Computers and
       People 25 (December 1976): 7-9, 21, 26.

2493. Wilken, Earl W. "Technology and events—1976." Edi-
       tor and Publisher 109 (10 January 1976): 29-30.

2494. Willener, Alfred, et al. Videology and Utopia.
       Trans. by Diana Burfield. London and Boston:
       Routledge and Kegan Paul, 1976. (171p)

2495. Wolseley, Roland. "The coming disappearance of
       printed journalism." Gazette 21 (Winter 1975):
       199-208.

9
Fine Art and Literature in the Technologized Society

A. THE ARTIST AND TECHNOLOGY

2496. Anderson, Arthur J. The Artistic Side of Photography, in Theory and Practice. London: S. Paul, 1910. (359p)

2497. Arnheim, Rudolf. "Art today and the film." Film Culture 42 (Fall 1966): 43-45.

2498. _____. Film as Art. London: Faber, 1969. (194p)

2499. "Art and photography." American Artist 44 (February 1980): 8, 42-85.

2500. "Art meets computers." New Scientist 84 (4 October 1979): 29.

2501. Bailey, Henry T. Photography and Fine Art. 2nd ed. Worcester, MA: Davis Press, 1922. (124p)

2502. Barr, Charles. "Cinemascope: before and after." Film Quarterly 16 (Summer 1963): 4-24.

2503. Barzyk, F. "TV as art as TV." Print 26 (January 1972): 20-29.

2504. Becker, Howard S. "Art photography in America." Journal of Communication 25 (Winter 1975): 74-84.

2505. Behne, Adolf. "Art, handicraft, technology." Oppositions, no. 22 (Fall 1980): 96-104.

2506. Belz, Carl. "The film poetry of Man Ray." Criticism 7 (Spring 1965): 117-130.

2507.   Benthall, Jonathan.   Science and Technology in Art
        Today.   New York: Praeger, 1972.   (180p)

2508.   Berkeley, E. C.   "Computer art and the eye of the be-
        holder."   Computers and People 26 (August 1977):
        6-23.

2509.   Berleant, A.   "Art, science, and technology in shaping
        the environment of the future; report on a symposi-
        um."   Journal of Aesthetics and Art Criticism 34
        (Summer 1976): 523-525.

2510.   Blake, Richard A.   "Reality and structure in film
        aesthetics."   Thought 43 (Autumn 1968): 429-440.

2511.   Bower, R. T. and L. M. Sharp.   "The use of art in
        international communication: a case study."   Pub-
        lic Opinion Quarterly 20 (1956/1957): 221-229.

2512.   Browning, Jon.   "Engineer-artist teams shape new art
        forms."   Chemical Engineering 75 (26 February 1968):
        102-104.

2513.   Burnham, Jack.   Beyond Modern Sculpture: The Effects
        of Science and Technology on the Sculpture of this
        Century.   New York: Braziller, 1968.   (402p)

2514.   _____.   "Problems of criticism: art and technolo-
        gy."   Artforum 9 (January 1971): 40-45.

2515.   Busch, Julia M.   A Decade of Sculpture: the 1960's.
        Philadelphia: Art Alliance Press, 1974.   (54p)

2516.   Caffin, Charles H.   Photography as a Fine Art; The
        Achievements and Possibilities of Photographic Art
        in America.   New York: Doubleday, Page, 1901.
        (191p)

2517.   Cahn, J. G., et al.   "Art by telephone; using the
        telephone together with a Xerox photocopier to
        transmit images."   Print 25 (January 1971): 69.

2518.   Camfield, William A.   "The machinist style of Francis
        Picabia."   Art Bulletin (September-December 1966):
        309-322.

2519.   Cassidy, Harold G.   The Sciences and the Arts; A New
        Alliance.   New York: Harper, 1962.   (182p)

2520.   Chandler, John.   "Art and automata: cybernetic seren-
        dipity, technology, and creativity."   Arts Magazine
        43 (December 1968): 42-45.

2521.   _____.   "Art in the electric age."   Art Inter-
        national 13 (February 1969): 19-25.

2522. Coburn, Alvin L.   "Photography and the quest of
       beauty." Photographic Journal 64 (April 1924):
       159-167.

2523. Cock, Elizabeth M.   "The influence of photography on
       American landscape painting, 1839-1880." Ph.D.
       dissertation, New York University, 1967. (264p)

2524. Coke, Van Deren. The Painter and the Photograph;
       From Delacroix to Warhol. Rev. and enl. ed. Albu-
       querque: University of New Mexico Press, 1972.
       (324p)

2525. Conant, Theodore R. "Art, the artist, and the new
       technologies." Journal of Broadcasting 25 (Winter
       1981): 92-94.

2526. Curl, David H. Photocommunication: A Guide to Cre-
       ative Photography. New York: Macmillan, 1979.
       (304p)

2527. Davis, Douglas. "Art and technology: the new com-
       bine." Art in America 56 (January/February 1968):
       28-47.

2528. _____. Art and the Future; A History/Prophecy of
       the Collaboration Between Science, Technology, and
       Art. New York: Praeger, 1974, c 1973. (208p)

2529. Davis, Douglas M. and Allison Simmons, ed. The New
       Television. Cambridge, MA: MIT Press, 1977. (289p)

2530. Dufrenne, M. "Aesthetic object and the technical ob-
       ject." Journal of Aesthetics and Art Criticism 23
       (Fall 1964): 113-122.

2531. Ehrlich, George. "Technology and the artist: a
       study of the inter-action of technological growth
       and nineteenth century American pictorial art."
       Ph.D. dissertation, University of Illinois, 1960.
       (248p)

2532. Eidsvik, Charles. Cineliteracy: Film Among the Arts.
       New York: Random House, 1978. (303p)

2533. Ellul, Jacques. "Remarks on technology and art."
       Social Research 46 (Winter 1979): 805-833.

2534. Feininger, Andreas. Roots of Art: The Sketchbook of
       a Photographer. New York: Viking, 1975. (176p)

2535. Fell, John L. Film and the Narrative Tradition. Nor-
       man: University of Oklahoma Press, 1974. (284p)

2536. Fong, Monique. "On art and technology." Studio In-
       ternational 177 (January 1969): 5-6.

2537.   Freund, Gelele. Photography and Society. Boston:
        D. R. Godine, 1980. (231p)

2538.   Friedlander, G. D. "Art and technology; a merger of
        disciplines." IEEE Spectrum 6 (October 1969): 60-
        68.

2539.   Fuller, John C. "The photographic image in England
        from 1839-1865: an integrated study of photography
        and painting showing the emergence of a new medium
        amid academic and pre-Raphaelite art." Ph.D. dis-
        sertation, Ohio University, 1968. (203p)

2540.   Gale, Peggy, ed. Video by Artists. Toronto: Art
        Metropole, c 1976. (223p)

2541.   Goldin, A. "Art and technology in a social vacuum."
        Art in America 60 (March 1972): 46-51.

2542.   Gowans, Alan. The Unchanging Arts; New Forms for the
        Traditional Functions of Art in Society. Phila-
        delphia: Lippincott, 1971, c 1970. (433p)

2543.   Gräff, Werner. Es Kommt der Neue Fotograf. Berlin:
        Reckendorf, 1929. (126p)

2544.   Green, Jonathan, comp. Camera Work: A Critical An-
        thology. New York: Aperture, 1973. (376p)

2545.   Haber, F. "American mythologies in painting; dis-
        covering the new landscape of technology." Arts
        Magazine 46 (February 1972): 32-35.

2546.   Hamilton, Edward A. Graphic Design for the Computer
        Age; Visual Communication for All Media. New York:
        Van Nostrand Reinhold, 1970. (191p)

2547.   Harten, J. "Open letter to the Bishop of Carlisle;
        or, what should the artist do in relation to indus-
        try and commerce." Studio International 183 (April
        1972): 146-148.

2548.   Hawkins, Henry W. "Art and technology: implications
        for art education in the technological society."
        Ph.D. dissertation, University of Oregon, 1973.
        (128p)

2549.   Herrman, R. D. "Art, technology, and Nietzsche."
        Journal of Aesthetics and Art Criticism 32 (Fall
        1973): 95-102.

2550.   Hertlein, Grace C. "NCC '76 art review, directions,
        and questions: the role of the computer in computer
        art." Computers and People 25 (August 1976): 6.

2551.   _____, ed. "Fourteenth annual computer art expo-
         sition, 1976." Computers and People 25 (August
         1976): 8-31. (More than 70 examples of computer
         art are reproduced here.)

2552.   Higgins, Dick. The Computers for the Arts. Somer-
         ville, MA: Abyss, c 1970. (17p)

2553.   Hoenick, P. K. "Robot art: using the rays of the
         son." Studio International 175 (June 1968): 306-
         309.

2554.   Holden, Constance. "Holoart; playing with a budding
         technology." Science 204 (6 April 1979): 40-41.

2555.   Hulten, Karl G.P. The Machine; As Seen at the End of
         the Mechanical Age. New York: Museum of Modern
         Art, 1968. (216p)

2556.   "Is photography among the fine arts?" Magazine of Art
         (1899): 102-105, 156-158, 206-209, 253-256, 369-373.

2557.   Jablonowski, J. "Sculpting via computer optics."
         American Machinist 123 (September 1979): 79-82.

2558.   Jay, Bill. "The romantic machine: towards a defi-
         nition of humanization in photography." Massachu-
         setts Review 19 (Winter 1978): 647-662.

2559.   Jules-Rosette, Bennetta. "Technological innovation
         in popular African art: a case study of some con-
         temporary art forms in transition." Journal of
         Popular Culture 13 (Summer 1979): 116-130.

2560.   Jussim, Estelle. "Icons or ideology: Stieglitz and
         Hine." Massachusetts Review 19, no. 4 (1978): 680-
         692.

2561.   _____. "Technology or aesthetics: Alfred Stieg-
         litz and photogravure." History of Photography 3
         (January 1979): 81-92.

2562.   Kelman, Ken. "Film as poetry." Film Culture 29
         (Summer 1963): 22-27.

2563.   Kepes, Gyorgy. The New Landscape in Art and Science.
         Chicago: Theobald, c 1956. (383p)

2564.   _____, ed. Structure in Art and in Science. New
         York: Braziller, 1965. (189p)

2565.   Kevles, Barbara L. "Slavko Vorkapich on film as a
         visual language and as a form of art." Film Culture
         38 (Fall 1965): 1-46.

2566.   Kies, Emily B. "The city and the machine: urban and
        industrial illustration in America, 1880-1900."
        Ph.D. dissertation, Columbia University, 1971.
        (290p)

2567.   Klein, H. Arthur. "Pieter Bruegel the Elder as a
        guide to 16th-century technology." Scientific
        American 238 (March 1978): 134-140.

2568.   Klein, Stanley. "Technology invades the arts." Ma-
        chine Design 40 (29 February 1968): 37-41+.

2569.   Klingender, Francis. Art and the Industrial Revolu-
        tion. London: Carrington, 1947. (282p)

2570.   Kouwenhoren, John A. The Arts in Modern American
        Civilization. New York: Norton, 1967, c 1948.
        (259p)

2571.   Kragen, Robert. "Art and TV." Radical Software 1
        (Summer 1970): 4.

2572.   Kranz, Stewart D. "Art technology and visual illu-
        sion." Ed.D. dissertation, Columbia University,
        1969. (411p)

2573.   _____. Science and Technology in the Arts: A
        Tour Through the Realm of Science and Art. New
        York: Van Nostrand Reinhold, 1974. (335p)

2574.   LeGrice, Malcolm. Abstract Film and Beyond. Cam-
        bridge, MA: MIT Press, 1977. (160p)

2575.   Lindgren, Nilo. "Art and technology I: steps toward
        a new synergism." IEEE Spectrum 6 (April 1969):
        59-68.

2576.   _____. "Art and technology II: a call for col-
        laboration." IEEE Spectrum 6 (May 1969): 46-56.

2577.   Lobell, J. "Developing technologies for sculptors."
        Arts Magazine 45 (Summer 1971): 27-29.

2578.   Loewen, Norma. "Experiments in art and technology:
        a descriptive history of the organization." Ph.D.
        dissertation, New York University, 1975. (430p)

2579.   London, Barbara. "Independent video: the first fif-
        teen years; chronology of video activity in the
        United States: 1965-1980." Artforum 9 (September
        1980): 38-45.

2580.   Luhr, William and Peter Lehman. Authorship and Nar-
        rative in the Cinema: Issues in Contemporary Aes-
        thetics. New York: Putnam, c 1977. (320p)

2581.   MacCann, Richard D.   "From technology to adultery."
        Films and Filming 9 (January 1963): 73-77.

2582.   Machine Art, March 6 to April 30, 1934.   Reprint ed.
        New York: Published for the Museum of Modern Art
        by Arno Press, 1969, c 1934.   (112p)

2583.   Mallary, Robert.   "Computer sculpture: six levels of
        cybernetics."   Artforum 7 (May 1969): 29-35.

2584.   Marcus, Fred H.   Film and Literature: Contrasts in
        Media.   Scranton: Chandler, 1971.   (283p)

2585.   Meeker, Joseph W.   "The imminent alliance: new con-
        nections among art, science, and technology."
        Technology and Culture 19 (April 1978): 187-198.

2586.   Moholy-Nagy, Laszlo.   Vision in Motion.   Chicago:
        Theobald, 1947.   (371p)

2587.   Moore, A.   "Jean Dupuy 'I use technology only to show
        the things that are invisible.'"   Artforum 13 (Oc-
        tober 1974): 72-74.

2588.   Morgan, Douglas N.   "Photography and philosophy: an
        essay on the esthetics of a new art medium."   Ph.D.
        dissertation, University of Michigan, 1948.   (307p)

2589.   Morison, Elting.   "The uncertain velation."   Daedalus
        109 (Winter 1980): 179-184.

2590.   Mueller, Robert E.   The Science of Art; The Cyber-
        netics of Creative Communication.   New York: John
        Day, 1967.   (352p)

2591.   Mumford, Lewis.   Art and Technics.   New York: Colum-
        bia University Press, 1952.   (162p)

2592.   Mussman, Toby.   "Early surrealist expression in the
        film."   Film Culture 41 (Summer 1966): 8-17.

2593.   Noll, A. Michael.   "Art ex machina."   IEEE Student
        Journal 8 (September 1970): 10-14.

2594.   _____.   "The digital computer as a creative medium."
        IEEE Spectrum 4 (October 1967): 89-95.

2595.   Noxon, Gerald.   "Cinema and cubism."   Journal of the
        Society of Cinematographers 2 (1962): 23-33.

2596.   Pierce, John R.   Science, Art and Communication.   New
        York: Potter, 1968.   (174p)

2597.   Pincus-Witten, Robert.   "Buky Schwartz: video as
        sculpture."   Arts Magazine 53 (February 1979): 93-95.

2598. Popper, Frank. "Movement and light in today's art."
       Arts and Architecture 81 (April 1964): 24-25+.

2599. _____. Origins and Development of Kinetic Art.
       Trans. by Stephen Bann. Greenwich, CT: New York
       Graphic Society, c 1968. (272p)

2600. Powell, Earl A., 3d. "Morton Schamberg: the machine
       as icon." Arts Magazine 51 (May 1977): 122-123.

2601. Price, Jonathan. Video-Visions; A Medium Discovers
       Itself. New York: New American Library, A Plume
       Book, 1977. (232p)

2602. Raymond, Herbert D. "The persistence of illusion in
       American non-referential painting in the 1960's."
       Ph.D. dissertation, New York University, 1970.
       (158p)

2603. Reese, Teresa. "Holography at hand; the 3D visual
       reproduction process." Print 33 (January 1979):
       45-57.

2604. Reichardt, Jasia, ed. Cybernetic Serendipity: The
       Computer and the Arts. New York: Praeger, 1969,
       c 1968. (101p)

2605. Richardson, John A. Modern Art and Scientific Thought.
       Urbana: University of Illinois Press, 1971. (191p)

2606. Richardson, Robert. Literature and Film. Blooming-
       ton: Indiana University Press, 1969. (150p)

2607. Richter, Hans. "The film as an original art form."
       Film Culture 1 (January 1955): 19-23.

2608. Rondthaler, Edward. Life with Letters, As They
       Turned Photogenic. New York: Hastings, 1981.
       (190p)

2609. Roth, Moira. "Harold Cohen on art and the machine."
       Art in America 66 (September 1978): 106-110.

2610. Schneider, Ira and Beryl Korot. Video Art: An An-
       thology. New York: Harcourt, Brace, Jovanovich,
       1976. (286p)

2611. Schrader, Paul. "Notes on film noir." Film Comment
       8 (Spring 1972): 8-13.

2612. Sheridan, Sonia L. "Tools and the artist: work-
       spaces; of time and telecopiers." Afterimage 9
       (Summer 1981): 23-25.

2613. Sitney, P. Adams. Visionary Film: The American Avant-
       Garde, 1943-1978. 2nd ed. New York: Oxford Uni-
       versity Press, 1979. (463p)

2614. Sparshott, F. E. "Basic film aesthetics." Journal
        of Aesthetic Education 5 (April 1971): 12-34.

2615. Stephenson, Ralph and J. R. Debrix. The Cinema as
        Art. Baltimore: Penguin, 1967. (268p)

2616. Strand, Paul. "The art motive in photography." Brit-
        ish Journal of Photography 70 (5 October 1923):
        612-615.

2617. Tait, Jack. Beyond Photography; The Transformed
        Image. New York: Hastings House, 1977. (144p)

2618. Tashjian, Dickran L. "Henry Adams and Marcel Duchamp:
        liminal views of the dynamo and the Virgin." Arts
        Magazine 51 (May 1977): 102-107.

2619. Taylor, Henry. "Poetry of the movies." Film Journal
        1 (Fall/Winter 1972): 36-49.

2620. Theil, Linda. "Color xerography and the fiber artist."
        Fiberarts 8 (September/October 1981): 59-63.

2621. Thomas, Alan. Time in a Frame: Photography and the
        Nineteenth Century Mind. New York: Schocken, 1977.
        (170p)

2622. Trachtenberg, Alan. "Reflections on art in photogra-
        phy." Afterimage 7 (April 1980): 10-11.

2623. Tuchman, M. Art and Technology; A Report on the Art
        and Technology Program of the Los Angeles County
        Museum of Art, 1967-1971. Los Angeles: Los Angeles
        County Museum of Art; dist. by Viking Press, New
        York, 1971. (387p)

2624. Tyler, Parker. "The film sense and the painting
        sense." Perspectives USA 11 (Spring 1955): 95-106.

2625. Waldman, Diane. "Critical theory and film: Adorno
        and 'The Culture Industry' revisited." New German
        Critique 12 (Fall 1977): 39-60.

2626. "Welding as photographic art." Welding Journal 57
        (June 1978): 21.

2627. Wosk, J. "Artists on technology." Technology Review
        82 (December/January 1980): 66-74.

2628. Zabel, Barbara. "The machine as metaphor, model, and
        microcosm: technology in American art, 1915-1930."
        Arts Magazine 57 (December 1982): 100-105.

B. THE WRITER AND TECHNOLOGY

2629. Adams, Ralph E. "The industrial novel in England:
       1832-1851." Ph.D. dissertation, University of Il-
       linois, 1965. (287p)

2630. Adler, Richard P. and Walter S. Baer, ed. The Elec-
       tronic Box Office: Humanities and Arts on the Ca-
       ble. Springfield, MA: Praeger, 1974. (139p)

2631. Allen, Richard E. "Charles Kingsley and the Industrial
       Revolution." Ph.D. dissertation, Washington Uni-
       versity, 1956. (249p)

2632. Amelinckx, Frans C. "Man, machines and moral order:
       technology and values in French romanticism." Iowa
       State Journal of Research 54 (1979): 249-255.

2633. Ausband, Stephen C. "The whale and the machine: an
       approach to Moby Dick." American Literature 47
       (1975/1976): 197-211.

2634. Basile, Joseph L. "Man and machine in Thoreau." Ph.D.
       dissertation, Louisiana State University and Agri-
       cultural and Mechanical College, 1972. (191p)

2635. Bedell, Jeanne F. "Romance, adventure, and mechaniza-
       tion: attitudes towards technology in espionage
       fiction." Lamar Journal of Humanities 5, no. 2
       (1979): 54-62.

2636. Bellow, Saul. "Literature in the age of technology."
       In Frontiers of Knowledge, pp. 3-25. Garden City,
       NY: Doubleday, 1975.

2637. Beum, Robert. "Literature and machinisme." Sewanee
       Review 86 (Spring 1978): 217-244.

2638. Bierman, J. H. "Walt Disney robot dramas; General
       Electric Carousel of Progress." Yale Review 66
       (December 1976): 223-236.

2639. Booth, Thornton Y. "Criticisms of machinery and mech-
       anism by four Victorian writers." Ph.D. disserta-
       tion, Stanford University, 1951. (184p)

2640. Broderick, John C. "Thoreau's principle of simplicity
       as shown in his attitudes toward cities, government
       and industrialism." Ph.D. dissertation, University
       of North Carolina, 1953. (345p)

2641. Brunetta, Gian Pietro. Letteratura e cinema. Bologna:
       Zanichelli, 1976. (163p)

2642. Clark, John R. "Machine prevails: a modern techno-
       logical theme." Journal of Popular Culture 12
       (Summer 1978): 118-126.

2643. Clough, Raymond J. "The metal gods: a study of the
       historic and mythic aspects of the machine image in
       French prose from 1750 to 1940." Ph.D. disserta-
       tion, State University of New York—Buffalo, 1973.
       (305p)

2644. Cohen, Lance N. "Contending for humanity in the
       technological age: the art and argument of Norman
       Mailer." Ph.D. dissertation, Columbia University,
       1975. (223p)

2645. Colacurcio, Michael. "The dynamo and the angelic
       doctor: the bias of Henry Adams' medievalism."
       American Quarterly 17 (1965): 696-712.

2646. Copek, Peter J. "The Five Towns novels of Arnold
       Bennett: a response to industrial society." Ph.D.
       dissertation, Northwestern University, 1973. (189p)

2647. Cronkite, G. "Walt Whitman and the locomotive."
       American Quarterly 6 (1954): 164-172.

2648. Davis, Paul B. "Industrial fiction, 1827-1850."
       Ph.D. dissertation, University of Wisconsin, 1961.
       (520p)

2649. Dick, P. K. "Man, android and machine." In Science
       Fiction At Large, pp. 199-224. Edited by Peter
       Nicholls. New York: Harper, 1976.

2650. Dodge, Robert K. "The influence of machines and
       technology on American literature of the late nine-
       teenth and early twentieth centuries." Ph.D. dis-
       sertation, University of Texas—Austin, 1967.
       (217p)

2651. Drachmann, Aage G. The Mechanical Technology of
       Greek and Roman Antiquity: A Study of the Literary
       Sources. Madison: University of Wisconsin Press,
       1963. (218p)

2652. Dudek, Louis. Literature and the Press: A History
       of Printing, Printed Media, and Their Relation to
       Literature. Toronto: Ryerson, 1960. (238p)

2653. _____. "Poet of the machine age." Tomerack Re-
       view 6 (1958): 74-80.

2654. Eastwood, Wilfred, ed. Science and Literature: The
       Literary Relations of Science and Technology. Lon-
       don: Macmillan, 1957. (295p)

2655.   Edelheit, Steven J. "Dark prophecies: essays on Or-
        well and technology." Ph.D. dissertation, Brandeis
        University, 1975. (191p)

2656.   Eidsvik, Charles. "Demonstrating film influence."
        Literature-Film Quarterly 1 (April 1973): 113-121.

2657.   Engelhart, Carl W. "The reaction against industrial-
        ism in American literature, 1800-1860." Ph.D. dis-
        sertation, University of Minnesota, 1952. (199p)

2658.   Enzensberger, Hans M. The Consciousness Industry; On
        Literature, Politics and the Media. New York: Sea-
        bury, 1974. (184p)

2659.   Erickson, J. D. "Cheikh Hamidow Kane's l'adventure
        ambigue." Yale French Studies no. 53 (1976): 92-
        101.

2660.   Esslin, Martin. Mediations: Essays on Brecht,
        Beckett, and the Media. Baton Rouge: Louisiana
        State University Press, 1980. (248p)

2661.   Fairbanks, H. F. "Hawthorne and the machine age."
        American Literature 28 (May 1956): 155-163.

2662.   Fisher, Marvin. "The iconology of industrialism,
        1830-60." American Quarterly 13 (Fall 1961): 347-
        364.

2663.   Folsom, James K. "Magic and technology as opposing
        values in science fiction." Iowa State Journal of
        Research 54 (1979): 257-265.

2664.   Fontanella, Lee. "The mortality of types: technology,
        language, and prose in romantic Spain." Ph.D. dis-
        sertation, Princeton University, 1971. (501p)

2665.   Frederick, John T. "Industrial imagery in The House
        of the Seven Gables." Nathaniel Hawthorne Journal
        (1974): 273-276.

2666.   Geduld, Harry M., ed. Authors on Film. Bloomington:
        Indiana University Press, 1972. (303p)

2667.   George, Albert J. The Development of French Romanti-
        cism: The Impact of the Industrial Revolution on
        Literature. Syracuse: Syracuse University Press,
        1955. (193p)

2668.   Giannone, Richard. "Violence in the fiction of Kurt
        Vonnegut." Thought 56 (March 1981): 58-76.

2669.   Ginestier, Paul. The Poet and the Machine. Trans.
        by Martin B. Friedman. Chapel Hill: University of
        North Carolina Press, 1961. (183p)

2670. Granin, Daniel A. "Literature and the scientific
       and technological revolution." Soviet Literature
       no. 12 (1980): 124-131.

2671. Grant, Elliott M. "The relations of poetry to indus-
       try under Louis Philippe and Napoleon III." Ph.D.
       dissertation, Harvard University, 1923. (248p)

2672. Griffin, R. J. and William A. Freedman. "Machines
       and animals: pervasive motifs in The Grapes of
       Wrath." Journal of English and Germanic Philology
       62 (1963): 569-581.

2673. Griffith, Patricia A.T. "The technoscape in the mod-
       ern novel: Aleksandr Solzhenitsyn's The First Cir-
       cle and Ralph Ellison's Invisible Man." Ph.D.
       dissertation, University of Southern California,
       1976.

2674. Gugielminetti, Marziano. "Magia e technica nelle
       poetica di Tomaso Campanella." Revista di Estetica
       9 (1964): 361-400.

2675. Guillory, Daniel L. "Leaving the Stocha Station:
       contemporary poetry and technology." Triquarterly
       no. 52 (Fall 1981): 165-181.

2676. Harbison, Robert D. "Industrial diamonds: the Eng-
       lish proletarian novel, 1840-1890." Ph.D. disserta-
       tion, Cornell University, 1969. (223p)

2677. Harvie, C. "Sons of Martha: technology, transport,
       and Rudyard Kipling." Victorian Studies 20 (Spring
       1977): 269-282.

2678. Hillegas, Mark R. The Future as Nightmare: H. G.
       Wells and the Anti-Utopians. New York: Oxford
       University Press, 1967. (200p)

2679. Hilton, George. "The social importance of the machine
       in France as seen in nineteenth century French lit-
       erature." Ph.D. dissertation, University of Illi-
       nois, 1941. (323p)

2680. Hutchins, Patricia. "James Joyce and the cinema."
       Sight and Sound 21 (August/September 1951): 9-12.

2681. Kirschner, Paul. "Conrad and the film." Quarterly
       of Film, Radio and Television 11 (Summer 1957):
       343-353.

2682. Klass, P. "Innocent in time: Mark Twain in King Ar-
       thur's court." Extrapolation 16 (December 1974):
       17-32.

2683. Koch, Stephen. "Fiction and film: a search for new sources." Saturday Review 52 (27 December 1969): 12-14+.

2684. Kovacevich, Ivanka. "The mechanical muse: the impact of technical inventions on eighteenth-century neoclassical poetry." Huntington Library Quarterly 28 (1965): 263-282.

2685. Leonard, Neil. "Theodore Dreiser and the film." Film Heritage 2 (Fall 1966): 7-16.

2686. Lewis, Arthur O., ed. Of Men and Machines. New York: Dutton, 1963. (349p)

2687. Lewis, Wyndom. "The machine poets." In his Enemy Salvoes, pp. 173-176. New York: Barnes and Noble, 1976.

2688. McCauley, Carol S. Computers and Creativity. New York: Praeger, 1974. (160p)

2689. Maggs, W. Randall. "Tradition and technology in the poetry of E. J. Pratt." Ph.D. dissertation, University of New Brunswick, 1977. (N/A)

2690. Marx, Leo. "American literary culture and the fatalistic view of technology." Alternative Futures 3 (Spring 1980): 45-70.

2691. _____. "Hawthorne and Emerson studies in the impact of machine technology upon the American writer." Ph.D. dissertation, Harvard University, 1950. (N/A)

2692. _____. The Machine in the Garden; Technology and the Pastoral Ideal in America. New York: Oxford University Press, 1964. (392p)

2693. Meakin, David. Man and Work: Literature and Culture in Industrial Society. New York: Holmes and Meier, 1976. (215p)

2694. Neuburg, Victor E. Popular Literature: A History and a Guide. New York: Penguin, 1977. (301p)

2695. Neufeldt, Leonard N. "The science of power: Emerson's views on science and technology in America." Journal of the History of Ideas 38 (1977): 329-344.

2696. Noxon, Gerald. "The anatomy of the close-up: some literary origins in the works of Flaubert, Huysmans and Proust." Journal of the Society of Cinematographers 1 (1961): 1-24.

2697. _____. "Pictorial origins of cinema narrative." Journal of the Society of Cinematologists 3 (1963): 29-43.

2698.   _____. "Some observations on the anatomy of the
         long shot: an extract from some literary origins
         of cinema narrative." Journal of the Society of
         Cinematographers 5 (1965): 70-80.

2699.   Oakman, Robert L. "Using the computer in literature:
         reflections on the state of the art." Literary Re-
         search Newsletter 5 (1980): 3-14.

2700.   Parrish, S. M. "Computers and the muse of litera-
         ture." In The World of the Computer, pp. 312-324.
         Edited by John Diebold. New York: Random House,
         1973.

2701.   Perez de la Dehesa, Lily L. "A dream of Arcadia:
         turn of the century anti-industrialism in Spanish
         literature, 1895-1905." Ph.D. dissertation, Uni-
         versity of California—Berkeley, 1972. (N/A)

2702.   Prusok, Rudi A. "The use of science and technology
         in the novels of Thomas Mann." Ph.D. dissertation,
         Washington University, 1967. (193p)

2703.   Rogers, P. "Gulliver and the engineers." Modern
         Language Review 70 (April 1975): 260-270.

2704.   Ruhe, Edward. "Film: the 'literary' approach."
         Literature-Film Quarterly 1 (January 1973): 76-83.

2705.   Schneider, Ben R., Jr. "Using the computer in literary
         research: the basic advantages." Literary Research
         Newsletter 5 (1980): 15-20.

2706.   Shenk, Robert. "McKenna's 'The Sand Pebbles' and
         the poetry of machinery." Critique 23, no. 1 (1981):
         67-81.

2707.   Shi, David E. "Advertising and the literary imagina-
         tion during the Jazz Age." Journal of American
         Culture 2 (Summer 1979): 167-175.

2708.   Shusterman, David. "The Victorian novel of industrial
         conflict: 1832-1870." Ph.D. dissertation, New York
         University, 1953. (345p)

2709.   Silberman, Marc D. "Literature of the working world:
         a study of the industrial novel in East Germany."
         Ph.D. dissertation, Indiana University, 1975. (284p)

2710.   Solecki, Sam. "D. H. Lawrence's view of film." Lit-
         erature-Film Quarterly 1 (January 1973): 12-16.

2711.   Spindler, Michael. "John Dos Passos and the visual
         arts." Journal of American Studies 15 (December
         1981): 391-405.

2712.   Sussman, Herbert L.   "The response to machine tech-
        nology in Victorian literature."   Ph.D. disserta-
        tion, Harvard University, 1963.   (N/A)

2713.   _____.   Victorians and the Machine; The Literary
        Response to Technology.   Cambridge: Harvard Uni-
        versity Press, 1968.   (261p)

2714.   Sypher, Wylie.   Literature and Technology; The Alien
        Vision.   New York: Vintage Books, 1971, c 1968.
        (257p)

2715.   Tashjian, Dickran L.   "Hart Crane and the machine."
        In his Skyscraper Primitives; Dada and the American
        Avant-Garde, 1910-1925, pp. 143-164.   Middletown,
        CT: Wesleyan University Press, 1975.

2716.   Tillotson, Geoffrey.   "Morris and the machine."   Fort-
        nightly Review 141 (April 1934): 464-471.

2717.   Valgemae, M.   "Broken world of Aro Valton's Eight
        Japanese Girls."   Books Abstract 47 (Autumn): 653-
        657.

2718.   Van Nostrand, Albert.   The Denatured Novel.   Indiana-
        polis: Bobbs-Merrill, 1960.   (224p)

2719.   Wagner, Geoffrey.   The Novel and the Cinema.   Ruther-
        ford, NJ: Fairleigh Dickinson University Press,
        1975.   (394p)

2720.   Waldron, Randall H.   "Armour's Iron Brace: the ma-
        chine in major American novels of World War II."
        Ph.D. dissertation, University of Kentucky, 1968.
        (241p)

2721.   Walkover, Andrew.   The Dialectics of Eden.   Stanford:
        Humanities Honors Program, Stanford University,
        1974.   (98p)

2722.   Warburg, Jeremy.   "Poetry and industrialism."   Modern
        Language Review 53 (April 1958): 161-170.

2723.   _____, ed.   The Industrial Muse.   London: Oxford
        University Press, 1958.   (174p)

2724.   Warrick, P. S.   "Images of the man-machine intelligence
        relationship in science fiction."   In Many Futures,
        Many Worlds, pp. 182-223.   Edited by Thomas D.
        Claveson.   Kent, OH: Kent State University Press,
        1977.

2725.   Weber, Daniel B.   "John Muir: the function of wilder-
        ness in an industrial society."   Ph.D. dissertation,
        University of Minnesota, 1964.   (285p)

2726. Werlin, Robert J. "The English novel and the indus-
      trial revolution: a study in the sociology of lit-
      erature." Ph.D. dissertation, Harvard University,
      1968. (N/A)

2727. West, Paul. "Symbol and equivalent: the poetry of
      industrialism." Essays in Criticism 9 (1959): 61-
      71.

2728. West, Thomas R. Flesh of Steel; Literature and the
      Machine in American Culture. Nashville: Vanderbilt
      University Press, 1967. (155p)

2729. Winge, John H. "Brecht and the cinema." Sight and
      Sound 26 (Winter 1956/1957): 144-147.

2730. Woodward, Robert H. "Automata in Hawthorne's 'Artist
      of the Beautiful' and Taylor's 'Meditation 56.'"
      Emerson Society Quarterly 31, no. 2 (1963): 63-66.

2731. Wylie, Harold A. "Machine imagery in French litera-
      ture to 1900: the music of the cogs." Ph.D. dis-
      sertation, Stanford University, 1965. (392p)

2732. Zolla, Elemire. The Eclipse of the Intellectual.
      Trans. by Raymond Rosenthal. New York: Funk and
      Wagnalls, 1969, c 1968. (301p)

Author Index

Robinson, Michael J.   2157
Rocca Torres, Luis   2023
Roche, Bruce W.   1003
Rockett, L. R.   998
Rogers, Bob   149
Rogers, Katharine M.   1712
Rogers, P.   2703
Rohr, Louis O.M.   556
Rollin, Roger B.   150
Rollings, Harry E.   1650
Rondthaler, Edward   2608
Root, Marcus A.   495
Rosaldo, Renato   1349
Rose, A. M.   1651
Rosen, Irwin C.   1383
Rosen, Jay   1538
Rosen, Marjorie   1867
Rosenberger, Gary   2474
Rosenbloom, Henry   2024
Rosenblum, Barbara   151
Rosentraub, M. S.   2064
Ross, Bonnie L.   1591
Ross, Dale H.   1093
Ross, Rhonda P.   2386
Ross, S. S.   1004
Rössel-Majdan, Karl   1408
Rossell, Christine H.   1652
Rossiter, John R.   2260,
  2387-2389
Rosten, L. C.   1071,2092
Roth, Herbert   1623
Roth, Moira   2609
Roth, Rachel   1943
Roth, William D.   2093
Rotha, Paul   557
Rothschild, Michael L.   2025
Rotzoll, Kim B.   2261
Roucek, J.   1159
Rourke, Francis E.   1982
Rowden, D.   2098
Rowell, C. H.   1005
Rowse, Arthur   830
Ruben, Brent D.   152
Rubin, Alan M.   1539,1540
Rubin, Bernard   831,2158
Rubin, David M.   1006
Rubin, Richard L.   2026
Rubinstein, Eli A.   1449,
  1541,1542
Ruckmick, Christian A.   1371
Rue, Vincent M.   1543
Rugh, William   2027
Ruhe, Edward   2704
Rupp, Leila J.   2028
Russell, Nick   2475
Rutherford, E.   1286

Rutstein, Nat   1544
Ruud, Charles A.   2065
Ryan, Michael   832
Ryan, Roderick T.   558
Ryant, Carl G.   1765

Sabine, Robert   407
Sackler, Arthur E.   1007
Sackman, Harold   153
Sadoul, Georges   559
Saenger, G.   1653
Sahay, B. N.   1307
Said, Edward W.   833
Saldich, Anne R.   2159
Salt, Barry   154
Salter, Patricia J.   889,
  1731
Sampson, Henry   2262
Sandbank, C. P.   2476
Sanderson, R. A.   560
Sandman, Peter M.   1642
Sanoff, A. P.   834
Sargent, John A.   1072
Sarris, Andrew   155,2094
Scanlon, T. Joseph   156
Schafer, Judith K.   2333
Schaffert, R. M.   496
Schaffner, Taleaferro P.
  409
Schattenberg, Gus   835
Schatz-Bergfield, Marianne
  2029
Schechter, Harold   1868
Scheibe, Cyndy   2390
Schenck-Hamlin, William J.
  1841
Scher, Jacob   836
Schicke, C. A.   255
Schiller, Dan   1008
Schiller, Herbert I.   1300
Schillinger, Elisabeth H.
  1820
Schlesinger, Laurence E.
  1009
Schickel, Richard   1384
Schmidbauer, M.   2477
Schmidt, Dorothy   1350
Schnabel, Reimund   2111
Schneider, Ben R., Jr.   2705
Schneider, Ira   2610
Schoof, Jack F.   1766
Schrader, Paul   2611
Schramm, Wilbur L.   157-160,
  837,1301,1545
Schreiber, E. M.   1933
Schudson, Michael   161

Subject Index

About the Compilers

BENJAMIN F. SHEARER is Library Director, Spring Hill College, Mobile, Alabama. His earlier books include *Periodical Literature on United States Cities: A Bibliography and Subject Guide* (with Barbara Smith Shearer, Greenwood Press, 1983) and *Finding the Source: A Thesaurus-Index to the Reference Collection* (Greenwood Press, 1981).

MARILYN J. HUXFORD is Assistant Professor of Social Sciences at McKendree College, Lebanon, Illinois. Her previous works include the bibliography *Man, Technology and Society,* compiled with co-author Benjaman F. Shearer, and *Saint Louis Statistical Abstract.*